THE
IMPERIAL
MANTLE

THE
IMPERIAL
MANTLE

*The United States, Decolonization,
and the Third World*

DAVID D. NEWSOM

*Indiana
University
Press*

BLOOMINGTON AND INDIANAPOLIS

This book is a publication of
Indiana University Press
601 North Morton Street
Bloomington, IN 47404-3797 USA

http://www.indiana.edu/~iupress

Telephone orders 800-842-6796
Fax orders 812-855-7931
Orders by e-mail iuporder@indiana.edu

The paper used in this publication meets the minimum
requirements of American National Standard for Information
Sciences—Permanence of Paper for Printed Library Materials,
ANSI Z39.48-1984.

MANUFACTURED IN THE UNITED STATES OF AMERICA

Library of Congress Cataloging-in-Publication Data
Newsom, David D.
The imperial mantle : the United States, decolonization, and the Third World / David D. Newsom.
p. cm.
Includes bibliographical references (p.   ) and index.
ISBN 0-253-33834-4 (alk. paper)
1. United States—Foreign relations—Developing countries. 2. Developing
countries—Foreign relations—United States. 3. Decolonization. I. Title.

D888.U6 N49 2000
327.730172'4—dc21   00-040754
1 2 3 4 5   05 04 03 02 01 00

*In the last half of the twentieth century
in many lands it was not always easy or safe to
be a friend or adviser to a United States diplomat.
To those in several lands who had the confidence and
the courage to help me understand their lives,
their politics, and their views of my country,
this book is dedicated.*

Mantle—Something that covers, envelops, or conceals.
—The Random House Dictionary
of the English Language

CONTENTS

Acknowledgments ix

INTRODUCTION A Voyage of Discovery 1

PART 1
THE IMPERIAL AGE
ONE The March of Empire 13
TWO The Nature of Imperialism 29

PART 2
INDEPENDENCE
THREE Independence 43
FOUR Freedom in Asia 55
FIVE Fictional Independence:
Protectorates, Mandates, and Influence 71
SIX The Gulf and the Peninsula 87
SEVEN Africa I: Where Blacks Prevailed 95
EIGHT Africa II: The Settler Countries 109

PART 3
THE THIRD WORLD AND THE UNITED STATES
NINE The Legacy of the Twentieth Century 123
TEN Economics 134
ELEVEN The Cold War 147
TWELVE Africa, Race, and Politics 159
THIRTEEN The General Assembly 176
FOURTEEN The Twenty-First–Century Agenda 191

Appendix: Backgrounds of Liberation Leaders 203

Notes 215

Bibliography 225

Index 233

MAPS

MAP 1. The Century That Ended Colonial Rule   12
MAP 2. Asia   54
MAP 3. The Mediterranean and the Middle East   70
MAP 4. Sub-Saharan Africa   94

ACKNOWLEDGMENTS

Although this is my personal account, many have contributed to it. I owe a special debt to those in the lands where I served or visited who, often in the face of antagonism against Americans, spoke honestly and helped me to draw back the veils on their cultures, their politics, and their views of the United States.

I am particularly grateful to Professor Philip Zelikow, director of the Miller Center of the University of Virginia, and to the late Marshall Coyne of the National Capital Foundation in Washington, D.C. Grants from these sources made possible essential research.

Colleagues and former colleagues in diplomacy and academia took time to read drafts and make insightful comments and constructive suggestions. J. Wayne Fredericks, former deputy assistant secretary of state for African affairs, and Ambassador Donald Easum helped me recall my African days. Ambassador George C. McGhee generously drew on his experiences as ambassador and undersecretary of state in the turbulent 1950s. Professors Elliott Skinner and Gwen Mikell, distinguished African scholars, urged me forward and provided valuable comment. Ambassadors Richard Parker, Roger Kirk, and James Blake shared their knowledge and opinions stemming from their own foreign service experiences. Ambassadors Teresita and Howard Schaffer made more current my impressions of South Asia. Pamela Brement shared her insights into Philippine history. Early in the project I consulted with Ambassador Donald McHenry, now at Georgetown University, on the experiences of the United States in the UN General Assembly and with Dr. Carol Lancaster on her recent study of U.S. economic assistance to Africa. David Barnes at the University of Wales at Cardiff introduced me to the work of Peter Calvocoressi.

Among my colleagues at the University of Virginia, I am especially indebted to Professor R. K. Ramazani, who gave me early and continuing encouragement and valuable comments, and to Professors John Echeverri-Gent, Alfred Fernbach, and Inis Claude and to Ms. Helena Cobban who provided me detailed critiques on the work. Professor Robert Fatton, chair of the Department of Government and Foreign Affairs, was ever ready to help and advise. At Alderman Library, reference assistant Muhammed S. Yusuf responded quickly to my often unusual questions. History student Taylor Fain, who shares with me an interest in the Buraimi oasis incident, helped me recall details I had forgotten.

Valuable perspectives by non-Americans were provided by Major General Indar Rikhye, (Indian Army retired), former director of the International Peace Academy, and by retired British ambassador and scholar Adam Watson. My good friend Sir Donald Maitland sent ideas and positive comments from Murhill Farm in Limpley Stoke, England. British diplomat Andrew Stuart provided insights into colonial administration. Indian Diplomat Sunil Lal, an associate of the Institute for the Study of Diplomacy at Georgetown University, helped me understand contemporary Indian views on the colonial past.

Four students at Virginia—Thomas Brister, Stephen Norris, Christopher Sutton, and Luciana Lavalee—took time from their studies to help with research. I am grateful for their valuable contributions.

And none of this would have been possible without my wife, Jean, who read each word, did the initial editing, and provided valuable comments in the process.

Charlottesville, Virginia
December 11, 1999

THE
IMPERIAL
MANTLE

INTRODUCTION

A Voyage of Discovery

Life can only be understood backwards;
But it must be lived forwards.
—Soren Kierkegaard

The premise of this book is simple. Solutions to some of the most significant foreign policy problems of the United States in the twenty-first century will require coming to grips with the emotions, attitudes, and disorder of those nations that, in much of the twentieth, were colonies of the West. Call them developing nations, new nations, emerging nations, or the Third World, their preoccupations, conflicts (internal and external), and sensitivities represent both opportunities and inhibiting factors in the pursuit of U.S. national interests.[1] These nations vary widely in age, size, strength, and policies, but they share common experiences.

The collapse of the European empires in the mid-twentieth century resulted in cataclysmic transformations and tragedies as subject peoples threw off imperial rule and resisted the dominant positions of the European powers and Japan. In terms of the displacement of peoples, casualties, and social revolutions, the process of decolonization in the twentieth century has probably been unmatched in history, yet in a century overshadowed by wars both hot and cold, the full implications of these volcanic changes have never been fully understood in the United States. At the beginning of a new century, with the world still conscious of the ethnic cleansing and massacres of a shattered Yugoslavia, an East Timor, or a Rwanda, the dimensions of the human disasters of a half century before are forgotten.

More than one-half of the peoples of the world saw their political, social, and economic conditions transformed within a period of two decades:

An estimated twelve million Hindus, Sikhs, and Muslims were killed or moved across borders when Pakistan was created and India became independent.

Over 700,000 Palestinians fled or were expelled as Arabs and Israelis fought at the end of the British mandate in Palestine. An estimated 3,000,000 refugees remain in 1999, 1,000,000 of whom are in camps maintained by the UN Relief and Works Agency (UNRWA).

Algeria's eight-year war of independence against France resulted in 600,000 deaths. Tragically, these internal conflicts continued in Africa and Asia into the twenty-first century.

A Personal Journey

This book represents a personal journey, a voyage of discovery, but it is not a memoir. Although I draw on my experience, the intent is to present a dimension of U.S. foreign policy that is seldom understood and appreciated and that has led to numerous disasters in the last half century. In presenting the story, I have augmented my own experiences by research into the events and crises of the segment of history through which I have lived.

As a Pulitzer Travelling Scholar journeying in Asia, Africa, and Latin America in the early years of World War II and as a post-war diplomat and professor, I have been an observer and occasional participant in the breakup of empires.

In Japan in 1940, already center of an empire that included North China, Manchukuo, Formosa, and Korea, sidewalk loudspeakers were blaring "The Greater East Asia Co-Prosperity Sphere March"; the expansion into Indochina had already begun. In North China, Japan ruled. I saw recuperating Japanese soldiers in white kimonos occupying the Summer Palace outside Peking.

Jittery Dutch East India officials carefully examined every passenger as we arrived in Surabaya. I glimpsed Batavia, now Jakarta, little knowing that thirty years later I would return as U.S. ambassador.

Singapore was bright under the Union Jack. In a talk with Teddy White, the famous correspondent, I found no hint of the city's doom, then a year away.

In Ceylon, now Sri Lanka, a bored U.S. consul wondered what possible interest I had in touring that part of the world. Undeterred, I continued by train to India and to my introduction to the pressures for independence. Through a fortunate letter of introduction to Robert Stimson, assistant editor of *The Times of India* in Bombay, I met an Indian justice and diplomat, Sir Benegal Rama Rau, and his family and leaders of the Indian Congress Party, including Mohandas K. Gandhi and Jawalharal Nehru. In November 1940, in their preliminary maneuvering toward independence, Congress Party leaders were debating whether to oppose the British war effort. My lifelong interest in decolonization began at that point.

I saw another facet of colonial life when, during my stay, Santha Rama Rau, daughter of Sir Benegal, just back from university in London, could not enter the Bombay Yacht Club because she was Indian.[2]

As a diplomat, I was to return eight years later to the subcontinent—to an independent Pakistan—and to witness the end of the British Raj as troops of the Black Watch regiment, bagpipes playing, marched through the streets of Karachi to ships waiting in the harbor to take them home.

East Africa was colonial, from Mombasa in Kenya in the north to Portugal's Lorenzo Marques (now Maputo), the playground for stolid South Africans. South Africa, then part of the British Empire, still reflected the tensions between British and Boers. Apartheid was a decade away.

The glimpses I saw represented but a portion of the European imperial outreach. At a distance, our ship passed other colonial outposts. In the Philippines, the U.S. had already taken steps toward granting independence. France still held tight to Indochina, Belgium to the Congo, and Italy ruled Ethiopia and shared Somalia with Britain.

Later, in 1950, returning from Karachi, our ship stopped for a week in Haifa. At the adjoining dock, men, women, and children, thin and haggard, were arriving in the new state of Israel from the concentration camps of Europe. Anxious people on the pier scanned their faces for lost relatives. Proceeding on toward Nazareth, I saw the newly created Israeli farms, where agricultural methods contrasted with the Arab method of tilling the rocky soil in an age-old way. It was a heart-rending and revealing introduction to another post-imperial problem, the conflict between Jew and Arab in Palestine. That, too, would preoccupy me in later years.

Assigned to Baghdad in 1951, I saw the other side of the coin. Humiliated by their defeat at the hands of the Israelis following the Arab-Israeli war of 1948, Iraqis lost no opportunity to remind U.S. diplomats of Washington's responsibility for "the tragedy of Palestine." The Iraqis, freed from Ottoman rule under a British mandate, also felt they had the fiction of independence without the reality.

With the introduction of Secretary of State John Foster Dulles's policy of containment of the Soviet Union and the creation of the ill-fated Baghdad Pact, I became involved as well in the Cold War and its implications for the newly independent world.

During two years in London in the early 1960s, I followed the decolonization of British Africa and the traumatic end of the Belgian Congo. Subsequently, as director of North African affairs, I saw the departure of the French from Algiers and, in October, 1962, arranged the visit to Washington of Algerian president Ahmed Ben Bella, unaware that the Cuban Missile Crisis was unfolding around me, or that Ben Bella would displease his American hosts by going, thereafter, directly to Cuba.

The return to Indonesia in 1973 and a subsequent appointment to the Philippines, our own former colony, in 1977 completed my post-imperial journey.

A normal assumption would be that this was a happy journey. The United States, after all, had been a colony. With its democratic ideals and its devotion to freedom, the U.S. would seem a natural ally of the newly independent countries. Yet this was not to be.

A Troubled Relationship

My story represents an effort to put in one place brief descriptions of the events that have helped define the relationship between the United States and the Third World over the past two centuries and have been at the base of issues that still preoccupy Washington's policymakers. The story is far from complete. The emphasis is on the European empires in Asia and Africa, with only brief references to the Americas. Nor have I tried to deal with the Russian empire that has broken up in the last decades of the twentieth century. I am certain, however, that many of the post-imperial reactions described here will apply also to the peoples and nations of Latin America and Central Asia.

Two questions have constantly been posed to me over these years. Those in new nations have asked, "Why does the United States, with its own record of independence, not understand the attitudes of the Third World?" In the United States, people ask, "Why do the new nations exhibit such anti-American sentiments when we oppose imperialism and provide substantial help to them?"

In an article entitled "The Bewildered American Raj," which was written after an extensive stay in the United States, British historian Michael Howard reflected this query:

> Why, Americans ask, are our achievements not universally recognized and admired? Why does American generosity not evoke more gratitude? Why have American economic and military strength not brought more influence in the world? Why are small countries in Southeast Asia and the Middle East able to defy the United States, and to gain such widespread support when they do? Why is the United States always in a minority at the United Nations, which it did so much to create and still does so much to sustain?[3]

The fact is that throughout the last half century, the United States has had a troubled relationship with much of what, for want of a better term, we call the Third World.

One answer to the question of why the United States has had such difficulties with the Third World lies in looking at attitudes and issues created in the age of imperialism. For in the early years of the twenty-first century, the United States, with its economic and military power and global reach, is seen as the inheritor of the imperial mantle in much of the world. While I was information officer at the U.S. Embassy in Karachi from 1948 to 1950, I described some of the perceptions of the United States that I was encountering in an article for the University of California at Berkeley alumni magazine:

> "America is a land of monopolies where all wealth and privilege are concentrated in a few hands."

> "America is an imperialistic nation interested only in exploiting the less developed nations of Asia."

> "The European Recovery Program [the Marshall Plan] is merely a device through which America seeks to rule the world."[4]

This review of history will be familiar ground to many, but to new generations for whom these events are distant or unknown, some background is necessary to understand why those in the Third World may feel the way they do about contemporary actions of the Western powers. A new generation may not be familiar with the Amritsar massacre in India or the Boxer Rebellion, but Indians and Chinese remember—just as Texans remember the Alamo.

Racism inescapably enters this picture. I have included doggerel and comments denigrating non-whites not because I agree with the attitudes reflected, but because some knowledge of how the empire builders regarded "the natives" is essential to understanding the residual feelings that have flowed from that period.

Well into the mid-twentieth century, the fate of millions in Asia, Africa, South and Central America, and the Caribbean was determined in distant capitals. Under colonial regimes people accommodated or schemed to make the most of their situation. A few protested. At the beginning of World War II, independence was, for many, still a distant dream.

Recollections of the past are kept alive through rhetoric and commemorations. The direct U.S. experience with imperialism was more than two hundred years ago. But for those outside Western Europe and North America, the imperial age was yesterday. Peoples dispossessed by the imperial reach are still alive and aware of kingdoms destroyed and traditions suppressed. However idealized their recollections of their past may be, that past was kept alive during the imperial period and remains important to them and to succeeding generations. Newer catastrophes not attributed to the European imperialists, such as the Indonesian takeover of East Timor in 1975, may blot out colonial episodes, but the more distant episodes never fully fade from local lore.

This study carries through to the end of empires and pays less attention to what followed independence. Nevertheless, it is important to note that the period that followed the imperial age has left its own problems:

The global victory over the Soviet Union left tragic debris in unresolved conflicts in Angola and Afghanistan.

In five of the countries with which the United States once had close Cold War relationships—Ethiopia, Iran, Iraq, Libya, and Sudan—anti-U.S. revolutions overthrew friendly regimes.

In 1999, the United States had economic sanctions of one kind or another against seventy countries—with few results to show for the pressure.

The United States lost control of the UN General Assembly and found itself in a minority on issues of Chinese representation, apartheid, Rhodesia, Palestine, and decolonization.

The Vietnam war was seen in much of the Third World as an effort to maintain France's imperial control; Washington's hopes of enlisting widespread support foundered.

New nations, presumably tutored by democratic Europe, became non-aligned and adopted internal socialist policies; many tilted toward the Soviet Union. A New International Economic Order and the Group of 77 (later expanded to 130) demanded concessions and resources from the richer north. A New World Information Order challenged Western concepts of press freedom.

Americans became prime targets of growing transnational terrorist movements. Between 1960 and 1998, 3,415 American citizens were victims of terrorist acts perpetrated by nationals of Third World countries: 830 were killed and 2,588 wounded.

Especially in Africa, tribal rivalries, hidden or suppressed in colonial times, erupted into disasters such as Somalia, Rwanda, Sierra Leone, Liberia and Congo. Well-intended humanitarian interventions were assaulted and terminated.

The powerful U.S. armed forces retreated from two weak countries, Lebanon and Somalia, and were prevented by political considerations from fully defeating the Iraqi dictator Saddam Hussein in the Gulf War. At this writing, the outcome of the protracted commitment in the Balkans is still in doubt.

Even when assaults on U.S. embassies in Nairobi and Dar-Es Salaam killed scores of Africans, neither Kenya nor Tanzania endorsed the retaliatory U.S. raids on Afghanistan and Sudan.

Global efforts to curb weapons of mass destruction were set back seriously when India and Pakistan, to the surprise of Washington, detonated nuclear devices. The United States should not have been surprised. Such actions grow out of a search for pride, status, and security common throughout the decolonized world— although this does not extend to a desire to possess such weapons in every Third World country.

The Indian and Pakistani detonations have not been the only surprises. The American public and officials have been unprepared for each of the major revolutions in the Third World as well as for individual events such as terrorist acts. James Reston, *New York Times* columnist, commented on this at the time of the hijacking of TWA flight 847 in Lebanon in 1983:

> Still we have to wonder why, from administration to administration of whatever political party, we are constantly taken by surprise in a world we are trying to help but don't quite understand.
>
> We were infuriated by the latest hijacking of T.W.A. Flight 847; but Washington is trying to deal with a world it knows little about, thinking it's dealing with the liberation of a plane and its passengers when it's up against not merely terrorists but a struggle for personal power in the Arab world and a clash of philosophy about nothing less than the meaning of life, here and hereafter.[5]

Each setback has numerous causes, but all have one element in common. They represent U.S. confrontations with nations that have, in the last fifty years, whether through independence or revolution or both, reduced the influence of major Western countries in their affairs.

Many of these difficulties lie in the problems Washington has had in accepting and responding to the attitudes and sensitivities developed in the breakup of empires and the subsequent creation of independent states. When I was in Jakarta as ambassador, dealing with the then priority issue of reconciling Third World and U.S. attitudes toward commodity agreements. I wrote the Department of State on November 5, 1974:

> Our current efforts to engage in a satisfactory discussion with the developing countries on resources are a matter of high priority. The Secretary [Henry Kissinger] is obviously deeply concerned with this and is making progress in his bilateral discussions with key world leaders.

> Seen from Jakarta, however, and on the basis of a number of discussions with recent visitors from the United States, there seems to be an insufficient public understanding of the historical background and atmosphere in which we must conduct these discussions.[6]

As the new century dawns, the enmities of world wars have faded, the ideologies of fascism and communism have been discredited, and the Cold War has thawed, but the perceptions and ambitions generated in the imperial upheavals of the previous decades continue to present obstacles to the fulfillment of U.S. policy objectives. This will continue to be the case well into the twenty-first century when the diplomatic agenda, more than ever before, will include global issues in which management and resolution will require Third World cooperation.

Policymakers and pundits in Western Europe and North America have viewed developments in the Third World variously with alarm, denigration, and ridicule. During the Cold War one heard the claims—sometimes justified, sometimes unfounded—that they were Soviet inspired.

Despite large ethnic minorities throughout the United States, senior U.S. policymakers—whether in the executive or legislative branches—who have understood and been sympathetic with Third World conditions have been rare. Many in the foreign policy community, especially during the Cold War, considered Africa and much of Asia and Latin America peripheral to U.S. interests. Problems in Asia and Africa were for the Europeans to deal with.

The turbulent and anti-democratic politics of many Third World countries baffled and dismayed Americans and undermined early post-independence sympathies.

Comments by officials and media in Western capitals, often seen as patronizing, have insisted that such initiatives were detrimental to the nations involved and that they would not succeed. Some Western governments have tried to reverse Third World actions they have considered contrary to their interests. But few of these efforts have been successful in the long run. The necessity to confront the attitudes of the new nations of the twentieth century remains.

That situation has not changed in twenty-five years.

A Global Clash

Others have written of a global clash of civilizations or cultures.

A global clash exists, but it is a confrontation of sensitivities and perspectives between the industrialized north and the Third World more than it is one of religion or culture. Each of these elements enters the picture, but as interrelated parts of a whole; none represents the principal divide. Some describe the world scene as a confrontation between Islam and the West. Islam, because it is the dominant religion in Africa and Asia and is associated with memories of past glories and conquest, occupies an important place in the equation, but it is but one of many elements in today's North-South divide.

Whoever writes about the expressions and actions of the Third World faces immediate problems of credibility from both sides. It is not easy to determine how individuals in many developing countries feel about the United States. Some will publicly denounce "Yankee imperialism" and then come privately and say, "We don't really mean this, but we have to say these things to be politically credible." I have never been sure which is the true voice. Looking back at events I have observed I have often felt the only honest voices were those that told us the same things privately they said publicly—things we often did not want to hear.

It is equally difficult to convey to many in Washington how people in the Third World feel toward the United States. Those who seek to explain vagaries of the newer nations are called apologists. The irrelevant question, "Whose side are you on?" is frequently asked. In addition, objections are raised to the premise of a North-South division, beginning with denial of the existence of a Third World:

> The Third World is gone. It has been vanishing for a long while, but now it has completely disappeared. Oh, the countries once assigned to the Third World are still there, but the concept of the Third World is no longer connected to any reality.
>
> We still deal (quite obviously) with the Brazils, Indonesias, Nigerias, and Indias. But the ideas that these many nations represent anything like a single bloc with similar characteristics is shattered forever.[7]

Robert Samuelson, columnist for *The Washington Post,* who wrote these lines, insists that, with the end of the Cold War, the Third World nations no longer have the leverage they once had. Other arguments similarly seek to discredit the concept of a group of developing nations:

Many of the nations are artificial creations with rulers who lack legitimacy;

Foreign policy cannot be built on claims of victimization;

Western interests cannot be subordinated to the demands of the corrupt and the powerless;

Globalization and the rise of technically sophisticated elites are diminishing the North-South gap;

Tensions existing between and among Third World nations are as serious as those between North and South.

Each of these statements has elements of truth, but to the degree they deny the underlying force of Third World attitudes, they do a disservice to policy making.

An understanding of today's divide must begin with a look at how history has formed perspectives on both sides. As a free, democratic, multi-ethnic nation, the United States displays its awareness of power while at the same time placing in the shadows legacies of the expulsion of native Americans and slavery. Peoples of the newly independent nations have come out of a long history of hierarchical tribal societies, poverty, and submission to the power of imperial domains. They find the U.S. system of government complex and difficult to understand. Those not conditioned to the freedom of press and expression often react angrily to U.S. comments and find it hard to distinguish between official and unofficial expressions.

Individuals who write about U.S. foreign policy also face a dilemma—especially if he or she has been involved in the policy-making process. The critical audience of scholars, journalists, and politicians await disclosures of new and, perhaps, sensational insights into the process. Inherently suspicious of the U.S. government, they believe that officials have made mistakes and someone must be to blame. Yet for the practitioner, the matter is not that simple. Policy making in Washington requires the constant adjustment of the myriad of interests—official, legislative, private, corporate—that affect the results. Seldom is there a clear and desirable choice.

This book will analyze U.S. attitudes and circumstances in other countries with which some, in both the United States and abroad, will disagree, perhaps strongly. My analyses are in no way intended to denigrate the strong and generally envied position of the United States in the world. They are, rather, an effort to help the American reader see us as others see us and the foreign reader to recognize that even Americans, in trying to understand their point of view, do not exclude other interpretations.

This is not intended to evoke sympathy for or an excuse for the deprivations and failings of newer nations. It is intended to show why the United States, a prosperous, advanced, assertive nation, has often had unexpected problems with the Third World and why these problems remain relevant today and into the future. The history of the United States in many ways parallels their histories, but at some point in the nineteenth century the United States switched sides. George III's oppressed colony evolved into an aggressive imperialist in its own right. The first major white settler communities were in North America—well ahead of those that later appeared in Africa.

Any analysis must acknowledge the imperfections of all societies. Heroes and heroines as well as villains are to be found in the story of decolonization. Criticism of Europeans for not recognizing the force of nationalism and opposing independence should not obscure recognition of the many men and women in imperial bureaucracies who espoused self-government and independence, often with great courage, and worked diligently to bring empires to an end when given the opportunity. As this history demonstrates, the task of disengaging from colonies was not an easy one, either for the colonizers or the colonized.

How individuals are seen depends on perspective. The courageous missionary preaching the gospel in the jungles of Africa is seen as a brave crusader in the West; he may be perceived as a destroyer of indigenous cultures in Africa and Asia.

No one party in the story has a basis for arrogance. The peoples of Asia and Africa have committed atrocities against their own peoples even as they blame the West for their tragedies. The United States has little basis for criticizing the often brutal European colonization of Africa. The British wars with the Zulus and others to open the way for gold and settlers occurred in the nineteenth century—at exactly the same time the United States was taking the southwest from Mexico and warring against the Sioux and Cheyenne of the northern plains. France exiled Queen Ranavalona III and established a protectorate over Madagascar in 1896, three years after the United States overthrew Queen Lilioukalani and proclaimed a protectorate over Hawaii.

My descriptions of the attitudes and sensitivities that had their roots in the colonial and post-colonial period and that persist today in the Third World are not intended to suggest that these are dominant in the politics of all such countries. It does suggest that they lie dormant in most countries that became independent in this century and are vulnerable to exploitation by demagogic leaders in times of political crises. It suggests, also, that a full understanding of these attitudes requires an understanding of what went before in the imperial and decolonization eras, eras of brutality, duplicity, and struggle.

In both Europe and America, two tendencies have lived side by side—a brutal assertion of power and a compassion for the weak. In the nineteenth century, although the latter tendency was always present, the exercise of often inhuman power prevailed, whether in the conquests of Africa by Europe or in the winning of the American west. The twentieth century has seen a shift in the balance toward a more concerned and compassionate view of the native peoples of America and of the Third World. The same shift has been apparent in Europe as the nations of the continent have turned away from the militant policies of the colonial period to a greater emphasis on humanitarian concerns.

The story begins with the imperial age.

Part 1

THE
IMPERIAL
AGE

This is what England must either do or perish: she must found colonies as fast and as far as she is able, formed of her most energetic and worthiest men; seizing every piece of fruitful waste ground she can set her foot on, and there teaching her colonists that their first aim is to advance the power of England by land and sea.
—John Ruskin (quoted in Lapping, *End of Empire*, 448)

The Century That Ended Colonial Rule

In 1900, Europe's major colonial powers had expanded their empires into every corner of the world. By the middle of the century, the Europeans were on the retreat, and as the century closes, hardly any overseas territories remain under their control.

The world in 1900:

Britain, the largest colonial power, held its colonies, as well as dominion over Canada and Australia. Southern Asia was colonized too, and the coasts of China and India were dotted with small European enclaves. The Americas had all been colonized as well. But nearly all of those possessions had become independent by 1900.

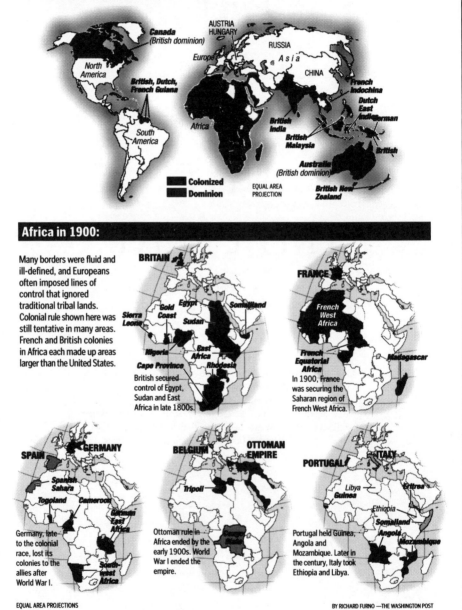

Africa in 1900:

Many borders were fluid and ill-defined, and Europeans often imposed lines of control that ignored traditional tribal lands. Colonial rule shown here was still tentative in many areas. French and British colonies in Africa each made up areas larger than the United States.

British secured control of Egypt, Sudan and East Africa in late 1800s.

In 1900, France was securing the Saharan region of French West Africa.

Germany, late to the colonial race, lost its colonies to the allies after World War I.

Ottoman rule in Africa ended by the early 1900s. World War I ended the empire.

Portugal held Guinea, Angola and Mozambique. Later in the century, Italy took Ethiopia and Libya.

EQUAL AREA PROJECTIONS

BY RICHARD FURNO —THE WASHINGTON POST

Map 1. The Century That Ended Colonial Rule.
© 1999, The Washington Post. Reprinted with permission.

ONE

The March of Empire

On a day in 1434 Portuguese Captain Gil Eannes sailed his 70-foot ship south beyond the much-feared Cape Bojador and landed on the coast of Africa. His was the sixteenth attempt by his fellow countrymen to pass beyond this seemingly formidable barrier. Success was due not only to pressure from his patron, Prince Henry the Navigator, but also to the capacities of the caravel, a ship designed to carry men beyond the confines of the Mediterranean. As Daniel Boorstin writes in *The Discoverers*, "The caravel was a ship especially designed to bring explorers back."[1] Technology drove history in the fifteenth century, as it has in the twentieth. The voyage also opened the way to the age of European imperialism that was to reshape Asia, Africa, and America in the coming five centuries. At the end of the twentieth century, the global community is still dealing with issues rooted in that age: Indochina, East Timor, Cyprus, Palestine, Angola—to name but a few.

The world into which the Portuguese sailed was not empty. The empires of Songhai, Mali, and Ghana dominated the West African coast; farther south were the Kongo and Ovimbundi states. The East Coast was dominated by Arab principalities. Farther to the east, the Moghul empire still ruled in the Indian sub-continent and the Majipahit empire ruled in Sumatra and Java. The Ming Dynasty was at its height in China, and beyond the Pacific were the significant civilizations of the Aztecs and Incas.

The Europeans, however, treated the world as if it were empty. Explorers led the way, followed by missionaries, merchants, administrators, soldiers, and settlers. They recognized that the indigenous peoples were there—but to be converted, exploited, enslaved, massacred, and controlled as the imperial powers saw fit. The stages of intervention and conquest of America, Africa, and Asia began—moving from trade to markets to slavery to white settlements.

The Imperial Game

With the Portuguese in the lead with their new technology of ships, compasses, maps, and weapons, these ancient principalities were soon to feel the severe cultural and economic impacts of the more advanced and aggressive West. The imperial race, a global competition among European powers for the spoils of an "empty" world, had begun. The traditional societies in this empty world were divided and weak in European terms; they had few means to resist the Western onslaught.

The Portuguese ventured farther and farther down the African coast and beyond, searching for gold and spices (primarily pepper, nutmeg, cloves, and cinnamon). In 1475, forty years after Eannes sailed beyond Cape Bojador, they reached the Gold Coast (now Ghana) and established a trading post.

Two decades later, in 1497, Vasco da Gama took the Portuguese flag on his historic 12-year voyage around the Cape of Good Hope to India. By the end of the sixteenth century, the Portuguese had established trading posts in Mozambique (1505), Malacca(1511), the Moluccas (1511), Timor (1520), Ceylon (later Sri Lanka, 1505), Cochin (1500), and Goa (1510). The latter became the capital of the Portuguese empire in India in 1590. But the full Portuguese presence in India was destined to be short-lived.

Five years before Vasco de Gama set out, Christopher Columbus, in 1492, flying the Spanish flag, went westward with well-known results. Sensing future rivalry, Portugal and Spain two years later signed the Treaty of Tordesillas, which divided the non-Christian world between them by an imaginary line in the Atlantic 370 leagues (about 1,300 miles) west of the Cape Verde Islands. Portugal could claim everything east of the line and Spain everything to the west. The agreement permitted Lisbon's acquisition of Brazil, finally completed in 1549; the rest of the Western hemisphere was left to Madrid. A papal bull issued by Pope Leo X in 1514 confirmed this arrangement and forbade others to interfere with Portuguese possessions.

Following Tordesillas, Spain turned its attention primarily to the New World of America, ultimately conquering the Mayan, Aztec, and Incan domains; the stage was set for the delicate relationships three centuries later between the future American republics and the Yankee colossus of the north.

In 1565, Spain made its sole successful sortie into Asia from New Spain (now Mexico). Forty-four years after Ferdinand Magellan died in Cebu on his round-the-world voyage, Miguel de Legazpi founded the first Spanish settlement in the Philippines in that city. Manila was established six years later and, by the end of the sixteenth century, most of the island chain was under the rule of New Spain, administered from Mexico.

For nearly a century, however, although other adventurers such as Sir Francis Drake and Magellan visited the regions, it was the Portuguese who dominated the Indian Ocean and Pacific areas and the lucrative trade in spices. In 1515, they wrested the island of Hormuz at the mouth of the Persian Gulf from the Persian ruler, Shah Ismail, only to lose it to Shah Abbas the Great at the end of the century.[2]

By this time other major European nations, England and Holland, were beginning to develop their power and to sense the opportunities. A small island in modern Indonesia, Ternate, is a symbol of the imperial rivalry in the Indies. Ternate in the Moluccas is 42 square miles in area, two-thirds the size of the District of Columbia. The first in the Moluccas to accept Islam, the Sultan of Ternate controlled the clove trade, a monopoly that lasted from the twelfth to the seventeenth centuries. Ternate became a natural objective of European explorers seeking spices. Today one can still see the sultan's palace and, in the center hall, the crown that once symbolized his authority. The island jungle covers the ruins of four forts built by the Portuguese, Dutch, Spanish, and British. The Portuguese were the first to arrive in Ternate, coming in 1512 in a ship under Admiral Alfonso de Albuquerque's command. In that same year, Magellan's remaining ship, returning from Cebu, visited Ternate, as did Sir Francis Drake fifty years later.

The names are familiar to Americans; these same explorers touched the shores of North America. The United States itself was a product of this imperial age. America's Spanish heritage is a permanent reminder of Spain's explorations and settlements in the New World. The British settlement at Jamestown, Virginia, in 1607 coincided with the Dutch entry into Java. The British and Dutch were establishing colonies that later became Massachusetts and New York at the same time that they were jousting for lands and riches in the Asian Indies. Drake, on his voyage around the world, visited the California coast in 1579. Five years before the Pilgrims landed at Plymouth in 1620, the British established their first trading rights in India.

The Portuguese presence in Ternate ended when the sultan expelled them and granted the Dutch a spice monopoly in 1606. Ternate became a vassal of the Dutch East India Company and remained Dutch until Indonesian independence, except for the few years in the early nineteenth century when the British took over the Dutch East Indies in the Napoleonic Wars. Sir Stamford Raffles, one of the remarkable figures of the imperial period, ruled Java from 1811 to 1815.

Seventeenth-century exploration was carried out primarily by chartered companies that, in effect, became states within a state. They raised their own military forces, were empowered by their kings to conclude agreements with foreigners, and, where they could, monopolized trade. The British East India Company was organized in 1600 and the counterpart Dutch East Indies Company in 1601. Both effectively challenged the Portuguese.

The Dutch determined to dominate the Indies and to eliminate rivals, particularly the Portuguese and the British. The Dutch first reached Sumatra in 1596 and Bantam in Java in 1607. The Portuguese were able to hang on only to a trading post on the eastern half of the island of Timor. The British had established a warehouse (or "factory") on a small island in the Moluccas, Amboyna. When, in 1623, the Dutch seized the factory and killed all the inhabitants. Britain turned its attention to India.

The British East India Company acquired Madras in 1639, meanwhile destroying the Portuguese position at the Strait of Hormuz in 1622. In what became a pattern among European royalty, the British gained Bombay in 1661 as part of the dowry of the Portuguese queen, Catherine of Braganza, who married Charles II. Portugal held on to the enclave of Goa until forced to relinquish it three centuries later to an invading independent India.

The only serious challenge to British dominance in India came from France. France, with its strong military, its wealth, and its population, had the potential to be a leading colonial power in the seventeenth and eighteenth centuries. Preoccupied with European affairs, Paris conducted only an occasional imperial sortie—mostly in North America and the Caribbean.

The weakening of the Moghul empire with the death of the Emperor Aurangzeb (1707) spurred rivalry between the French and the British. In the Seven Years War (1756–1763), the French captured Madras but were forced to relinquish it in the Treaty of Paris of 1763. France retained five small enclaves: Pondicherry, Yanaon, Karikal, Mahe, and Chandernagor. It was not until the next century that France expanded its Asian empire in another direction. Cochin China was taken in 1862 and protectorates were created over Cambodia (1863), Annan (1884), and Tonkin (1884). A union of Indochina was established incorporating the four principalities in 1887. Laos was added in 1893. Thus the seeds of the later tragedy of Vietnam were planted.

In the latter half of the eighteenth century, through arrangements with local princes and the control of other regions, the British gained full authority in India. In 1773, the British parliament passed the Regulating Act which made Calcutta supreme over Madras and Bombay and appointed Warren Hastings, an employee of the East India Company, as the first governor general.

With British authority in India consolidated under Hastings, the East India Company became a power in its own right, acting at times without London's authority. Such was the case when Britain acquired Singapore and, later, Malaya. One man's determination made a difference.

After Waterloo in 1815, the Dutch regained Malacca, Java, and other colonies and, to exclude the British, signed treaties with the Malay sultans. Raffles, banished to Bengkulu on Sumatra after the Dutch regained Java, felt that British interests had been damaged. He persuaded Hastings to support an expedition to the Malacca Strait; Hastings agreed, provided Raffles abstained from all negotiation if the Dutch were already established. When the East India Board in London learned of this, they immediately asked Hastings to call it off. But it was too late. Raffles was on his way.

He visited the small island of Singapura at the tip of the Malay peninsula in January 1819, found it virtually deserted, and saw it as a possible stronghold and trading port. The island was under the sovereignty of the sultan of Johore. Not to be deterred, Raffles found a dispossessed brother and offered him British protection and 5,000 Spanish dollars a year to sign for the sultan. Raffles left an officer in charge with 300 men and ten big guns. The Dutch decided not to challenge this coup, and Singapore and the Straits Settlements became British. Subsequently, in 1874, when a British merchant was the victim of river piracy in a Malay state, the governor of the Straits Settlements made the sultans agree to accept British advisers. Malaya, too, became British.

Except for Indochina, by the end of the eighteenth century the major Asian colonies that were to become independent parts of the Third World had been established in roughly their present form: India, Indonesia, Malaya, Singapore, and the Philippines. On the other side of the world, the American colonies gained their freedom, the nations of Latin America took shape under Spain, and the British and French contested Canada.

The eighteenth century saw major changes in European colonial policy, principally resulting from the industrial revolution. Early imperial expansion had been primarily through the establishment of trading posts to purchase spices and slaves. As the *Encyclopedia Britannica* explains:

> Spices, sugar, and slaves became less important. The pressure for markets and raw materials prevailed. This involved a major disruption of social systems over wide areas of the globe. It required an overhaul of existing land and property arrangements, including the introduction of private property and the expropriation of land; the creation of a labor supply through forced labor; the introduction of land rents and the curtailment of production and export by native producers.
>
> India had been an exporter of cotton goods; by mid-19th century, India was receiving one-fourth of all British exports of cotton piece goods and had lost its own markets. This required new patterns of administration and greater imposition of the culture and language of the dominant power. The expansion of the late 18th century and 19th instituted a search for land in place of trading posts. This meant a displacement of the local population and a transformation of their existing societies. New technologies in arms, communication, and transportation facilitated Western dominance.[3]

The concentration of the imperial surge of the next century would be on the "scramble for Africa."

The Scramble for Africa

A popular idea exists that Africa south of the Sahara in 1800 was an empty quarter, unknown and ripe for the taking. The contrary is true. Vibrant kingdoms and mini-empires dominated the continent. The Europeans who entered to create the nations of the twentieth century did so only by making treaties with, subjugating, or destroying existing African authorities and societies.

The process had begun two centuries earlier in southern Africa. As the sixteenth century dawned, the Portuguese established themselves in Mozambique (1505) and Angola (1574). They had touched South-West Africa and the Cape of Good Hope in the fifteenth century but did not remain. They found the coast inhospitable and few settled tribes with which to trade. It would be 150 years before the Dutch, who by then had displaced the Portuguese in the Indian Ocean, would establish themselves at Table Bay at the Cape. In 1652, the Dutch East Indies Company sent Jan van Riebeck and thirty settlers to set up a station. They took land and imported slaves from Malaya and other Asian countries; the Afrikaaner presence was established.

In another hundred years, in 1795, the British arrived and pushed the Afrikaaners north; in turn, the Afrikaaners fought and displaced settled African tribes. Then appeared upon the scene one of the more remarkable characters in imperial history—Cecil Rhodes of England, the only individual to give his name to a colony in Africa, although the name disappeared upon independence. Because the territories he founded were to become major issues in the decolonization of Africa, his story deserves to be told.

Through profits in diamonds and gold in South Africa, Rhodes became a multi-millionaire before he was thirty. But he had a dream beyond riches. He wanted to create a solid band of British territory from Cape Town to Cairo. At Oxford, he had been inspired by a lecture by the naturalist John Ruskin, whose words epitomized the imperial vision:

> This is what England must either do or perish: she must found colonies as fast and as far as she is able, formed of her most energetic and worthiest men; seizing every piece of fruitful waste ground she can set her foot on, and there teaching her colonists that their first aim is to advance the power of England by land and sea.[4]

In 1885, the British acquired Bechuanaland (later Botswana). Beyond that lay a high plateau land called Zambesia, dominated by the Matabele, a tribe driven north by the Boers, the descendants of the Dutch settlers who colonized the Cape area in 1652.

The British government at the time did not endorse Rhodes's dream but it approved Rhodes's request to seek claims in central Africa to keep out the Boers and the Portuguese. With this encouragement, Rhodes obtained from Lobengula, king of the Matabele, an exclusive mineral concession in Zambesia. He then set about obtaining the formal backing of the British government. By appointing respectable men to the boards of his companies and making generous donations to political parties, he obtained a royal charter for his British South African Company (BSAC). The charter gave the company the power to "govern, raise its own police force, fly its own flag, construct roads, railways, and harbors, establish banks, and allocate land to settlers."[5]

Although Lobengula had been assured that "no more than ten white men"[6] would enter the territory, Rhodes had no intention of abiding by such restrictions. His objective was to found a white colony in Zambesia. He recruited white "pioneers" and sent a column of 200, protected by the British Bechuanaland police, into the territory. On September 13, 1890, they raised the British flag in their capital, naming it after the British prime minister, Lord Salisbury.

For a time African rivalries impeded settlement. The Shona nation of Zambesia (to whom the whites turned for labor) had traditionally been preyed upon by the Matabele. The European settlers demanded action to prevent such raids. Lobengula sent a peace mission, but BSAC company troopers killed its members. The

British government urged a peaceful solution, but Rhodes made himself unavailable while a force was assembled that attacked Bulawayo, the Matabele capital, and destroyed its army. Rhodes pressed for more settlers and inaugurated a forced labor system, using the Shona to work the new white farms.

Pressures in London for more responsible treatment of the Africans were turned aside by the political power of the company. Zambesia became Southern Rhodesia—a colony without a Colonial Office presence—governed, in reality, by the white settler minority.

Two adjoining territories, Northern Rhodesia and Nyasaland, escaped the company's rule and became colonies ruled from London. In the late 1940s, Southern Rhodesia floated the idea of an amalgamation of the three territories, but London and black Africans, who saw the attempt as an effort to extend white settler rule, strongly opposed the idea. Instead, London proposed a federation—which African populations initially supported. Various obstacles were overcome and the Federation of Rhodesia and Nyasaland came into being on August 1, 1953. But the federation was short-lived; its three components were to come separately to independence as Zimbabwe, Malawi, and Zambia, involving the international community in the process.

Europeans had not always been the conquerors of Africans. Peoples from North Africa, participating in the expansion of Islam, had joined in the conquest of Spain in A.D. 711. As John Henrik Clarke writes in his essay, "Time of Troubles," "the Gothic kingdom of Spain was laid low by Africans who had been converted to the Islamic faith, not by Arabs."[7]

In the seven centuries that followed, Islamic dynasties waxed and waned, primarily centered in Morocco, but extending as far south as Ghana. Dynastic conflicts weakened the North African Moors and, with the fall of Granada in 1492, they had lost all of Spain. The Moroccans, anticipating treasures of gold and silver, turned their attention to the Songhai kingdom of the Western Sahara, conquering Gao in 1591 and destroying the university city of Timbuktu in 1594. In the place of, and around, the Songhai empire, a number of kingdoms began to emerge in the area that is now Nigeria. These included state structures incorporating the Yoruba, Ibo, Borgu, and Nupe peoples.

The Slave Trade

Always at the forefront of the African scene of the seventeenth, eighteenth, and part of the nineteenth centuries was the tragic trade in slaves. Slaves were a part of ancient societies—usually captives from wars. As commerce and industry expanded, so did the need for disciplined labor. Slaves did most of the work in the empires of Greece and Rome. When these empires declined, the practice in Europe declined as well, but it continued in the Mediterranean area, where prisoner slaves were a recognized feature of the continuing conflicts between Muslims and Christians. North and East African Arabs also enslaved black Africans.

After the Crusaders discovered sugar, plantations were established on various Mediterranean islands, creating a need for intensive labor. At first slaves were brought from Russia and other European countries. Beginning in the fourteenth century, slaves bought or captured from Arabs replaced the Europeans. The opening of the plantations of the New World in the 1500s and the decimation of the Indian populations of the Caribbean created the demand for black slaves. At the same time, the Reformation removed the inhibition against violating the papal division of the world between the Portuguese and the Spanish. The British, the French, and the Dutch now felt free to explore and trade in the Americas.

From the fifteenth to the early nineteenth centuries, Europeans shipped an estimated 12 million black slaves from Africa to America. The majority of the slaves were brought to Brazil, Cuba, Jamaica, Haiti, and other sugar colonies. About 6 percent went to North America. One-third of the slaves came from Angola.

Traders obtained slaves in large measure directly from African rulers, who provided criminals, domestic slaves, victims of raids on neighboring peoples, or prisoners of war. Although some African rulers sought to end the practice, others, who became addicted to European goods "had no choice but to sell their fellow men to attain them."[8]

The Portuguese initiated the slave trade as they pioneered in trade in spices. They were quickly followed by other Europeans—until the trade was eventually ended in the early nineteenth century as a result of antislavery movements in Europe and North America. Three African colonies, Liberia, Sierra Leone, and Libreville (Gabon), were established by freed slaves. But the slave trade forever weakened major African political and social structures. Historic West African states of Benin, Dahomey, and Ashanti collapsed in the conflicts over slavery. The disintegration of these societies opened the way for European colonization.

Colonization proceeded in a pattern. A European nation would open a trading post, often by agreement with a local ruler. As the demands for slaves increased, the European traders advanced more and more inland. Ultimately the traders' demands for protection led to colonization by a European power. Ironically, efforts to stop slavery as well as slavery itself hastened the European intervention. Missionaries and antislavery elements came; they too demanded the help and protection and intervention of their governments.

Britain, under pressure from antislavery groups, encouraged new crops to replace slavery in the economy of the Gold Coast (Ghana), one of the principal centers of the trade. British developers of the new crops requested London's aid, and eventually the British government declared the coastal area a colony. To define this area and protect it from other Europeans, the British conquered the areas beyond Ashanti, naming it the Northern Territories. In the neighboring area that would later become Nigeria, Britain annexed Lagos in 1861, but it did not complete the conquest of the country until early in the twentieth century.

With Britain's conquest of Ghana, other European countries, fearing a British monopoly of trade, began to stake their claims. The French established themselves in Senegal in 1640 but did not expand until four centuries later. In 1885 it proclaimed a protectorate over Madagascar. In 1895, French colonies on the African continent were consolidated into French West Africa, consisting of Senegal, Soudan (Mali), Upper Volta (Burkina Faso), Guinea, Niger, the Ivory Coast, Dahomey, and Mauritania. It was not until 1910 that France completed its sub-Saharan African empire with the establishment of French Equatorial Africa, consisting of Chad, Congo Brazzaville, Gabon, and the Central African Republic. Togo and French Cameroon, former German colonies, were added after World War I.

King Leopold of Belgium, not wanting to be outdone but fearing opposition in Belgium to his plans, began the conquest of the Congo as a personal fiefdom in 1870. In 1885 he announced the consolidation of his rule and the establishment of the Congo Free State.

The Berlin African Conference

In 1884, to establish some order in the European race for African colonies, German Chancellor Otto von Bismarck called a conference of European nations, the Otto-man empire, and the United States in Berlin. The conference created rules that pre-vented further serious conflict among the European nations, although the arti-ficial boundaries created were to be the roots of trouble in later years. At the Berlin conference, Germany announced that it had established protectorates over Togo-land, Kameroon, South-West Africa (later Namibia), Rwanda, Burundi, and Tan-ganyika. Germany subsequently lost these colonies in the Treaty of Versailles in 1919. One half of Togoland became a British mandate and, ultimately, part of independent Ghana. The other, mandated to the French, became independent in 1960 as the Republic of Togo. The Ewe people who inhabited both countries were thus permanently divided. A portion of Kameroon (Cameroon) became a French mandate, South Africa became the League of Nations mandate power for South-West Africa (later Namibia), Belgium acquired Rwanda and Burundi, and the Brit-ish acquired northern Cameroon and Tanganyika.

In East Africa, the primary challengers to the Europeans were Arab sultans who had long had a monopoly over the region's trade, including slaves. The prin-cipal sultanate was in Zanzibar. The British, troubled by the role of Zanzibar in the slave trade, proclaimed a protectorate over the island in 1890.

Britain's interest in East Africa came about not only because of the slavery is-sues, but also because of its involvement in Egypt. Having established its influence in Egypt in 1882, extended to Sudan in 1899, London wished to protect the head-waters of the Nile. With that as the justification, the British signed a protectorate agreement with the ruler of Uganda in 1894. To gain access for a coastal outlet for a railroad to Uganda, Britain took over what subsequently became Kenya, known until 1920 as the East African Protectorate. With few other economic benefits from an unwanted colony, Britain encouraged white settlement in the attractive high-lands, making conflict with African tribes inevitable.

Italy, a latecomer to colonization, had long had an interest in Abyssinia (Ethio-pia). In 1873, they purchased from Ethiopia the Red Sea port of Assab. They later acquired the port of Massawa and, in a treaty with Ethiopia in 1889, were ceded the strip of coast that subsequently became Eritrea. Seeking further concessions from the emperor Memelik II, the Italians invaded Tigre province in 1896 and suffered a disastrous military defeat at Adowa. They retained Eritrea and Somalia, but it would be 1936 before they again attacked Ethiopia. This time they succeeded but made a world hero of Emperor Haile Selassi, whose impassioned pleas to the League of Nations caught world attention. The tangled Italian relations in the Horn of Africa, however, left unresolved boundary disputes and the seeds of irredentism that were to plague nations late into the twentieth century.

The End of the Ottoman Empire

As Europeans were expanding into Africa in the nineteenth century, one of the world's great empires, the Ottoman, was in decline. Morocco had resisted incorporation into the empire, but other North African states, in varying degrees, still acknowledged the authority of the sultan in Constantinople.

The Ottoman empire was authoritarian, byzantine, and loosely organized. It contained a variety of tribes and ethnic groups, of which the most prominent were Arab and Muslim. When it collapsed, France, Britain, and Italy were its principal heirs.

In 1878, Britain, concerned by a Russian threat to the Ottoman empire, expanded its imperial reach by leasing Cyprus from the Ottomans. This strategic island served as a valuable base for the British, but because of its Greek majority and Turkish minority it was to become a major headache for the Western powers in the next century.

France moved to dismantle the Sublime Porte's holdings in the Mediterranean when it seized Algeria in 1830. The coastal areas were settled by French and ultimately incorporated into metropolitan France. Tunisia, acknowledging only a religious tie to the sultan in his role as caliph, was in reality independent until unpaid debts provided a pretext for France to invade and establish a protectorate in 1881.

Although Napoleon briefly occupied Egypt in 1798, after his defeat Egypt returned to nominal Ottoman sovereignty. Debts incurred in the construction of the Suez Canal (1869) by Khedive Ismail again provided a pretext for European intervention. The British and French intervened and persuaded the khedive to appoint foreign advisors. Their presence in 1881 sparked an army revolt led by a colonel, Ahmad Bey Arabi, against foreign overlordship. In actions that seemed to presage events of a century later, when another Egyptian colonel opposed a foreign presence, Britain and France sent warships to Alexandria. The French subsequently withdrew, but the British carried out a bombardment that led to their occupation of Egypt.

Formally, Egypt remained part of the Ottoman empire, but Britain in effect established a "veiled protectorate."[9] The true power rested with the British agent and consul general. In 1904, Britain and France formalized their relationship in the Entente Cordiale: Britain had free rein in Egypt; France in Morocco. When Turkey sided with Germany in 1914, the British set aside the fiction of khedive sovereignty and established a protectorate.

As the British were establishing their control in Cairo, a threat to Egyptian influence arose in the south—in Sudan, where a fervent Muslim leader, the mahdi, was attacking Egyptian troops and seeking to detach Sudan from Egypt. In an effort to resolve the problem, General Charles Gordon, who had previously served the khedive in Khartoum, was sent to Sudan. But Sudanese and Islamic emotions were aroused; Gordon and his men were surrounded and killed by the mahdi's forces. To avenge Gordon's death, the British sent a force under General Sir Herbert Kitchener, who defeated the mahdi at the battle of Omdurman in 1899. Britain gained control not only of Egypt but of Sudan as well.

In 1911, in a war with Turkey, Italy gained a foothold in Libya. Overcoming a prolonged resistance from the Senussi brotherhood, an Islamic religious order, and its allies, Italy gained control of Tripolitania and Cyrenaica. In 1934 the two provinces were combined with the Fezzan in the south and proclaimed an Italian colony. After the settlement of some 40,000 colonists, Italy in 1939 declared Libya to be a part of Italy.

The Near East

Some uncertainty has always existed about what to call the crescent of countries that lie at the east end of the Mediterranean Sea. Near East, or Middle East, or Proche Orient have, to the peoples of the region, seemed Europe-oriented. West Asia, however, has never caught on. For our purposes, we will use the designation of the Department of State, the Near East.

In this region colonies did not exist, but imperial influence was exerted through protectorates and mandates. This situation was to lead to serious conflicts in the period of decolonization. What was said by a Malaysian leader could apply equally to the British and French presences in the Near East:

> Alan Lennox-Boyd, Colonial Secretary when Malaya became independent, recalled a conversation with Tunku Abdul Rahman, Malaya's first Prime Minister:
> I said, "You weren't a colony. Your brother the sultan of Kedah was an independent ruler in a treaty relationship with us." The Tunku answered, "That didn't stop you from treating us like a colony."[10]

Ottoman rule was maintained in Syria, Lebanon, Palestine, and Iraq until World War I. After the defeat of the Turks, League of Nations mandates with authority to govern and prepare territories for independence were created and in 1922 awarded to France for Syria and Lebanon and to Britain for Palestine and Iraq. A secret agreement, the Sykes-Picot agreement, between France and Britain divided the eastern Mediterranean between them. The British created a new entity, Transjordan, to provide a realm for Abdullah, one of the sons of Hussein, the former

Sherif of Mecca, who had been defeated by Saudi Arabia, thus establishing the Hashemite dynasty.

Iraq, Transjordan, and Palestine were made British mandates. In Egypt, the British presence was based on British rights in the Suez Canal. By its mandate in Palestine, Britain also inherited the problem of Zionist claims to ancient Israel, a problem that was to bedevil Western diplomacy for many decades afterwards.

The mandates were colonies with the fiction of independence. Britain arranged for members of the Hashemite family, descendants of the Sherif of Mecca, to become kings over both Iraq and Transjordan, but in effect London controlled the destinies of these territories. Only Saudi Arabia and Yemen, through the astute protectiveness of their royal families, escaped the imperial yoke.

The principalities of the Persian Gulf represented still another form of empire. Created out of nineteenth-century "truces" designed to control piracy, they became important to the British as steppingstones to India. They were ostensibly ruled by emirs chosen out of traditional tribes, but the British Resident in Bahrain was the true power in the region. That power became vital to Britain when vast oil resources were discovered in the region.

The British jealously guarded their rights and access to the rulers. The region, as they saw it, was vital to the security of their empire, to their access to oil, and as markets for arms and other manufactured goods.

At the opposite, southwest, corner of the Arabian Peninsula lay Aden and its significant harbor. For centuries, the Sultan of Aden had thrived on taxing cargoes to and from India; Marco Polo wrote of the wealth of Aden in 1276. In January 1839, the British, feeling the need for a port to provide its navy with coal en route to India and concerned about French designs on the Red Sea, bombarded and seized the town and port after unsuccessfully trying to negotiate with the sultan. More than a century later, in 1959, worried by threats from Yemen to the north, the British extended their influence through the organization of the small hinterland principalities into the Federation of Arab Emirates of the South.

Iran

Given the preoccupation with access to India that led the British into the Gulf and the Arabian Peninsula, London could not ignore Iran—or, as many British still call it, Persia. Further, Iran lay on the border of another potential rival for regional supremacy, Russia. As Russia's influence spread south in the late nineteenth century, Britain extended its influence in Tehran through generous assistance to the Iranian throne.

In the early nineteenth century, Persia fought two wars with Russia, resulting in the Treaty of Turkmanchai of 1828. The latter is considered by Iranians to be one of the most humiliating documents ever signed by an Iranian government, for it established the precedent of capitulatory (or extra-territorial) rights for foreigners in the country. Feelings about this were to be echoed a century later when Iranians objected to granting immunity to U.S. military advisors in the country.

Faced with the threat from Germany, the two imperial rivals Britain and Russia signed a treaty in 1907 that effectively divided Iran into two spheres of influence: the Persian government was informed but not consulted. Thereafter, until the Bolshevik revolution, London and Moscow manipulated the internal affairs of Persia, ensuring that the composition of the Persian Majlis (parliament) would not threaten their interests.

The importance of Iran for Britain grew substantially before World War I, when the Royal Navy switched from coal to oil and when, in May, 1908, oil was discovered there. The Anglo-Persian (later Anglo-Iranian) Oil Company was founded with British government participation. Although London's effort to negotiate a treaty with Tehran failed, the British nevertheless continued to exercise significant influence.

In 1921, dissatisfied with the ruling regime, they were instrumental in placing Reza Shah Pahlavi on the throne. Far from being a puppet, however, Reza Shah confronted both the power of the *ulema,* or religious leaders, and of the Anglo-Iranian Oil Company. When, in 1941, however, he declared Iran neutral in the war with Germany, the British reacted again and arranged that he be replaced by his son, Mohammed Reza Shah. In 1952, a popular nationalist leader, Mohammed Mussadeq, nationalized the Anglo-Iranian Oil Company, and when the Shah was unwilling to dismiss Mussadeq the British acted again, this time with the help of the U.S. CIA. Mussadeq was overthrown and a new prime minister, General Ardeshir Zahedi, was installed. After a brief exile, the Shah returned to remain in power until another revolution erupted in 1979 that the British and Americans were unable to stop. There is some basis for the Iranian belief articulated by Abol Hassan Bani Sadr, briefly president after the 1979 revolution:

> A great number of Iranians blamed the British all the time. If it rained it was because the British wanted it; if that character was Prime Minister, it was because the British put him there. In towns across Iran, if something happened, even a crime, it was thought the intrigues of the British were always behind it.[11]

Imperial Claims in Asia

To the east, in Asia, two other nations—China and Japan—helped shape the attitudes of future Third World nations.

If the Iranians, for historical reasons, have cause to be suspicious of the actions of Western powers, so does another major Asian nation, China. Although only two colonies were formally established on Chinese territory, Hong Kong and Macao, the Chinese have experienced the power and devastation of imperialism in many ways. They, too, though never fully a part of an imperial empire, associate themselves with the sentiments of the former colonies and they played a prominent part in the Bandung conference of newly independent states in 1955.

When, in 1839, China objected to the illegal importation of opium by the British and raided a British warehouse in Canton, the British went to war. The First

Opium War (1839–1842) resulted in the Treaty of the Bogue. Britain acquired Hong Kong, the use of five other Chinese ports for British trade and residence, and the right of Britons to be tried in local British courts. Other Western powers, with the British rights as precedents, also obtained the same privileges. In the 1858 Treaty of Tientsin, the French obtained residence in Peking for foreign diplomats, the opening of eleven new ports, the right of foreign travel in the interior, and freedom of movement for foreign missionaries. When the Chinese refused to sign, allied troops resumed hostilities, burned the Summer Palace, and captured Peking. The Chinese capitulated and signed the Peking Conventions with Britain and France.

Seizing on the pretext of a Chinese insult to the British flag, Britain went to war a second time in 1856. After the Second Opium War (1856–1861), China was forced to cede Kowloon, across the bay from Hong Kong. Three decades later, in 1898, Britain pressured China to lease the adjacent New Territories (later part of Hong Kong colony) for 99 years.

Two years later, in 1900, in what became known as the Boxer Rebellion, a Chinese militia, the Boxers, with support from factions in the imperial court, began an anti-foreign crusade. The murder of the German minister, Baron von Ketteler, and a siege of legations in Peking led to the intervention of foreign troops, including Americans. The Boxer Protocol signed September 7, 1901, by China and twelve powers demanded indemnity, the fortification of the legation quarter, the razing of forts, and the establishment of foreign garrisons on the road to Peking.

The application of extra-territoriality (permitting foreign citizens to operate under their own laws) was a particularly galling form of imperial presence, applied not only in China but in many other areas of the world where the imperial powers had important trade interests.[12]

Alerted to the threat of European colonialism by the First Opium War in 1839, the Japanese restricted European access to their country. They were able to maintain some immunity from the Europeans because the imperial powers were preoccupied with China, the Indian Mutiny, the Crimean War, and the French bid for influence in Morocco.

Japan began its own colonization program in 1874 with the incorporation of nearby islands—Ryukyu, Kuril, Bonin, and Hokkaido. A naval victory over China in 1895 paved the way for the Japanese conquest of Korea, South Manchuria, Formosa (Taiwan), and the Pescadores. Russian efforts to block Japanese expansion were thwarted in the Russo-Japanese War (1904–1905). In 1915, Japan secretly presented China with a list of twenty-one demands. These included giving Japan rights in Shantung formerly held by the Germans, extending leases in southern Manchuria and giving Japan commercial freedom there, providing rights to key mining areas, and agreeing that no part of China's coast would be leased or ceded to any other power.[13] In 1918, Japan was rewarded for declaring war on Germany by receiving the German ports in Shantung province and a mandate over the German North Pacific Islands.

The widest expansion of Japan's empire, subsequently proclaimed "The Greater East Asia Co-Prosperity Sphere" began with the invasion of Manchuria in 1932, the capture of Nanking in 1937, and the successive conquests of Indochina, Malaya, Singapore, the Dutch East Indies, and the Philippines in World War II.

Although of relatively short duration, the Japanese empire left a profound mark in the region—a mark that was to stimulate the march to independence of Asian nations and to complicate later U.S. efforts to involve Japan in Asian security arrangements.

The impact was particularly strong in Korea. Japan's "paramount interest" in Korea had been recognized in the Treaty of Portsmouth (1905) that ended the Russo-Japanese War. The Japanese reacted strongly to Korean efforts to resist Tokyo's hegemony. The emperor was forced to abdicate, Korea's army was abolished, the Korean language was outlawed, and Korean officials were replaced with Japanese officials. In 1910, Japan formally annexed the country, renaming it Chosen.

The United States

Just as Japan asserted itself as a rising power, so also the once colonial United States shifted over the nineteenth century from a weak nation at the mercy of Algerian pirates and the European impressment of its sailors to an assertive power in its own right. The nineteenth century saw interventions in Canada and Mexico, the latter ultimately leading to the Mexican War of 1848 by which the U.S. acquired most of the west and southwest.

Although the Monroe Doctrine of 1823 accepted existing European colonies in the Western hemisphere, it asserted that "the American continents, by the free and independent condition which they have assumed and maintain are not to be considered as subjects for future colonization by any European powers."[14] By the end of the century the concept of "manifest destiny" that had applied to expansion in the North American continent was being applied to the Caribbean and the Pacific. Hawaii was annexed in 1898. In that same year a further impulse toward imperialism was fed by a revolt against the Spanish rule in Cuba and the blowing up in Havana harbor of the U.S. battleship *Maine*. Admiral George Dewey's defeat of the Spanish fleet in Manila Bay led to the occupation of the Philippines. Following the war with Spain that ensued, the United States became an imperial power. Cuba was declared independent and Puerto Rico placed under U.S. sovereignty. After a congressional debate spurred by an anti-imperialist minority, the United States agreed to purchase the Philippines from Spain for $2 million. The island archipelago became a U.S. colony.

Under President Theodore Roosevelt, the imperial thrust was exercised again and again. In 1903, he engineered the coup that separated Panama from Columbia in anticipation of the building of the Panama Canal. In 1904, he declared a "Roosevelt Corollary" to the Monroe Doctrine: "Chronic wrongdoing or an impotence which results in a general loosening of the ties of civilized society . . . may force the United States, however reluctantly, in flagrant cases of such wrongdoing or impotence, to the exercise of an international police power."[15] On the basis of this corollary, the United States intervened over the next decade in the Dominican

Republic, Haiti, Honduras, and Nicaragua. In one final flourish of power, Roosevelt sent the U.S. Navy—"The Great White Fleet"—around the world in 1908–1909. The United States had become an imperial nation; at the same time the stage was set for a series of issues in the American hemisphere and the Pacific that were to pre-occupy future generations.

Such were the circumstances behind the multicolored maps that gave several generations of schoolchildren the impression that the world was owned by a few great powers.

TWO

The Nature of Imperialism

What were the conditions of this imperial age? Are the claims of repression and exploitation that sparked independence movements justified? Or was it a period of national and societal development that might not otherwise have occurred? As in many a human story, the picture was mixed.

In both Europe and America, the brutality of conquest (to the extent it was known) was tolerated side by side with humanitarian concerns for the victims. Admittedly, facts were not always easy to determine. Colonial administrations tended to discourage outside observers, and stories that did reach other capitals were at times colored by the advocates of independence. For example, reports of the Black Hole of Calcutta, in which 146 British men, women, and children allegedly died of heat and suffocation in the locked cell of an Indian prison were later determined to have been exaggerated. In *End of Empire*, Brian Lapping notes: "Later some of those named as dead were found to be alive, casting doubt on the whole story."[1]

The nations that emerged into the Third World of the twentieth century varied widely in size, resources, history, and forms of colonial rule. Each colonial power applied its own style of rule to the territories. These different styles were to be reflected later in the character, stability, and outlook of the independent nations that emerged.

The legacy of imperialism was not all negative. Infrastructures were created and improved. Education and literacy increased in many colonies. The introduction of world languages such as English, French, and Spanish provided communication with the rest of the world. Modern governmental procedures were introduced. And there are still those in the post-independence period who will insist that life was better for all under colonialism. Within each imperial country, political differences existed not only over colonial policy but even over whether colonies should be acquired. Nevertheless, the enduring impression of imperial rule, particularly among the political elites of the Third World, is negative.

To the peasant benefiting from good crops and good prices, the colonial presence was benign. But that same peasant who believed his work was being exploited for the benefit of a distant government or corporation, or who was dispossessed from land, became an enemy of the imperial power and ripe for pro-independence exploitation. A young, educated person deprived of employment or jealous of the perquisites of the colonial masters was even more ripe for anti-imperial manifestations. It was from the dissatisfied educated elite, often in exile, that the later leadership of independence movements was to emerge.[2] (See Appendix: Backgrounds of Liberation Leaders.)

Maintaining Control

The objectives of imperial rule varied from the exploitation of resources to national prestige to markets to settlement. But whatever the colonial motive, the imperial power sought to maintain unchallenged control.

Virtually supreme authority was often delegated to viceroys and governors, especially in earlier years when distance and poor communications made such delegation inescapable. In Spanish Manila, for example, "the governor general was so powerful that he was often likened to an independent monarch. He dominated the Audiencia, or high court, was captain general of the armed forces, and enjoyed the privilege of engaging in commerce for private profit."[3]

The authority of a colonial governor at times enabled such an entity to conceal from the home government the true conditions of the colony. In the mid-nineteenth century, the novel *Max Havelaar* by Eduard Douwes Dekker, a former district officer in the Dutch East Indies, shocked the Netherlands into a realization of the reality of their prized overseas possession. Dekker, under the pseudonym Multatuli, writes:

> The Government of the Dutch East Indies likes to write and tell its masters in the Motherland that everything is going well. The Residents like to report that to the Government. The Assistant Residents, who, in their turn, receive hardly anything but favorable reports from their Controleurs, also prefer not to send any disagreeable news to the Residents. All this gives birth to an artificial optimism in the official and written treatment of affairs, in contradiction not only to the truth but also to the personal opinion expressed by the optimists themselves when discussing those affairs orally, and—stranger still!—in contradiction to the facts in their own written statements.[4]

Colonial authorities had the discretion to decide between direct rule or indirect rule through local potentates. At the beginning, arrangements for trade and facilities were frequently made through treaties with local rulers. In many cases, these arrangements continued for many years; in others, the colonial power became impatient with the restrictions of such treaties, abruptly abrogated them, and assumed full power.

In India during British times, a portion of the subcontinent was under the rule of princes who had made treaty agreements with the government of India; the remainder of the territory was directly under the viceroy. It was the disposition of one of these princely states, Kashmir, that led to sour relations between Pakistan and India in the twentieth century.

In Indonesia, the Dutch gave prominence to traditional sultans, especially on Java, but such rulers were little more than surrogates of the Dutch Resident. They exercised petty power, often at the expense of the people of their region.

In Morocco and Tunisia, the French established protectorates with local rulers in place. Paris was not averse to exiling those rulers who showed streaks of independence. The banishment of Mohammed V of Morocco to Madagascar in 1953 demonstrated the limits of French tolerance. Habib Bourguiba, a young independence advocate in Tunisia, spent many years in prison.

In sub-Saharan Africa, the French built an empire on education, a professional civil service, a military presence, close financial ties, and the creation of a French-speaking elite. The capacity to speak French was a greater key to prestige than race. Two Africans, Felix Houphouet-Boigny of the Ivory Coast and Leopold Senghor of Senegal, were active in French politics. Houphouet-Boigny became a minister in a French cabinet. Senghor, a poet and writer, was recognized in the academies of Paris.

One American observer of the African scene comments on another aspect of the French presence in the continent:

> One unique dimension of the French presence in Africa was the role played by the *petit commercant* who has no British counterpart. Whereas British settlers made major commitments to grand enterprise in East Africa (and of course) Rhodesia, the small-scale French businessmen/traders/technicians/teachers settled in francophone Africa in much greater numbers, sent their children to local French-language schools at least through lycee, and made significant contributions to *la francophonie* which still continue. There are many more French today [1999] in Cote d'Ivoire, for example, than there were during any part of the colonial era. A continuing "British presence" in anglophone Africa is harder to define and certainly much more transient.[5]

The openness of French universities to Africans helped create the elite that subsequently preserved French ties in the period of independence. An ambassador from the Malagasy Republic in Washington had had two uncles killed by the French in a massacre in 1947. Once I asked: "You obviously are bitter toward the French for what happened to your family, yet every time you have a few free days, you go to Paris. How do you explain that?"

"You see," he replied, "I hate the French, but I love France. The French were wise. Any student in Madagascar who could qualify could enter a university in France. When I was a student in the early 1950s, there were five thousand African students in France. I went to visit a friend in Cambridge, England. There were twenty African students in Cambridge, all sons of chiefs."

The French were aided in the creation of the elite by their approach of "assimilation." French colonists could be as arrogant as any others—but more often their arrogance was cultural rather than racial. The French were, more than the British, prepared to accept fully educated Africans as equals and bring them into their political process.

An African from a British colony once said to me, after he had attended his first all-African conference, that he found the French Africans difficult to talk to, even if they spoke a common language. "We were trained as administrators," he said, "they were trained as poets. There is a big difference."

Educational policy was important to the character of a colony and to its future. Each country followed a different policy. The Dutch, Belgian, and Portuguese did the least to create a cadre of educated indigenous people. All imperial powers faced the dilemma that even the minimum of education for literacy risked spurring demands for change by opening the eyes of people to their political circumstances. Those demands grew when local peoples were educated abroad, met other colonial peoples, and saw the possibilities of demands for independence. Although many from British colonies were educated in the United Kingdom, the British emphasized the creation of educational institutions in the colonies. They anticipated ultimate independence, although on timetables more extended than the independence leaders demanded.

The British emphasized administration—the maintenance of law and order. For over forty years, one man, Ralph Funze, chose civil officers for the empire. He looked for stable, unimaginative types that would not "rock the boat." I once spoke with a retired British colonial officer who had served in Ghana as a commissioner in the home district of Kwame Nkrumah, who became the fiery leader of Ghana's independence movement. I asked if he had known Nkrumah. His answer: "I recall him only as a disturber of the peace."

The British contributions were remarkable in the development of national infrastructures and in the creation of stability over vast regions of the world. English was established as the lingua franca of a major portion of the globe. At the same time, the empire left behind recollections of discrimination, patronizing attitudes, and exploitation that are still reflected in its former colonies.

The empire was not egalitarian, either for the British or for the indigenous peoples. Rigid class distinctions from Britain carried over into the colonies; those who came out as government officials were clearly different in status from those who came out to build and run the railroads. The British accepted and recognized the local distinctions in class, although not even Brahmins in India were admitted to British clubs. And those of mixed blood occupied a sad middle status: they had pretenses to British identity, but they were not fully accepted by either the British or the local elites.

In many ways India captured Britain as much as the British captured India. Pomp and ceremony adapted from the Moghuls was part of the pageant of British India and of the princely states. The empire was built and sustained by elaborate demonstrations of its inherent power. No one who has witnessed a parade in New Delhi during the days of the British "Raj," with the ostentatious passage of decorated elephants, elaborately uniformed horsemen, and striding pipers, could fail to be impressed with this show of power.

A minor manifestation could be seen in the rigid colonial protocol which extended into the post-colonial period. In 1948, my wife and I were guests of the last British governor of the North-West Frontier Province (a province of Pakistan), Sir Ambrose Dundas. He had been retained, after independence, by the new government of Pakistan. In strict order of precedence, we assembled with the other guests in a circle at the foot of the staircase of the mansion, awaiting "His Excellency and his lady." The governor and his wife slowly descended the staircase and went around the circle, greeting each guest, after which we went in to dinner. In 1970, ten years after Nigerian independence, the United States ambassador, John Reinhardt, and I attended a dinner at the mansion of the Nigerian governor of Rivers State; we were treated to exactly the same protocol: the circle, the staircase, the formal greetings.

These demonstrations also represented another side of imperial rule: a patronizing air toward the "natives," the idea that, in the absence of other benefits, "circuses" will satisfy them. But the "natives" who joined the British officers in the parades could not be invited to the British clubs and were rarely invited to British homes.

Racial discrimination was an inevitable part of colonial rule and of the inescapable clash of cultures. Although the Portuguese and the French did more to create local elites and to tolerate the mixing of races, the sense of superiority of the conquering race was never far from the surface. It was natural that colonial officials and their families, benefiting from their privileged positions, would look down on the indigenous peoples. It was equally natural that such attitudes would breed deep and lasting resentment among proud Asian and African peoples. Such discrimination increased with white settlement in the colonies and as wives of officials joined their husbands.

Culture and Religion

Perhaps the most unsettling aspect of colonialism was cultural. If Europeans did not ban or discourage the cultural practices of the indigenous peoples, by example they made their way of life a model to imitate. The result throughout the imperial world has been, for many, a crisis of identity. With pretenses to becoming European, indigenous people turned their backs on ancient rites and religions, causing rifts in families and personal dilemmas and crises. As a Filipino once said to me, "I do not know who I am. I was four hundred years in a monastery [under the Spanish] and fifty years in Hollywood [under the Americans]."

If a cultural clash existed, so did a religious one. Throughout this story of empires, colonies, and, ultimately, independent states runs the theme of Islam. This religion which burst out of the Arabian Peninsula in the seventh century had, by the time of the European colonists, occupied a corner of Europe in Spain and spread to most corners of Asia and Africa. The first European explorers, the

Crusaders, sought to defeat it and eliminate it. Later explorers encountered it as a strong and binding force to be reckoned with in most of the countries that became parts of European empires.

Christianity sailed with the European conquerors. The papal grants to Portugal's Prince Henry in 1454 and 1456 gave Henry the lands and the power over the missionary bishops therein. Jesuit Francis Xavier reached Goa in 1542. He built a college there to train priests and established Christian communities throughout India. Another Jesuit, Matteo Ricci, reached China in 1582. In India, Jesuits were welcomed to the court during the reign of the Moghul emperor, Akhbar. In 1663, the Foreign Missionary Society of Paris was directed to reach out to non-Christian peoples in Vietnam, Cambodia, Laos, and Thailand.

The proclamation of Queen Victoria accepting the responsibility for governing India upon the dissolution of the East India Company in 1873 began: "Firmly relying ourselves on the truth of Christianity, and acknowledging with gratitude the solace of religion, We disclaim alike the right and the desire to impose Our convictions on any of Our subjects."[6] Stephen Neill, author of *A History of Christian Missions,* goes on to explain that "this proclamation was intended to restore the confidence of Hindus and Muslims; but it was also a charter of liberty for Christians—they were henceforth to be free from the hostile prejudices and discrimination of which they had been the objects under the Company's regime."[7]

Protestant missionaries were less a formal adjunct to colonialism than Catholicism, but they saw opportunities to propagate the faith as colonies were founded. The expansion of Protestants to North America with the colonists is part of American history. The Dutch East India Company trained ministers to both serve their employees overseas and to proselytize the natives. The German Lutheran Pietists in the seventeenth and early eighteenth centuries sent missionaries to South India, Greenland, and South Africa. Other Protestant missionary societies were organized in England, Scotland, and the Netherlands in the late seventeenth century.

In areas where the British and French were in competition, the rivalry extended to the Protestants and Catholics native to each colonial power. Neill writes:

> The country later known as the *Uganda Protectorate* was divided up among Protestant and Roman Catholic chieftains as the best way of keeping the peace between them. Msgr. Hirth, the French bishop[,] had not secured the predominance of French influence in the country, nor had he been able seriously to weaken the Anglican mission. . . . The French missionaries were not too pleased when the Mill Hill Fathers were sent in to divide the work of the White Fathers; once more European rivalries came from across the seas to perplex the minds of simple African Christians.[8]

Missionary efforts in sub-Saharan Africa gained world attention when explorer Henry M. Stanley went in search of the Scottish missionary David Livingston, who was ultimately found in Tanzania in 1871. Protestant missionaries were working in most of West and Central Africa in the nineteenth century. According to the *Encyclopedia Britannica,* by 1980 more than half of the population of sub-Saharan Africa were Christians, many of them in indigenous non-white churches.[9]

Although Christian proselytizing in Islamic countries often produced meager results, the missionary impact was nevertheless felt in education, medicine, and humanitarian services. In the Federation of Rhodesia and Nyasaland in Africa in 1960, it was estimated that 90 percent of children were being educated in missionary schools. In the former Ottoman territories, U.S. missionaries founded significant colleges: the American University of Beirut, the American University of Cairo, and Robert College in Turkey. Many independence movement leaders were educated in missionary schools.

The missionary identification with colonial administrations varied. Some missionaries worked with colonial administrators as translators and advisers. One served as an interpreter for Cecil Rhodes in his negotiations with the king of the Matabele. In the Kenyan Legislative Council a missionary was appointed to represent Africans. Missionaries of three denominations testified against Jomo Kenyatta in his trial in Kenya and were brought in to lecture to Mau Mau detainees on "conduct." In addition, both Catholic and Protestant missionaries frequently interceded with officials on behalf of the treatment of native peoples. The descriptions of conditions they sent home were often the only challenges to official views and undoubtedly contributed to a growing opposition to colonial rule in the metropoles.

Missionary movements also played an active role in efforts to stop the slave trade. Owing to the pressures of both Protestant and Catholic antislavery forces, the invitation to the 1884 Berlin conference on colonial questions expressly drew attention to the responsibility of the powers to "encourage missions and other enterprises which are likely to be of service in spreading useful knowledge."[10] All the powers undertook to suppress slavery and in particular to take steps for the extermination of the traffic in slaves.

Understandably, the efforts of missionaries to stop some of the native practices they considered particularly abhorrent were resented by local populations, whether they were efforts against suttee (widow sacrifice) in India or female circumcision in Africa. Nigerian writer Chinua Achebe's novel *Things Fall Apart* tells of a clan's wrath against a white missionary who objected to the exiling of twins and the mutilation of dead children.[11]

One African view of the missionary movement is contained in an essay by Professor Stanlake Samkange on "Wars of Resistance" in the *Horizon History of Africa*:

> The journeys [of travelers and explorers] had another merit to Europeans. They portrayed Africa as virgin land for the planting of Christianity. . . . So, European missionaries went to Africa to preach the gospel. They wore out soles to save souls and found themselves not only agents of life through death but of peace through war, accord through discord, education through Westernization, civilization through dehumanization, construction through destruction. Europeans were soon persuaded that only by waging ruthless wars of conquest or pacification (as

such wars are euphemistically called) could peace reign in Africa. Only through discord—inherent in the injection of Christianity and rejection of African ideas of god—could accord be achieved. Only through keeping Africans ignorant of the good in their culture and of the greatness in their history by teaching them Western values and the superiority of Europeans could they be educated. . . . Only through the total destruction of African ideas, values, and mores could a new Africa be built.[12]

Although colonial rule in many areas brought the benefits of education and literacy, it was often modeled on the system of the mother country. Indians learned about the history of the British kings rather than of their own pasts. The French, in particular, discouraged any education in local languages. The French government accepted the U.S. Peace Corps into Francophone Africa but officially protested when volunteers began to teach in local vernaculars.

India was, of course, the crown jewel of the empire. Here the British demonstrated a pragmatic approach, dealing with absolute and often ruthless potentates in the Indian states while establishing a measure of benign rule in the rest of the country. In the two centuries of British rule in India, they built roads and railroads and gave the vast country communications and stability. They established a highly professional cadre of administrators in the Indian Civil Service (ICS) and a modern, independent judicial system.

Indians will still recall favorably many of the district commissioners. A Pakistani, a former ICS officer, remarked once to me, "The British began to lose India when they replaced the British district commissioners with Indians. It was, of course, a necessary step, but it meant that there was no longer a recognizable British presence in their midst."

The Best and the Worst

Imperialism brought out the best and the worst in people. Many colonial administrators labored diligently for the benefit of the local population. Missionaries sacrificed to build hospitals, improve agriculture, and educate. But the conscientious administrator and missionary often labored side by side with petty officials and local rulers who, emboldened by a sense of power over "the natives," were autocratic, arrogant, and, at times, sadistic.

The writer of *Max Havelaar* describes the particular license given to local chiefs (or regents) by the Dutch authorities:

> Most attribute this unofficial protection of the Chiefs to the ignoble calculation that the latter, who have to display pomp and circumstance in order to exercise over the population that influence which the Government needs in order to uphold *its* authority, would require a higher remuneration than they receive now if they were not left at liberty to supplement it by unlawful use of the property and labor of the people.[13]

The Nizam of Hyderabad, the wealthiest of the Indian rulers, reportedly demanded that his subjects bring gold objects to audiences with him; the purity of the gold was tested before the audience was granted. One story I heard in India when I was there in 1940 recounted that on one occasion the nizam who personally oversaw the counting of jewels and money coming to his treasury was busy when a shipment of rupee notes arrived. He had the trucks locked in a garage until such time as he could oversee the accounting of the cash; before he could do so, white ants had eaten the entire contents.[14]

If corruption and favoritism became common in the post-colonial states, the roots of such practices were planted during imperial rule. Oppressed and restricted by foreign authority—or by those acting for such authority—colonial subjects often tried to challenge or "beat" the system by smuggling, informal barter, and bribes. Such arrangements were lucrative; profits were shared with members of a family or tribe. It was expected that those in authority or favored positions would share their benefits with their own circle.

If problems later arose between a majority population and a minority in post-colonial states, the reason lay in part in colonial exploitation of existing ethnic and religious differences. To enhance support for the colonial regime, authorities in many instances favored a minority group, providing them with the perquisites of trade or military careers, often because of the particular talents or interests of the group. Such favoritism inevitably created resentment within the majority. The Chinese in the Dutch East Indies were given favored positions in commerce. Indians brought into East Africa to work on the railroads stayed to monopolize much of the local trade. Families favored by the Spanish in the Philippines continued to play significant roles in politics and commerce into the American period and after. I recall realizing, as I prepared to assume the U.S. ambassadorship in Manila, that the United States was ruling through the same family structure used by the Spanish; only the United States gave the structure a democratic facade.

In each of the colonies, the British created military and police establishments. At its height, the British empire embraced one-quarter of the world's population and area. Considering the extent of the territory, their military presence was remarkably small. The numbers of British troops (not counting the air force and the navy) in India never exceeded 77,000, the total in 1903.[15] The Indian army, with its British officers and Indian ranks, became vital to Britain in two world wars. In the formation of military organizations, the British tended to favor certain ethnic or religious groups likely to be loyal to the Crown. The Gurkhas of Nepal became mainstays of British colonial forces throughout the Asian colonies. The Sikhs were favored in India. These divisions continued into independence.

A former British colonial official once explained to me why colonial authorities appeared to "divide and rule" by playing favorites among tribes. Colonial development, he explained, began at the local level. District officers tended to seek favors for their peoples, not realizing that in the eyes of others they were seeking favors for a particular tribe. The degree of animosity among tribes was hidden or controlled during the colonial period; the violent conflicts among tribes that caught the world's attention after independence were not new. He acknowledged that at times, authorities did "play one off against another," but insisted this was not policy. He had served in Uganda where, after independence, the assertion of the Acholi tribe brought the brutal Idi Amin to power.[16]

The establishment and maintenance of imperial control had a darker side. Empires were not democratic. Rule was by administrative decree, a practice continued in many post-colonial independent countries. Research into the imperial age contradicts any view of a benign era of peace and stability. In nearly every colonial territory, resistance in some form continued from the day of conquest. Colonial policy and the lack of today's invasive communications hid from the world acts of brutality and violence. The often brutal use of force accompanied the conquest of territories and the suppression of threats to imperial rule. Examples exist in the history of every colonial power and are still recalled by peoples of the former colonies today. Admittedly, the brutality of the colonial masters was often no worse than that indigenous peoples inflicted upon each other in their own continuing conflicts, but such acts by the foreign invader created deep resentments against the colonial powers and their allies that have not totally disappeared in these regions today.

For example, In India, in 1857, a portion of the Indian troops in the British army rebelled. An estimated 800 men, women, and children, including Indians, died in a siege of the British Residency in Lucknow. In retaliation:

> The British shot and slashed their way back into full control and wrought a bloodthirsty vengeance on the mutineers, both proved and suspected. . . . Nobody knows how many Indians were hanged, run through, shot or disembowelled, how many villages were burned, how many temples desecrated, or how much was looted from innocent Indians.[17]

In 1919, Brigadier Reginald Dyer, in response to mob action in which three British were killed, led a force that massacred 379 unarmed Indians in Amritsar. In Madagascar in 1940, the French suppressed a rebellion at the cost of 11,000 Malagasy lives. The British and Dutch conquests of southern Africa were at the cost of numerous wars that eliminated African kingdoms and slaughtered thousands of their subjects.

In the East Indies, the Dutch used force not only to suppress revolt, but also to compel agricultural production. When inhabitants of Greater Banda Island resisted Dutch efforts to increase spice production in 1621, the governor, Jan Picterazoon Coen, ordered the massacre of 2,500 and the banishment of 800 more. To increase the monopoly of cloves in Amboina, he ordered the destruction of 65,000 clove trees in the Moluccas.

In 1899, Philippine casualties were heavy when the United States suppressed the revolt of Emilio Aguinaldo against American rule in that country. When forty-eight Americans were killed by rebels on the island of Samar in 1899, the U.S. Army officer in command ordered a village to be leveled and all men of "military age" (over ten years) killed.

Whatever the degree of suppression in the imperial world, subject peoples were never totally conquered. In nearly every colony, revolt against authority rose periodically. Finally, by the mid-twentieth century, the task of maintaining the imperial hold became too burdensome and the age of independence dawned.

Part 2

INDEPENDENCE

When these events occurred [The Dutch surrender to the Japanese],
I was a girl of eighteen years. I had been entirely Dutch educated
and knew very little about my own culture or the political structure
of the country, and on January 12, 1942, I wrote in my diary:

> Will the time ever come that I can proudly say: these are our
> soldiers, our king and our country?

Later, on March 9, the day after the capitulation and after Mr.
Dachlan Abdulah had been appointed Mayor of Batavia, I wrote
again in my diary:

> Should I not be happy with a totally Indonesian government,
> or do I not care at all, because I can't see it happen? Have I
> grown up to be so Dutch? Do I not have any ideals about a
> Free Indonesia? But can it ever happen with such a
> heterogeneous population? But it must happen! But when???

—From *Reminiscences of the Past,* by Mien Soedarpo[1]

THREE

Independence

In March 1960, a group from the U.S. National War College visited Luanda in then Portuguese Angola. During a briefing for the group a Portuguese official stated with confidence, "We have been here for 500 years and, by God's grace, we will be here another 500." He was wrong. When the Portuguese briefer in Luanda spoke, the process of decolonization was already advanced in Asia and beginning in Africa. In fifteen years, Angola would be independent.

This book seeks to retell briefly the story of this global transition for the recollection of those who lived through it and the enlightenment of generations for whom the story is but part of history. The story, on a broad canvas, is one of variety, both in time and in the individual national experiences, and yet common patterns of resistance and hope are woven through the fabric.

No brief historical telling can possibly fully portray the ins and outs of what were often complex and tedious negotiations between imperial powers and nationalists, extending over months if not years. The ultimate resolution often involved military actions, threats of conflict, domestic politics in Europe, and pressures from abroad, particularly from the United States.

Proceeding regionally and largely chronologically from the developments in Indonesia and India to the Middle East and Africa, the stories will be brought to the point of independence. The emphasis will be on Asia and Africa. In Latin America, except for the Guyanas, Belize, and islands in the Caribbean, independence came in the nineteenth century. Nevertheless, the nations of Latin America, still feeling the weight of the colossus to the North, share many of the post-imperial attitudes of nations in the eastern hemisphere.

What Is Independence?

In any discussion of independence, it is reasonable to ask, "What is independence?" In many countries, the population merely changed allegiance to a distant monarch for subservience to local oligarchies that were less efficient and, often, more corrupt. In others, the imperial power retained substantial influence through mandates and treaties; in such cases, independence in the eyes of the political elite came only through revolution. And in today's world of technological interdependence and efforts at regional consolidation, no country is completely independent.[2] But, whatever the circumstances, independence ultimately meant the departure of the imperial government, the substitution of a new flag for an old, and membership in the United Nations. New leaders wanted their own opportunities for patronage and prestige unhindered by imperial watchdogs. Having spent most of their lives fighting the imperialists, anti-imperialism became the basis of their politics. Even when the imperialists had left, they continued to see the hand of the foreigner behind many of their difficulties.

The imperial age created modern state structures, generally with boundaries different from those that defined peoples before the Europeans came. Those that assumed power at independence were determined to inherit and maintain those state structures with their bureaucracies, their privileges, and their power, even in cases in which those structures were artificial distortions of historic ethnic divisions. In cases such as the Buganda in Uganda, old entities had to be subsumed within the new. Ironically, imperialism created the conditions of the nationalism that ultimately undermined the European power. The history of Africa, particularly, has been the history of efforts to resist returning to pre-imperial jurisdictions.

Inescapably, the military was to play a major part in most of the new nations. Liberation movement guerilla forces turned into the armies of the independent country. Not only were the armed forces often the best-organized and best-trained elements in the new lands, but their prominence in the struggle for independence gave them political power. Where their officers did not become leaders, they waited in the wings. In some cases, such as Uganda, coups were led by a non-commissioned sergeant, Idi Amin.

Independence inescapably set up struggles for power, often dividing the new military and the leaders that had led the fight for independence. Coups representing the continual struggle for power became a pattern in a majority of Third World countries.

In Africa, more than seventy successful military coups took place between 1952 and 1999. Asia has been less prone to successive coups; nevertheless, in the years since World War II, successful overthrows of governments by the military have taken place in Indonesia, Pakistan, Bangladesh, South Korea, Laos, Myanmar, and Vietnam. Not all can be attributed to former colonial rule; independent Thailand had seventeen military coup attempts between 1932 and 1991.[3]

Independence also meant the incorporation into new nations of territories considered natural parts of the nation-state. Thus Indonesia insisted on the incorporation of West New Guinea (Irian Jaya) and, ultimately, East Timor. India pursued the return of Goa and Pondicherry. And China sought Hong Kong and Macao.

What followed was not automatically better for everyone. New countries found themselves strapped economically as colonial subsidies declined and trade preferences withered. They found themselves locked into arbitrary colonial boundaries that divided peoples and resources. Traditional chiefs and rulers battled new elites for power; ethnic and personal feuds that had been hidden or suppressed during the colonial period erupted.

> While the old established states, particularly those of Western Europe and North America, have been transforming themselves from belligerent to benevolent entities, many of the newer states, particularly those brought into being by the dissolution of European empires, have been unable to liberate themselves from the grip of internal hostilities that pre-date colonization, or from external animosities against former colonial neighbors that the rule of empire held in check.[4]

It was common for colonial officials to argue that "the natives were not ready for self-government." Britain's Prime Minister Harold Macmillan, who did much to bring about the "winds of change" in Africa, obviously reacting to this argument, quoted Thomas Babington Macauley, one-time member of the Executive Council in India, who wrote in 1851:

> Many politicians of our time are in the habit of laying down as a self-evident proposition that no people ought to be free until they are fit to use their freedom. The maxim is worthy of the fool in the old story who resolved not to go into the water until he had learned to swim. If men are to wait for liberty until they become wise and good in slavery they may indeed wait forever.[5]

Meg Greenfield, columnist for *The Washington Post*, presented a later rationale after a visit to three southern African countries in 1982:

> To some degree this [unreadiness for rule] is of course the case, although the reason for it is not the one advanced. The creation of widespread managerial skill in a population with virtually no experience in running anything other than some one else's kitchen or a guerilla operation cannot be an easy or immediate thing. Many of the current leaders have given over much of their professional lifetimes to resistance, combat, political organization and/or incarceration by the British.[6]

In most cases, transitions were marked by formal ceremonies with imperial officials bedecked in uniforms while eager new leaders looked solemn as they waited for their flag to be raised. In other cases, retreating colonials left without ceremony, fleeing out the back door as new power came in the front.

The breakup of the European (and American) empires was predictable. Populations in Europe and America became restless as the human costs of empire became clear in reports from journalists and missionaries—and the occasional disaffected colonial official. In a world of more open communications, European and American societies proved less tolerant toward the excesses of colonial rule that now came to light.

But the European powers were not to give up quickly. Colonies—especially rich areas such as the Netherlands East Indies—were considered economically indispensable. A study commissioned by the Netherlands government in 1945 estimated that one-sixth of the Dutch national wealth was invested in the East Indies.[7] Moreover, the substantial empires gave nations such as Britain, France, the Netherlands, and Portugal prestige, power, and profits they might not otherwise have had.

The transition from empire to independent state was far from easy. The pressures of troubled populations, excited by ambitious elites, collided with the expectation of most imperial powers that their empires would endure. European capitals were slow to recognize how World War II changed the imperial equation, weakening the metropoles and giving unexpected strength to demands for independence. Surprisingly few in the imperial leadership recognized the power of nationalist leadership and their capacity for political organization. This was especially true in areas of European settlement where race was a factor, as in Rhodesia (later Zimbabwe) and the Kenya highlands. There is a remarkable repetition in the approaches—and failures—of the colonial authorities; cycles involving military action, arrests of nationalist leaders, and searches for malleable leadership alternatives were followed by the release and negotiation with the original leaders. Efforts at compromise often came too late with too little. The process was often delayed by bitter divisions among nationalist leaders; for them, the struggle was one for power.

Attitudes of imperial settlers, colonial administrators, and, often, foreign representatives frequently blinded individuals to the growing power of anti-colonial movements. Foreign consuls, both by inclination and the restrictions of the colonial power, moved largely in the circle of the Europeans. They met over pink gins or gimlets at exclusive clubs after tennis and before bridge. Their dinners were formal with few "natives" present. On weekends they rode to the hounds or hunted in the jungles. They saw the indigenous peoples as servants, ball boys, porters, beaters. The colonial authorities looked with suspicion on diplomats who met with politically active indigenous people and at times expelled such "troublemakers." It is little wonder that the pre-war U.S. consul-general in Batavia (now Jakarta), Walter A. Foote, advised General Douglas MacArthur in early 1944 that, based on his experience with his servants, "the natives were docile, peaceful, contented, and apathetic toward politics." He continued:

> Their main interests in life are their wives; children; rice fields; carabaos; chickens; a bamboo hut in a garden of banana and coconut trees, and occasional visit to the motion pictures (especially when "Westerns" are shown);[and] a new sarong now and then, especially around their New Year.[8]

Charismatic, demagogic, ideological nationalist leaders such as Sukarno, Gandhi, Nkrumah, and Ho Chi Minh came on the scene to mobilize populations against colonial rule. To the patronizing European and American they did not fit the stereotype of the "docile native." To some they were impressive; to others enigmatic and dangerous.

Although the organization of anti-colonial forces began early in the twentieth century, the period after World War I saw growing pressures on the remaining empires. By 1945, the situation for imperial powers, especially in Asia, had changed radically. The Japanese occupation had exploited and released nationalist elements throughout Asia. Moreover, the Japanese victories had destroyed any myth of the invulnerability of the white European. Modern communications lifted the veil on what was happening in imperial lands. Ho Chi Minh was advancing in Vietnam. Mao Tse Dung was leading the Long March in China. Britain was moving toward independence for India. And within a year, the Philippines would gain its independence from the United States.

Although the timetable varied by region, seeds of demands for independence were planted the day conquerors arrived. Exiles from colonial territories gathered in Paris and London to build hopes and plans for liberation even in the nineteenth century. The actual movement to independence for European colonies, however, only began in the twentieth century with two of the largest of the imperial dependencies, Indonesia and India. Demands for independence were stimulated not only by European fatigue but, as each new country became independent, the pressure also increased on the remaining empires. Membership of major new countries such as Indonesia and India in the United Nations, the growing numbers of Third World countries in the British Commonwealth, and the growth of meetings of anti-colonial groups increased the difficulties of those opposing change. The trend began that was ultimately to bring to an end colonialism in Asia, Africa, and the Caribbean.

The Role of the United States

The U.S. role in the breakup of empires was significant, but ambiguous. Rather than emerge as the champion of independence—as its early history and much of its rhetoric might have suggested—the United States, in the view of many, became the new imperialist. Caught between European reconstruction and sympathy for nationalism, America lost its anti-colonial credentials and became, in the period after World War II, the prime target of pressures and protests from much of the Third World.

The overwhelming power of the United States at the end of the war made it a natural candidate to inherit the imperial mantle. But that very power also lessened the outward manifestations of hostility as independence movements and the newly freed nations looked to Washington for material help and political support. Nevertheless, a broad sense of disenchantment set in and continues to feed attitudes toward the United States in Asia, Africa, and Latin America at the turn of the twenty-first century.

The relationship of the United States to the breakup of empires was a complex mix of principles, interests, and attitudes, frequently in conflict with each other. To peoples of the colonial world the rhetoric from America provided hope, but it also led to disappointment. In European capitals, Washington's rhetoric and actions were often unwelcome burrs under imperial saddles, and they also created suspicions that the United States was seeking to displace the colonial powers for its own benefit. Nevertheless, at least its early history, its educational activities in the

Middle East, the independence it gave to the Philippines, and pronouncements of its leaders gave the United States the strongest anti-colonial credentials of any major power.

In his book on U.S.-Indonesian relations, *Shared Hopes, Separate Fears,* Paul Gardner quotes a statement made by Vice President Mohammad Hatta of Indonesia six days after that nation declared its independence:

> World War One . . . saw the birth of a new idea summed up in the word "self-determination." The author of that idea was the late President Woodrow Wilson. That concept took firm root in the minds of the subject peoples, and it was on this central issue that they based their struggle for freedom. . . .
>
> The six year war just concluded saw history repeat itself. Both sides proclaimed high ideals; but it was the Atlantic Charter which succeeded in holding all men's minds in thrall. For does not the Atlantic Charter carry the solemn assurance of the Big Powers that they "recognize the right of all peoples to live under a government of their own choice?"[9]

There can be no doubt that the nationalists of Indonesia, and those of many other colonies as well, were inspired to make their own demands for independence by the history and declarations of the United States. In his book *Colonialism and Cold War,* Robert J. McMahon writes that "American pronouncements during World War II . . . had a profound impact on Asian independence movements," and notes that Ho Chi Minh, Communist and leader of the Vietnamese nationalist movement, believed the United States would oppose the reimposition of colonial rule in Asia.[10]

Throughout the Middle East—in Beirut, Damascus, Cairo, Istanbul, and Athens—Americans established schools and colleges that stimulated nationalist sentiments.

America's Credentials

Despite its apparent preference for the status quo, the United States was and is a country with revolutionary influence. It was the United States, after all, that not only inspired the Atlantic Charter, but also won its own war of independence. Its Declaration of Independence declared that "All Men are created equal" and that whenever government is not by consent of the governed, "it is the right of the People to alter or abolish it." It was also, in the Philippines, one of the first of the major powers to grant independence to a colony.

Many of those seeking independence, recognizing the overwhelming power of the United States in the immediate post–World War II period, also believed that if the United States genuinely wanted freedom for colonial peoples it could bring it about.

In reality, the United States did contribute substantially to decolonization in Asia and Africa, both as an individual nation and as a member of the UN Security Council. The pressures, however, were not always visible, and the results were rarely sufficiently prompt or dramatic to satisfy more extreme expectations. Further, because of complications in U.S.–Third World relations after independence, and particularly during the Cold War, the United States reaped few lasting rewards for its anti-colonial efforts. Any harsh judgement, however, should be softened by the genuine—if not always appreciated—efforts the United States made to press for and facilitate transitions to independence, especially in the case of Indonesia.

As a predominantly white nation in which many of its citizens shared with Europeans patronizing attitudes toward peoples of color, the United States was continually trapped between its inherent identity with the glories of empire and fundamental interests in European stability on one hand and anti-imperial tendencies and desires for open world trade on the other. Further affecting the nation's dilemma were the pressures of émigrés from countries seeking independence and the particular concerns of the African American community toward independence in Africa.

True, the words of Jefferson, Wilson, and Roosevelt represented the sincere beliefs of many Americans, but a look at the words in the context of U.S. history as well as the concerns at the end of World War II should have created skepticism in the minds of those looking for miracles from Washington. For America's anti-colonial credentials were not as solid as they may have seemed.

The words of the Declaration of Independence were written without regard to the institution of slavery—which would last another eighty-seven years. The nineteenth century saw not only the westward expansion and the Indian wars, marked by the capricious attitude toward treaties, but also the acquisition of large territory after the war with Mexico. The Spanish-American War and further acquisition of territory closed the century.

It is true that Cuba was granted independence and that, subsequently, so were the Philippines. But, in the latter case, the United States fought a bitter war with the incipient independence movement. And the beginning of the twentieth century ushered in the somewhat imperialistic acquisition of the Panama Canal.

Wilson's Fourteen Points established the principle of self-determination, but there is little evidence that either the full implications of that doctrine or its application to the European empires of the time were considered. In an example not uncommon in presidential rhetoric, words were chosen to fit the needs and the emotions of a moment without full consideration of the longer term significance. Walter Lippmann, who helped in the drafting of the Fourteen Points as a statement of allied purposes at the end of World War I, writes in *Public Opinion:*

> It would be a mistake to suppose that the apparently unanimous enthusiasm which greeted the Fourteen Points represented agreement on a program. Everyone seemed to find something that he liked and stressed this aspect and that detail. But no one risked a discussion. The phrases, so pregnant with the underlying conflicts of the civilized world, were accepted. They stood for opposing ideas, but they evoked a common emotion. . . .
>
> As long as the Fourteen Points dealt with that hazy and happy future when

the agony was to be over, the real conflicts of interpretation were not made manifest.[11]

Whatever Wilson's own interpretation of "self-determination" may have been, there is little in his explanations of the Fourteen Points to suggest that he envisioned the dismantling of the major European empires, other than the German one. In his address to Congress on February 11, 1919, he spoke in limiting terms:

> All well-defined national aspirations shall be accorded the utmost satisfaction that can be accorded them without introducing new or perpetuating old elements of discord and antagonism that would be likely in time to break the peace of Europe and consequently of the world.[12]

U.S. support for decolonization was not entirely dictated by idealism. American diplomats familiar with Asia and Africa insisted that grants of independence by the European powers were becoming increasingly important for U.S. interests and for the peace of the regions. China expert John Paton Davies wrote:

> We cannot afford to align ourselves in an Anglo-American bloc which would place us in opposition to the rise of nationalism in Asia. We must not put ourselves in a position where we cannot move with the historical stream rather than attempting to block a force which might prove too strong for us.[13]

Cordell Hull, secretary of state under President Franklin D. Roosevelt and a specialist in world trade issues, believed that discriminatory and monopolistic trade practices that were part of the imperial system had been elements bringing on world wars. He wrote in his autobiography that as early as World War I he had begun to realize that "unhampered trade dovetailed with peace; high tariffs, trade barriers, and unfair economic competition with war."[14] Hull had long chafed under the disadvantages to the United States of imperial preferences that discriminated against American goods. This was especially the case in southeast Asia. U.S. oil companies were granted access to resources in the Dutch East Indies only after the U.S. government threatened retaliation against Dutch interests in the United States. Britain, the Netherlands, and France colluded to control the export of rubber and tin from their colonies at a moment when a Pacific war threatened and U.S. needs for these commodities were growing.

But, beyond that, President Roosevelt himself, and other members of his administration, made it clear on many occasions that they believed the day of empires was over. On March 15, 1941, in a speech to White House correspondents, Roosevelt said, "There never has been, there isn't now and there never will be any race of people on earth fit to serve as masters over their fellow men. . . . We believe that any nationality, no matter how small, has the inherent right to its own nationhood."[15]

When, in August 1941, Roosevelt met with Winston Churchill to draft a statement on war aims, the two allies differed on the future of empires. In the opening words of what became the Atlantic Charter, Churchill drafted the phrase "respect the right of all peoples to choose the form of government under which they will live." Over Churchill's resistance, Roosevelt added "and they wish to see sovereign rights and self-government restored to those who have been forcibly deprived of them."[16] To make clear his meaning, Roosevelt declared in a radio address on February 23, 1942, that "the Atlantic Charter not only applies to the parts of the world that border on the Atlantic, but to the whole world."[17]

This document was quickly drafted to meet the needs of the moment without any lengthy consideration of its implications. In his biography of Roosevelt, James MacGregor Burns notes that "the lofty pronouncements were actually scribbled on pieces of paper and issued as a press release, but their reception by a people yearning for presidential leadership converted them into an historic act."[18]

In 1942, Roosevelt urged a reluctant Churchill to make a liberal statement of war aims for India. Churchill, agreeing that something needed to be done in the face of Indian nationalist resistance to the war effort, accepted a proposal to offer independence after the war in exchange for cooperation during the war. Sir Stafford Cripps was sent to persuade the Indians to accept. Roosevelt sent a special envoy, Colonel Louis A. Johnson, to help persuade the Indians, but, in correspondence with the viceroy behind Cripps's back, Churchill sabotaged the mission.

Roosevelt did not like the French and was opposed to the reintroduction of French imperialism in Indochina. Nevertheless, to avoid angering the French, he put off meeting with nationalist groups until after the war, a decision the president explicitly made clear in a letter to his secretary of state at the beginning of 1945, where he stated "I do not want to get mixed up in any Indochina decisions. It is a matter for post war."[19]

In *Present at the Creation,* Dean Acheson recalls Roosevelt's views:

> At the beginning of 1949 the French were still trying to re-establish their authority in Cambodia, Laos, and Vietnam. . . . President Roosevelt had been unsympathetic to the effort and during the war the United States had furnished aid to indigenous leaders, notably Ho Chi Minh, in the hope they would make difficulty for the Japanese.[20]

Acheson describes the dilemma facing the United States in its efforts to influence the French—comments that could as well be applied to any of Washington's European allies:

> Both during this period and after it our conduct was criticized as being a muddled hodgepodge, directed neither toward edging the French out of an effort to reestablish their colonial role, which was beyond their power, nor helping them hard enough to accomplish it, or even better, to defeat Ho and gracefully withdraw. The description is accurate enough. The criticism, however, fails to recognize the limits on the extent to which one may successfully coerce an ally. Withholding help and exhorting an ally or its opponent can be effective only if the ally can do nothing without help, as was the case in Indonesia. Furthermore, the result of withholding help to France would, at most, have removed the colonial power.

It would not have made the resulting situation a beneficial one either for Indo-China or for Southeast Asia or in the more important effort of furthering the stability and defense of Europe.[21]

Indochina was not the only region where the United States and France crossed on colonial issues. The French were particularly sensitive about North Africa and protested any contacts U.S. diplomats had with independence leaders in Algeria or Tunisia. Hooker Doolittle, a U.S. diplomat stationed in Tunis during the war, be-friended Habib Bourguiba, who would later become the leader of an independent Tunisia. Doolittle's actions drew protests from the French and suggestions from other U.S. officials in the area that he be replaced. In the immediate post-war period, William Porter, then director of the State Department's Office of Northern African Affairs, held frequent meetings in Washington with Algerian nationalists; when the French became aware of these meetings, they protested. Such efforts by U.S. diplomats to make contact with nationalist leaders was parallel to similar efforts by Irving Brown, European representative of the AFL-CIO. All such contacts were valuable to the United States when Tunisia and Algeria ultimately became independent and those in contact with the Americans emerged as key leaders.

Many such American meetings with nationalist leaders were taken on the initiative of State Department officers, probably without the knowledge of the White House. Roosevelt was, in fact, ambivalent about the idea of decolonization and might not have approved an activist U.S. policy. Taking the United States experience in the Philippines as a model, he favored a long period of preparation to be incorporated in an international trusteeship. His idea never caught fire because neither the Europeans nor the Asian nationalists accepted it. For the Europeans it represented interference in their affairs; for the nationalists it was a delaying tactic, putting off the goal of independence. Beyond that, as McMahon points out, "From the very inception, however, the trusteeship scheme was marred by the president's vague and often inconsistent proposals on the matter."[22]

Roosevelt, perhaps because of his Dutch ancestry, was more tolerant of the Dutch. At one point, in April 1942, he assured Queen Wilhelmina that, after the war, the Dutch East Indies would be returned to the Dutch. During a visit a year later, the Queen promised that "her government would announce immediately after victory in Japan, that they were going to grant the peoples of the Dutch East Indies first dominion status, with the right of self-rule and equality. Then, after their government had been established, if the people by free vote, decide they want complete independence, they shall be granted it."[23]

Although Roosevelt had left the scene and the conditions were different than the Dutch expected, it was in Indonesia that the United States was most involved in demonstrating its anti-colonial credentials. It was the one situation in which Washington was, ultimately, to play the card of economic pressure through the Marshall Plan.[24]

The independence transition unfolded not only against the backdrop of World War II but also against that of the Cold War. Attitudes and fears that stemmed from that confrontation were often intricately bound up with the anti-colonial struggle. Although some independence leaders obtained significant support from Moscow and saw in the Marxist-Leninist rhetoric echoes of their own protests, imperial powers used the communist label to discredit nationalist forces more widely than the facts justified. Ironically, in the United States, the perceived need to combat Communist influence probably stimulated more assistance to the new nations than might otherwise have been the case.

The full rush to independence, especially in Africa, came during the administration of John F. Kennedy. Kennedy was openly sympathetic with nationalist aspirations. When he was in the Senate, on July 2, 1957, he criticized U.S. support for France in Algeria in a famous speech, saying that it had "damaged our leadership and prestige."[25] In the brief period of his presidency he received many more Third World leaders than any of his predecessors. He was a strong proponent of foreign aid. His organization of the Peace Corps further symbolized his interest in the developing world. No U.S. president was more respected in the Third World; an Indian nationalist used the word "revered."

It is amazing, in 1999, to read the histories of the independence struggles, particularly concerning the Dutch and French in East Asia, and find how the governments of the time misread the strength of the nationalists. But they were depending on sources that told them what they wanted to hear, their own bureaucrats and colonial officials and local rulers and sycophants in their debt. They would not talk to those "extremists" who might have given them a sense of the reality of their situation.

Imperial powers in such cases were certain they could gain the sympathy and support of moderates in the colonies as well as of other major nations. Once the "extremists" were crushed, the status quo ante could be restored. The story of decolonization shows how wrong they were.

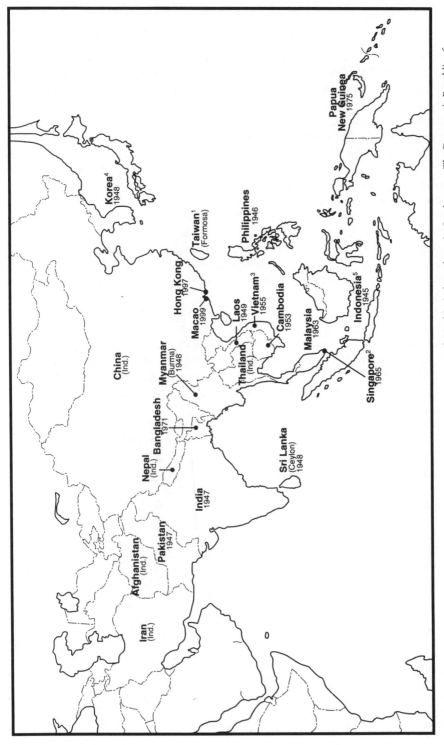

Map 2. Asia

1. Liberated from Japan 1945; status disputed but generally considered province of China.

2. Singapore, which originally gained independence as part of Malaysia, separated in 1965 to become the Republic of Singapore.

3. Vietnam was divided at the Geneva Conference in 1954. South Vietnam proclaimed its independence in October 1955. The Democratic Republic of North Vietnam proclaimed its independence in December 1959.

4. Korea was divided at the Potsdam Conference at the 38th parallel in July 1945. Separate republics were proclaimed in the north and south on May 1, 1948.

5. Indonesian nationalists proclaimed independence in August 1945, but the Dutch did not cede sovereignty until December 1949.

FOUR

Freedom in Asia

In Asia, the march to independence began following the defeat of Japan in 1945. The empires of four major nations would be involved: the United States, the Netherlands, France, and Britain. The imperial age ended, but not without serious struggles and post-independence problems that would bedevil the international community for decades afterward: Vietnam, Irian Jaya, East Timor, Kashmir.

Indonesia

The first to declare independence was Indonesia, which proclaimed the establishment of the Republic of Indonesia on August 17, 1945, three days after Japan's surrender. Although not fully in control of the nation, nationalist leaders decided to make their declaration to preclude an expected Japanese grant of independence. Already accused by the Dutch of being "quislings" because of their wartime cooperation, the leaders of the new nation did not want to begin life under apparent Japanese sponsorship. That declaration, however, was only the beginning of a five-year struggle, first with the British and then with the Dutch, before the government at The Hague finally accepted independence for their valuable colony.

Even before the rise of a successful nationalist movement, the peoples of the East Indies had demonstrated their restlessness under Dutch rule. When the Dutch sought to reclaim the islands in 1825 after the Napoleonic Wars and a brief interregnum under the British, they faced an Islamic revolt with nationalist overtures by a native sultan, Prince Diponegoro. Before the Dutch were able to suppress the insurrection five years later, nearly 15,000 Dutch and 200,000 Javanese had died.[1]

A peasant revolt that began in 1890 was not finally suppressed until 1917. An uprising staged by an incipient Communist party in 1926 was quickly put down. The Dutch did not finally conquer all of the Indies until the early twentieth century. Aceh, a strongly Islamic region in north Sumatra, was not fully subdued until 1903 and remained restive in 2000.

In 1873 as the Dutch approached, the Achenese sultan appealed for support to the U.S. consul in Singapore; Washington rejected the appeal.

Political parties had existed before 1927, despite the best efforts of the Dutch to quash them. The most effective and lasting, the Indonesian Nationalist Party, came into being that year under the leadership of a dynamic engineer named Sukarno. He was joined by two others who helped lead the nation to independence, Mohammad Hatta and Sutan Sjahrir. The Dutch authorities realized the potency of the new movement and, seeking to deflate it, arrested Sukarno in 1929. He was released in 1931 but was re-arrested in 1933. Hatta and Sjahrir were arrested the following year; all three were exiled to one of the outer islands, where they remained until they were released by the Japanese in 1942.

At the end of the war, the Dutch, ignoring the nationalist declaration of independence, fully expected that with the help of wartime allies they would regain control of the Indies. Released from German occupation only in May of 1945, Holland was in no position to send forces to take the Japanese surrender and restore Dutch rule. Although Indonesia, except for Sumatra, had been part of the U.S. command during the war, the responsibility for recovering Indonesia was passed to the British; the U.S. rationale was that all of its Pacific forces were needed to prepare for the anticipated invasion of Japan.

The British were unprepared for the task that awaited them. Although the Japanese surrendered on August 14, the British (including many Indian troops) and Australian forces and a few Dutch were not able to land until late September. In that interregnum, the Indonesian nationalists established a functioning administration; the British and Dutch faced not a defeated Japan but an Indonesia believing and acting as if it were independent. At the same time, the situation in Java was an often chaotic mix of departing Japanese, released internees (largely Dutch), incoming allied forces, and enthusiastic supporters of the Republic—in many cases armed by the Japanese.

Added to the mix were divisions within Islam in Indonesia, a country with the world's largest Muslim population. In areas such as West Java and portions of Sumatra and Sulawesi, militant Islamic groups opposed the secular nationalist leadership. For many years the Indonesian army, despite the 90 percent Muslim population, viewed some of the Islamic groups as their principal enemy.

In 1974, as U.S. ambassador to Indonesia, I paid an early call on the Minister of Home Affairs, Lt. General Amir Machmoud. I commented that I was pleased to serve again in another Islamic country. He replied, rather sharply, "Mr. Ambassador, Indonesia is not an Islamic country."

Following the Japanese surrender, the British were initially accepted to disarm the Japanese and release prisoners; they were not accepted as a surrogate to reestablish the authority of the Netherlands. Any doubts about the popular support for the new nationalist Republic were dispelled in a bitter battle for Surabaya, Java's second city, in October 1945, in which the British commander was killed.

Allied powers, including the British and the Americans, urged the reluctant Dutch to negotiate with the nationalist government already in place. Talks finally did take place in mid-1946, leading to an agreement establishing a United States of Indonesia of which the Republic would be but one part, an approach designed to separate Sukarno's nationalist Republic from the rest of the Indies. This agreement never went into effect. In July 1947, the Dutch, concluding that negotiations were fruitless, and determined to strangle the incipient republic, launched their first military "police action," capturing most of the ports of Java and Sumatra and confining the Republic to an area in Central Java.

But, by August 1947, a major change had taken place in the international climate for imperial action. India had become independent. One of the first actions of the new government in New Delhi was to join the Australians in bringing action against the Dutch in the UN Security Council. The United States, with Britain, proposed a cease-fire and urged mediation. A Consular Commission was formed to oversee the cease-fire and a Committee of Good Offices to promote negotiations. The United States was to be active in both. A U.S. warship, the USS *Renville*, became the site for the negotiations. The Dutch remained intransigent, losing the support of some of their strongest American allies. The government of The Hague continued to believe that, with sufficient force, the nationalist insurrection could be put down and imperial rule restored. The Dutch defied UNSC resolutions that called for a cessation of hostilities, release of prisoners, and a resumption of negotiations.

Further negotiations on the USS *Renville*[2] led to another cease-fire in January 1948. This, too, collapsed when the Dutch inaugurated their second police action on December 19, 1948, capturing the Republican capital of Jogjakarta and jailing the republican leadership, including Sukarno. Further UN action culminated in a roundtable conference in August 1949, at which the Dutch agreed to transfer power to a federated Republic of the United States of Indonesia. They still hoped to shut off the nationalist republic on Java from the other provinces. The new arrangement was also short-lived, as support for the Dutch federal plan outside of Java gradually collapsed. On August 17, 1950, the Sukarno-led government proclaimed a unitary Republic of Indonesia. Although this meant independence for most of the Indies, two problems remained to cloud the future.

West New Guinea (Irian Jaya) had been excluded from the roundtable agreement, to be negotiated at a later date. That later date proved to be August 15, 1962 when, after a decade of tortured negotiations, military threats, and international mediation, the Netherlands and Indonesia signed an agreement transferring sovereignty to Indonesia. The United States, through the mediation of Ambassador Ellsworth Bunker, played a significant role in the successful mediation.

One other issue, East Timor, not even mentioned in earlier negotiations, remained a problem at the end of the century. As noted in Chapter 1, the Portuguese and Dutch established trading posts on separate parts of the island of Timor in the sixteenth century. When Indonesia became independent, the Dutch half transferred to the new nation. The Portuguese colony remained. Separate development over several centuries had made it distinctly different in religion, language, and traditions from the rest of Indonesia.

In April 1974, a coup in Lisbon brought to power a Portuguese government determined to dismantle that country's age-old empire, including East Timor. Even before the changes in Lisbon, a liberation movement, FRETELIN, had been organized in the territory, demanding independence and seeking support from other liberation movements and sympathetic governments, including China. As the demand for Irian Jaya (West New Guinea) at the time of independence demonstrated, Indonesian nationalists felt very strongly about bringing the whole of the archipelago under Jakarta's rule. Moreover, the Indonesian military, with a long history of antipathy to the Chinese Communists, made it clear that they would not permit East Timor to become independent and fall under Beijing's influence. The United States, along with other governments friendly to Jakarta, urged negotiations with the Portuguese. Such negotiations began, but, with an unsettled situation in Lisbon, the Indonesians found it difficult to get decisions from the Portuguese.

On December 6, 1975, when I was U.S. ambassador to Indonesia, President Gerald Ford and Secretary of State Henry Kissinger visited Jakarta on their way home from a trip to China. In a meeting with them, President Suharto informed them that Indonesia believed it now had no choice but to take military action and annex the territory. Secretary Kissinger expressed the view that Indonesia would do what it needed to do but urged that weapons supplied by the United States not be used. The next day, the Indonesians invaded the colony and subsequently, through a transparently staged process, declared it incorporated into Indonesia.

Diplomats often look back and wonder whether different action might have deterred tragedy. In September 1999, as I write this, Indonesian militias are hunting down and killing those who voted for independence. Would a different reply have deterred the Indonesian action in 1975? I think not. Given the strong Indonesian fears that giving up any part of what they consider their territory could lead to national disintegration—a fear that is still strong—it is doubtful that any pressure could have persuaded them to let East Timor go at that time. If the Indonesians had shown greater tolerance for a different society during their occupation, the end of the story might have been different, but, tragically, they did not.

Dutch tactics in the face of pro-independence movements followed a pattern that was to be seen time and time again as other metropole powers struggled to maintain their possessions, whether in Indochina, Algeria, Kenya, or Zimbabwe. They were tactics designed both to maintain support at home and to garner support among Western allies.

Nationalists were to be discredited as "children" not yet capable of running a country or jailed as terrorists or Communists. In the case of Indonesia, because Sukarno and Hatta had worked with the Japanese, the Dutch sought to portray these leaders as "quislings." Efforts were made to find indigenous alternatives to nationalists, exploiting where possible power struggles within nationalist movements. Foreign critics, whether journalists or diplomats, were to be confined or expelled. Economic pressures were to be applied against areas under nationalist control. Military force was to be used when necessary. But whatever the tactics, in the end the result was the same: the breakup of empires.

The Philippines

The United States was always an ambivalent imperialist. U.S. popular opinion supported the Monroe Doctrine, the conquest of the American continent, and the concept of "manifest destiny" toward the former Spanish territories to the South. At the same time many, conscious of the colonial beginnings of the United States, were opposed to the acquisition of colonies. After the explosion that destroyed the battleship *Maine* in Havana harbor on February 15, 1898 and a jingoistic campaign by the Hearst newspapers, President William McKinley, encouraged by his vice president, Theodore Roosevelt, was led reluctantly into war with Spain.

With the defeat of Spain, the United States gained control over Cuba, Puerto Rico, Guam, and the Philippine islands. Cuba was granted independence under a U.S. protectorate, and Puerto Rico and Guam became U.S. possessions.

In the Philippines, sentiment against the status quo was already strong. By the 1880s, a group of Filipino students in Europe had formed the Propaganda Movement and, by various writings, promoted reform for the islands. The most prominent voice was that of José Rizal, who wanted Philippine representation in the Spanish Cortes (the Governor-General's Council); his two political novels, *The Social Cancer* (1886) and *The Reign of Greed* (1891), had a wide impact in the islands. When he returned from Europe in 1892, he was arrested, exiled to a remote island, and subsequently executed by the Spanish in 1896. His death led to the more militant organization of nationalists and preparations for armed revolt against the Spanish.

On May 1, 1898, the United States fleet under Admiral George Dewey defeated the Spanish and took possession of the naval base at Cavite and the fort at Corregidor. In mid-May, Dewey encouraged Emilio Aguinaldo, Philippine independence leader, to rise against the Spanish. Aguinaldo, in mid-June, proclaimed independence and a few weeks later formed the Malolos Republic, expecting U.S. support for Philippine freedom. In the meantime, American forces had taken possession of Manila. When the Treaty of Paris that ended the war (December 10, 1898), transferred sovereignty to the United States, a disappointed Aguinaldo took up arms against the Americans. The Filipinos were ruthlessly defeated in the ensuing conflict and Aguinaldo was captured. Three thousand Americans and 15,000 Filipinos died in the conflict. Aguinaldo subsequently took an oath of allegiance to the United States and retired to private life.

Although opposition existed in the United States to the annexation of the Philippines, economic and strategic considerations prevailed and the islands became a U.S. possession. From the beginning, however, Washington made it clear that it wished to prepare the Filipinos for ultimate independence.

Governor General Francis B. Harrison was sent to the islands by President Woodrow Wilson in 1913 with the specific charge to prepare the nation for ultimate independence. Legislation in 1916 calling for a specific date for independence was passed by the U.S. Senate but died in the House of Representatives. The legislation, however, did establish a 24-member Philippine Senate, almost wholly elected; with the previously established 80-member Philippine Assembly, the basis for Philippine democracy was established. Filipinos took on more and more of the responsibility for governing. Although Americans formed 51 percent of the civil service in 1903, that figure had dropped to 29 percent by 1913 and to 6 percent by 1923.

From the beginning the U.S. administration placed great emphasis on education. Trained by teachers sent from the United States, by 1927, nearly all of the 26,200 teachers in the public schools were Filipino. The United States made a genuine effort to prepare the island nation not only for independence but also for democracy, but that preparation was flawed. When I served in Manila briefly as U.S. ambassador in 1978, I realized that, despite a facade of democracy, the Philippines was still, as the Spanish had left it, an oligarchical society. "Latin America in Asia," as someone described it. An essay in *The Encyclopedia Britannica* presents an accurate picture:

> American preparation of the Philippines for democratic self-government suffered from an inherent contradiction, perhaps not recognized at the time. Transferring governmental responsibility to those capable of undertaking it was not consistent with building a social and economic base for political democracy. Self-government meant, of necessity, assumption of power by those Filipinos who were already in positions of leadership in society. But these men came for the most part from the landed elite; preservation of their political and economic position was incompatible with equalization of opportunity. Even the expansion of an educated middle class did not necessarily result in a transformation of the pattern of power. Most middle-class aspirants for political leadership adhered to the values and practices of the existing power elite.[3]

This social structure was to haunt the Republic through much of the first half century of its independence.

Nevertheless, the United States did not wait for a perfect circumstance or moment. Under pressure from Filipino leaders, the Tydings-McDuffie Act was passed in 1934, providing for a 10-year commonwealth period leading to independence. World War II delayed the timetable; independence was formally declared twelve years later on July 4, 1946, making the Philippines the first independent nation in Asia established with the consent of the imperial power. For the Dutch and the French, still locked in conflict with nationalists in Indonesia and Indochina, the Philippine example became one more unwelcome precedent pressing them to do the same.

If the ultimate transition in the Philippines was relatively smooth, the story in French Indochina was far different.

Indochina

France had emerged from German occupation in World War II determined to regain a position of world prestige. Led by General Charles de Gaulle, the resumption of French glory did not permit yielding sovereignty to the new forces of nationalism that were seizing power in Indochina. Not only were the French fearful that other major powers might move in, they were also convinced that the peoples of their territories were far from ready for self-government. Moreover, they believed their rule unique in that, by the creation of the French Union in 1946, they were providing the colonial territories a measure of autonomy and allowing for colonial representatives to sit in the French parliament.

After the defeat of the Japanese, the French regained control of southern Vietnam and created monarchies within the French Union in Laos and Cambodia. In North Vietnam, however, they faced a situation paralleling that in the Netherlands East Indies. Japanese occupation forces had encouraged nationalists, who had become a formidable force under the mobilizing power of a skillful leader, Ho Chi Minh.

The son of a poor country scholar, Ho left Vietnam in 1911 and wandered the world as a cook, gardener, sweeper, waiter, photo retoucher, and oven stoker. Moving to France in 1917, he became an active socialist and Vietnamese nationalist, addressing a petition for Vietnamese rights to the 1919 Peace Conference in Versailles. Inspired by the Russian Revolution, he joined the French Communist Party in 1920. Through the inter-war period, he worked actively in Russia, China, Hong Kong, and Thailand on behalf of Vietnamese nationalism. In 1930, at the same time as the French were suppressing an insurrectionary movement in Vietnam, Ho founded the Indochinese Communist Party in Hong Kong. He was condemned to death in absentia; the French requested the British to extradite him from Hong Kong, but he escaped to Moscow. He re-entered North Vietnam in 1941 (with help from Chiang Kai-shek) to establish the League for the Independence of Vietnam, or Viet Minh.

The defeat of the Japanese gave Ho and his followers the opportunity to establish their authority. Ho and a guerilla force entered Hanoi on August 19 and proclaimed the independence of North Vietnam on September 2, 1945. Ho then sought negotiations with the French leading to independence, but Paris refused to speak of independence. On March 6, 1946, Ho did sign an agreement with Paris recognizing Vietnam as a "free state with its own government, army, and finances," within the French Union, but the agreement did not hold.[4] In November, 1946, a French cruiser opened fire on Haiphong after a clash between French and Vietnamese soldiers. An estimated 6,000 Vietnamese were killed and the first Indochinese War had begun.

In 1948, the French, utilizing a familiar tactic, sought to weaken the Viet Minh nationalists by appealing to the traditional ruling class in Vietnam; they offered to return the former Vietnamese emperor, Bao Dai, who had abdicated in favor of the revolution in August 1945. But this approach was not successful. The war continued until the French were decisively defeated at Dien Bien Phu on May 7, 1954. A conference followed in Geneva which resulted in the "temporary" boundary between North and South Vietnam at the 17th parallel. Under the rule of Ho Chi Minh, and with substantial help from China and the Soviet Union, North Vietnam grew in power and began the infiltration of the south.

South Vietnam, established initially as part of the French Union under Emperor Bao Dai, entered a period of instability. Ngo Dinh Diem, the South Vietnamese prime minister, deposed Bao Dai, inaugurated himself as president, withdrew from the French Union, and declared an independent South Vietnam on October 26, 1955. An election, which had been agreed to in the Geneva conference, to decide on the future of the two Vietnams was never held. Circumstances were thus set for the tragedy of Indochina that was to unfold and involve the United States in the succeeding decades.

Malaya

To the south, another independence drama was unfolding in the Malay states. Although not formally a colony, the Malay states were effectively controlled by Britain before World War II through resident advisors attached to the principal sultans. Malays were favored in matters of land ownership and government service over the energetic Chinese minority which, as in Indonesia, controlled most of the commerce. Malaya was of great importance to the British, not only because it sat astride a major waterway, the Strait of Malacca, but also because it was a prime source of rubber and tin.

When Japan conquered the Malay Peninsula in 1941, Malays were initially attracted to Japanese proposals for a Malay state that would include the Peninsula and Sumatra. Japan, considering all Chinese to be potential enemies, treated the Malayan Chinese brutally. When the war ended, in a departure from other colonial areas, both the Malays and the Chinese welcomed back the British. Malays saw them as protectors against the Chinese; the Chinese, in turn, saw the British as protecting their favorable economic position.

The Malayan Communist Party (MCP), primarily composed of poor immigrant Chinese, had other ideas. For a time, when the Soviet Union turned against the Axis, the MCP linked up with British agents. Some 7,000 guerillas were trained to harass the Japanese. But when the British returned after the war, they found that the MCP was no longer an ally. In the two-week interregnum after the Japanese surrender and before the return of the British, the MCP sought to seize power. A former member of the MCP recalled the party's plans:

> Instead of calling for individual strikes as we'd been doing before, we were going to call for nationwide strikes by occupation. All the rubber workers would be pulled out, Malaya's major industry. Then all the tin workers would be pulled while the first strike was unsettled. So you would have the two major industries crippled. Then we would call all the transport workers out, then we would call all

the dock workers out and the country would be, after a few months, in a state of total economic chaos.[5]

Their efforts did not succeed and, by the end of 1948, the MCP decided that if they were to drive out the British, they should resort to guerilla warfare. The MCP assumed that, like the French in Indochina and the Dutch in Indonesia, the British would resist any efforts at independence for this rich dependency. But the British had declared in 1944 that their goal for Malaya was independence; that remained their policy. A promise to preserve Malay privileges in an independent state assured them the support of the majority.

That objective was threatened by the MCP guerilla tactics. A 12-year "Emergency" followed in which British forces, initially under the command of General Sir Gerald Templar, gradually closed off the Communist access to food and information by a policy of force and resettlement of poor Chinese. The result was one of the rare defeats of a guerilla force during the independence period. Independence for Malaya was declared August 31, 1957. The Emergency was officially ended in 1960. Malaya officially became Malaysia in 1963 when a newly independent Singapore and the former British North Borneo colonies of Sabah and Sarawak were added. Singapore subsequently went its own way and became separately independent as the Republic of Singapore in August 1965.

The Subcontinent

To the west another decolonization was taking place in India. It, too, was sparked by a remarkable figure, Mohandas K. Gandhi.

I met Gandhi while on a student fellowship in India in 1940. My letter home recounts the meeting on October 31, 1940:

> Gandhi's village is in a beautiful little valley now green with corn and cotton fields. It might be El Dorado County [in California] with its red soil, low brush foliage, scattered trees. It is a beautifully quiet spot, undisturbed by automobiles (An occasional one does come in. Gandhi rides in one.) or mechanical noises of any kind. The village of Sevagram, a little mud hut settlement of 600 souls, lies in the center of the valley. Gandhi's compound of about 15 dirt-floored, bamboo-walled and tile-roofed buildings lies about a quarter of a mile from the village. In the compound are a school, a weaving house, and the living quarters of about 40 followers. The school was one of the most interesting parts for me. It is Gandhi's idea that the village children should be taught first how to make and grow food and clothing. From that craft training springs, by illustration with the craft, all other training. For example, out of the simple workings of the spinning wheel the student learns the elements of physics, geometry, mechanics, as well as the craft itself. After wandering down through the village, I returned to talk to the men at the school and had tea sitting on the floor with them. After that, I went to meet Gandhi.
>
> It is a shock to meet Gandhi—the utter simplicity of the man is amazing.

Here is a man who is one of the greatest leaders in history. He is small, lying on a sheeted mat on the floor, clad only in his dhoti. He was reclining as he spoke to me because he had a mustard plaster on his stomach. He is in a room barely the size of our bathroom [12 × 18 ft.]—his entire living quarters. A small book case and his spinning wheel are the only furniture in the room. He speaks slowly—without any noticeable "fire" at all—in a quietly intellectual manner. His English is excellent, with only a trace of an Indian accent. The fact that he has no teeth causes him to lisp slightly.

The things I shall most remember are his ability to express himself and his sense of humor. He handles the language beautifully—directly and cleverly. He has a really engaging smile. One would not call him serious-minded. There is always a light of kindness and good feeling in his eye. We talked about three things—non-violence, industrialism, and the type of government he would envisage for an independent India. His statement on non-violence—or rather on the possibility of defending India by non-violence—was the clearest: "After an invader has chopped off a million heads, his soldiers would get tired of chopping off heads. We would have conquered without committing the sin of taking a human life." He was vaguest on the type of government he would establish in India. [Jawaharlal] Nehru (his right-hand man and probable successor) who makes sly fun of Gandhi (the two are not wholly in agreement) describes Gandhi's ideal of government as a "benevolent Christian anarchy."

I was fortunate that Nehru was also present. I had a second tea with him after my talk with Gandhi. Nehru impressed one much more than Gandhi. He is tall, very dignified looking, cultured (Harrow and Cambridge), with a sense of humor and a more practical outlook on the whole question of independence than Gandhi.

Gandhi and Nehru were both impressive, each in his way. Gandhi came across as a shrewd—and dedicated—political leader. Nehru was—or at least appeared to be—more the intellectual, although equally dedicated to the cause of independence.

Defying a ban of his caste against traveling over water, Gandhi went to London to study law as a young man. Returning to his Indian homeland as a dapper British-trained barrister, he found little opportunity and sailed off again—this time to South Africa. It was his witnessing of the white South African discrimination against the Indian minority that led him to his life of non-violent protest. He never forgot his personal experience in South Africa in 1894 when, even though properly ticketed, he was expelled from a first-class train compartment because of his color. Small instances of discrimination can have global consequences.[6]

When Gandhi returned to live again in India in 1915, the path to self-government, if not independence, had already been opened. That path, from its inception, was a tortured route, affected by deep divisions in British politics, Hindu-Muslim differences in India, and the unanticipated impact of violent events.

As early as 1869, the first Indians had been taken into the prestigious Indian

Civil Service (ICS). The possibility of greater autonomy for India had been raised in 1880 when Lord Ripon, appointed viceroy by the Liberal Prime Minister William Gladstone, instituted a general system of local self-government. He had to back off, however, when he sought to abolish the regulation that an Englishman could only be tried in courts by another Englishman. A ditty of the day expressed another view:

> Woe to the blinded statesman
> Who truckles to the base
> And sets above the nobler
> The feebler falser race.[7]

Five years later, a retired British official, Allan Octavian Hume, established the Indian National Congress "to channel the counter-surge of educated Indian feeling."[8] The Congress, which was later to become the principal organ of the independence movement, held its first meeting in Bombay in 1885 with seventy-five English-speaking Indians present.

In his book *India's Struggle for Independence*, Bipan Chandra, Professor of Modern History at Jawaharlal Nehru University, discusses why Hume, an Englishman, was identified as the founder of the Congress when, according to Chandra's account, the organization was the result of the work of a number of prominent Indians:

> If the founders of the Congress were such capable and patriotic men of high character, why did they need Hume to act as the chief organizer of the Congress? . . . But the real answer lies in the conditions of the time. . . .
>
> Courageous and committed persons like Dadadbhai Naoroji, Justice Ranade, Pherozeshah Mehta, G. Subramaniya Iyer and Surendranath Banerjea (one year later) cooperated with Hume because they did not want to arouse official hostility at such an early stage of their work. They assumed that the rulers would be less suspicious and less likely to attack a potentially subversive organization if the chief organizer was a retired British civil servant.[9]

In 1909, another Liberal government in London took office and, this time in consultation with Indians in the Congress, instituted further reforms, including the appointment of the first Indian member of the Viceroy's Council. Many in England saw this as the first irreversible step down the road to independence— which many did not like. Lord Morley, the secretary of state for India, wrote to King Edward VII that the appointment was necessary and expedient "for the contentment of Your Majesty's Indian dominions." Edward replied, "The King has thought it over quite as much as Lord Morley has. He remains of the opinion that the step is fraught with the greatest danger to the maintenance of the British Empire under British rule."[10] The appointment, nevertheless, went ahead.

As India moved toward self-government, the deep division between Hindu and Muslim that was so seriously to cloud the political future increasingly appeared. Muslims represented a quarter of the population, but they were still a minority. Also, they were generally less well off than Hindus, and because many Muslim schools, still following the practice of the Moghul empire, taught in Persian rather than English, their graduates were at a disadvantage in an increasingly English-dominated society. The Morley reforms of 1906 opened a further wound by proposing separate electoral rolls for religious minorities. The move was seen by both Hindus and Muslims as an effort to "divide and rule." That same year the Muslim League was established; among its original members was a young Muslim member of the Congress, Mohammed Ali Jinnah.

When Gandhi returned to India in 1915, the primary effort of his work was to raise the consciousness of Indians as one nation. He was still loyal to the British empire; he even helped recruit Indians for the British in World War I, hoping that active support for the war effort would speed British willingness to grant independence. But tumultuous events often change people and history. So it was with the Amritsar massacre of April 6, 1919.

On March 18, 1919, the Viceregal Council approved the Rowlatt Acts to extend indefinitely wartime restrictions on civil liberties. Gandhi called for a 1-day strike of protest for April 6. Added to the explosive mixture were Muslim protests against an allied agreement with Turkey that abolished the caliphate in Constantinople. Contrary to Gandhi's hopes for non-violence, the strike sparked demonstrations and riots in various parts of the country. In Amritsar, rioters set fire to buildings and three British were killed. Authorities banned public demonstrations, but the word did not reach all districts. Another crowd assembled on April 13. Brigadier General Reginald Dyer, commanding a force of 25 Gurkhas and 25 Baluchis, ordered his men to open fire. A total of 379 were killed and 1,137 wounded. Not content with this action, he issued a number of humiliating orders to bring Amritsar to its knees, including one requiring Indians to "go on all fours" in certain sections of the city. Dyer was censured and relieved of his command, but in Britain many came to his defense and praised his action.[11]

Gandhi, deeply affected by the massacre and, even more, by the humiliating measures introduced and the attitudes of many British, felt betrayed. He determined to follow non-violent protest measures he had learned in South Africa. He abandoned his European clothes and insisted on wearing clothes of homespun cotton; his followers were encouraged to do the same. He became the undisputed leader of the Congress. He created a new phenomenon in Indian politics—a mass movement behind the Congress Party.

From 1920 on he and his followers harassed the British with various campaigns of civil disobedience, including the march to the sea in 1930 to evade the salt tax. Gandhi was jailed twice during this period. His protests produced results. Two British prime ministers, Conservative Stanley Baldwin and Labour Ramsey MacDonald, concluded, over opposition, that further steps toward self-government for India were necessary if the empire was to be preserved. The result was a roundtable conference in London in 1930. Gandhi did not attend, but agreed to discuss with Lord Irwin,[12] the viceroy, conditions under which he would attend the second roundtable. On March 5, 1931, a pact between the two men was signed, and in the fall of 1931 Gandhi went to London for the second roundtable conference. His negotiations with Lord Irwin were bitterly assailed by Winston Churchill who, until the end, remained opposed to independence for India. It was in the context of India that Churchill said, "I did not become the King's Chief Minister to preside over the liquidation of the British Empire."[13] With respect to Gandhi's meeting with Lord Irwin, he commented:

> It is alarming and also nauseating to see Mr. Gandhi, a seditious Middle Temple lawyer, now posing as a *fakir* of a type well-known in the East, striding half-naked up the steps of the viceregal palace, while he is organizing and conducting a defiant campaign of civil disobedience, to parley on equal terms with the representative of the King-Emperor.[14]

The roundtable conference resulted in the India Act of 1935 that gave each of India's eleven provinces an autonomous government responsible to a parliamentary assembly elected on a qualified franchise. The Congress Party accepted these provisions and participated in the election that followed in 1937. Another portion of the act established a central government in New Delhi, subject to the approval of the Chamber of Princes.

Under British rule a third of the subcontinent consisted of separate states ruled by princes in treaty relationships with the United Kingdom. Encouraged by Churchill, the princes opposed the concept of a central government, and no central government was put in place.

The 1937 elections established Indian rule in the provinces, but the results were to blight the process and pave the way for partition and disasters that accompanied independence ten years later. Although the Indian National Congress prevailed in most provinces, the viceroy, Lord Linlithgow, urged the Congress leaders to include Muslims in the resulting governments. Nehru took the position that any direct effort to assign portfolios on the basis of religion would undermine his hopes for a secular state. He accepted Muslims who were members of the Congress, but not those who were members of the Muslim League.

In 1948, when I was assigned to the U.S. embassy in Karachi, capital of the new state of Pakistan, I would ask Pakistanis what principal act had led to the decision to press for partition. They invariably referred to the election of 1937, especially in the United Provinces where, in their view, Hindus had excluded Muslims from any role of authority. Not only did they see at that time no future in an undivided independent India but they felt that significant Muslim institutions would be endangered under Hindu rule.

When war broke out in Europe in September 1939, Britain, without consulting any Indian, declared war for India against Germany. In protest, the Congress governments in the various provinces resigned. Britain, recognizing the importance of India to their war effort (ultimately 2 million Indians were to serve Britain in World War II), proposed a promise of independence after the war if India would support the war effort. Congress refused, and, in August 1942, Congress, led by Gandhi, began a "Quit India" movement. Although Gandhi hoped protests would be peaceful, serious riots broke out in several cities. Britain, in the desperate hours when the Japanese were threatening India, had little tolerance for such actions. Gandhi and the Congress leadership were jailed and remained incarcerated until the end of the war. The way was open to Jinnah to build the Muslim League and support for ultimate partition.

The final decade of Britain's rule in India was spent in seeking to reconcile the irreconcilable. The Labour government in London which came to power in 1945 faced the emotional opposition of Churchill and other Conservatives to any thought of independence. Muslims were becoming disillusioned with their prospects in a united India. Gandhi, Nehru, and the Congress stood fast in their quest for independence in a united secular nation. The Sikhs in the Punjab were thinking of their own separate status as independence and partition approached. The desire of the princes to retain their privileges encountered resentment in the rest of India.

The man sent by London in 1947 to sort this out as the last viceroy was Lord Louis Mountbatten. After hectic weeks of consultations with all parties and several rejected draft plans, Mountbatten declared on June 4, 1947, that India would be independent and partitioned by August 14 of the same year. That schedule provided only two months for the enormous task of separating the administrations, army, and resources of British India. In most cases, whole provinces were to opt for Pakistan or for India. Two key provinces, Punjab and Bengal, were to be divided. The timetable held, but at tremendous cost.

Fear gripped the subcontinent. Hindus, seeing their advantage, sought to drive out Muslims and take their properties. In fear, Muslims fled east and west to the divided parts of Pakistan. Sikhs in the Punjab sought to preserve their rights and expand their power. An estimated 12 million people relocated. At least 600,000 died in a wave of killings that went on for sixteen months. With authority uncertain and partitioned, army and police were powerless to stop the carnage. Gandhi, effectively out of leadership and disheartened by partition, concentrated in the weeks before independence on stopping the killings in Calcutta; he had some success, but he could not be everywhere.

To determine the geographic divisions, Britain called on a judge, Sir Cyril Radcliffe. Radcliffe had never been in India; he worked with maps from an office in Simla and made decisions that determined the future for districts, villages, and houses. He made one fateful decision: the district of Gurdespur in the Punjab was allocated to India. Gurdespur represented the only feasible route from India into Kashmir, a Muslim majority state. The Hindu maharajah of Kashmir, under pressure from New Delhi and over strong protests from Pakistan, opted for India. Thus began a conflict that, in the middle of 1999, still threatens peace between the two halves of what was once British India. And, in Pakistan, whether justly or not, Radcliffe's decision on Gurdespur is seen as a sly British way of rewarding India at the expense of Pakistan.

My family and I were in Pakistan from January 1948 until April 1950; the question that frequently arose during that time was "Was partition necessary?" Given the circumstances of 1946–1947, the answer is probably "yes." But looking at the longer history and at the rigid positions of Winston Churchill, Mohammad Ali Jinnah, Mohandas Gandhi, and Jawaharlal Nehru over several decades, one cannot escape the feeling that many opportunities to prevent one of the world's great tragedies were lost.

Two other parts of the empire in the subcontinent followed India. In Burma the Japanese had also encouraged nationalist forces during their occupation. After the war, given the move toward freedom for India, the British acquiesced and granted Burma independence in January 1948. Ceylon (which became Sri Lanka in 1972) became independent in February 1948.

The story continues with the tangled affairs of territories that were not quite colonies.

1. Liberated from Japan 1945; status disputed but generally considered province of China.

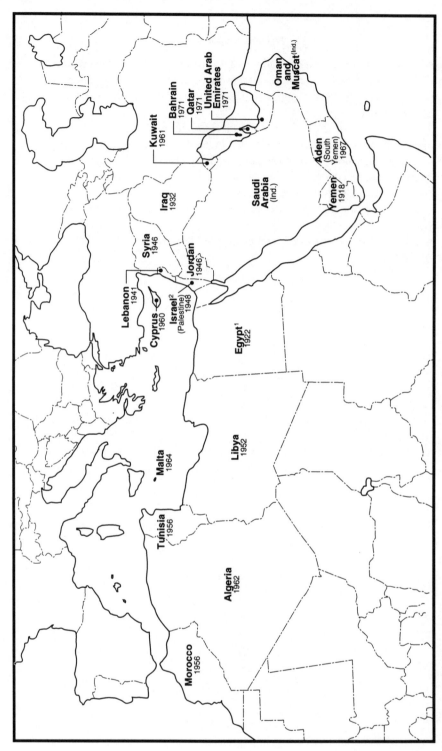

Map 3. The Mediterranean and the Middle East
1. The British mandate for Egypt ended in 1922, but Egypt remained bound by a treaty with Britain until 1951.
2. When the British mandate ended in May 1948, Israel proclaimed independence over a portion of the Palestine mandate. The remainder was occupied by Israel, but the final disposition of these territories remains subject to a peace agreement with the Palestine Authority.

FIVE

Fictional Independence:
Protectorates, Mandates, and Influence

To the west of the subcontinent, independent nations ostensibly existed under mandates, treaties, and various forms of indirect Western influence. For the populations of these nations, however, true independence meant the elimination of external domination, even where formal imperial relations did not exist. And, in much of the area, politics was intricately mixed up with oil. One such country was Iran.

Iran

Iran, although never formally a colony, was under the imperial reach of both Britain and Russia—and especially of the former. As noted in Chapter 1, Britain and Russia had occupied substantial areas of Iran in both world wars and both had been involved in the deposing of Reza Shah when he refused to expel Germans at the beginning of World War II. Russian influence faded at the end of the war, but the powerful economic influence of the Anglo-Iranian Oil Company, closely identified with the British government, established a sense of British dominance in Iranian affairs. As Professor R. K. Ramazani writes in *Revolutionary Iran*, "To Musaddiq [Muhammed Musaddiq, Prime Minister of Iran, 1952–1953] and his followers, the struggle against the British oil interests in Iran was not an economic or financial question, it was a struggle for Iran's independence. The reason for this nationalist belief, in Musaddiq's words, 'has been sure knowledge of the Iranian people . . . that the source of all the misfortunes of this tortured nation is only the oil company.'" [1]

As the British withdrew from east of Suez, Iran became more and more important as a Western bulwark against Soviet expansion. The fear of such expansion had been triggered when Russia sought to hold on to Azerbaijan at the end of

World War II. Pressure from the West and from the United Nations forced the Russians to withdraw support from a puppet regime, but the interest of the Soviet Union in Iran had been further demonstrated.

Iran's strategic position brought the shah in a close relationship not only with the British but with the United States as well. After the shah was returned to the throne after the coup against Musaddiq in 1953, the U.S. commercial, military, and political dominance of Iran resulted in increased Iranian alienation from the shah and the United States. According to R. K. Ramazani,

> The single most important event in this period that played into the hands of the opponents of the Shah and the United States was the Shah's conclusion of a status of forces agreement with the United States [in 1963]. [The status of forces agreement provided special immunities for members of the U.S. armed forces in Iran.] This agreement reminded Iran of the capitulatory rights that Western powers had imposed on Iran in the nineteenth century. More important, it was viewed as the single most important symbol of submission to American power at the expense of Iran's independence.[2]

A growing identity of the United States with Iran's security service, SAVAK, also weakened both the position of the shah and the United States. But the ultimate revolution against the shah, the British, and the oil interests came not from Musaddiq and his National Front, but from conservative *shiah* religious leaders under the Ayatollah Ruhollah Khomeini. They were reacting to what they saw as the excessive oppression of the shah's regime, which they associated with the British and the Americans—especially the Americans. To many in the country, the nation did not become truly independent until the revolution of January 1979 and the accession of the rule of the Islamic *ulema*.

The Ottoman Dilemma

In the Middle East and North African areas of the collapsed Ottoman empire, independence was more difficult to define. Britain, France, and Italy assumed hegemony over various parts of the Ottoman region after the Versailles treaty of 1919. In the minds of the local political elites, however, none of the post-Versailles arrangements constituted a true transfer of power. To them, independence would only come with the removal of Western domination, whether it be British, French, Italian, or, subsequently, American.

At the end of World War I, the British, who had conducted the major part of the military campaigns in the Eastern Mediterranean, including Iran, Mesopotamia, Syria, and Palestine, were the clearly dominant power. To them, in large measure, fell the responsibility to determine the future of the various Ottoman entities. But wartime diplomacy had complicated their task.

In the early twentieth century, an Arab nationalist movement gained momentum within the Ottoman empire.[3] Recognizing the importance of this movement and in order to gain the support of Arabs against the Turks, the British made an alliance with Sherif Hussein, the Hashemite ruler of the Hejaz in the western Arabian peninsula. To gain his support, the British promised that the Arab regions would become independent in an Arab nation after the war was over. As a result of the commitment, Arab forces, allied with the British, drove the Turks from the Levant.

Various interests sought to reshape the post-war map. Iraqis who had served in the Turkish army and had joined forces with the Arabs and the British demanded support for an independent Iraq in Mesopotamia. These included Nuri al-Said, later to become a strong figure in the Iraqi monarchy.

British members of the Indian Political Service who had been seconded to Mesopotamia during World War I espoused a post-war regime in which Mesopotamia, and perhaps other parts of the Near East, would be incorporated within the British empire under the viceroy of India. The British Middle East Command in Cairo, on the other hand, had supported Sherif Hussein and the Arabs and felt British interests in the region would be best served by endorsing an Arab nation.

Significant secret agreements, however, had been negotiated during the war. On April 26, 1915, Britain, France, Russia, and Italy signed the Treaty of London, designed to bring Italy into the war on the allied side. That treaty, among other provisions, transferred to Italy all rights and privileges belonging to the Ottoman sultan in Libya.

On May 16, 1916, to adjust their own claims to the Asiatic portions of the Ottoman empire, Britain and France concluded what became known as the Sykes-Picot agreement. It contained four provisions relevant to the Middle East:

- France was to obtain what is today modern Syria and Lebanon, eastern Turkey, and northern Iraq.
- Great Britain was to obtain southern Mesopotamia, including Baghdad, as well as the ports of Haifa and Acre in Palestine.
- The zone between the French and British territories was to form either a confederation of Arab states or one independent Arab state. This zone was to be further divided into a French and British sphere of influence. The French sphere was to include the Syrian hinterland and the Mosul province of Mesopotamia. (By a revision of the treaty in December 1918, Mosul was transferred to the British sphere of interest in exchange for a French share in the north-Mesopotamian oil deposits.) The British sphere was to extend over the territory between Palestine and the Iranian border.
- Palestine was to be internationalized.[4]

But complicating any implementation of the Sykes-Picot agreement was a letter to Lord Rothschild (who was representing the Zionists), which was approved by the British Cabinet on November 2, 1917 and signed by Lord Balfour, the foreign minister. It contained these commitments:

His Majesty's Government view with favour the establishment in Palestine of a national home for the Jewish people, and will use their best endeavours to facili-

tate the achievement of this object, it being clearly understood that nothing shall
be done which may prejudice the civil and religious rights of existing non-Jewish
communities in Palestine, or the rights and political status enjoyed by Jews in any
other country.[5]

Against this background, the Paris Peace Conference of January 1919 sought to
reconcile the various claims to former Ottoman territories. Under the pressure of
U.S. President Woodrow Wilson, who resisted any reestablishment of colonies, the
League of Nations was to allocate mandates to the major powers to govern desig-
nated territories. Such allocation was made in a further peace conference at San
Remo on April 24, 1920. France was given Syria (including Lebanon); Great Britain
was assigned Iraq and Palestine. All were Class A mandates, indicating that they
were temporary and were to lead to ultimate independence.

The Emir Feisal, son of Sherif Hussein of Mecca, had been established in
Damascus by the victorious Arab armies at the end of the war. In March 1920, he
was declared King of Syria. His outspoken Arab nationalist views were more than
the new French overseers were prepared to tolerate, and he was removed by French
forces in August.

Iraq

In that same month, Iraq erupted upon news of the mandate allocations and revelations of the secret treaties. It took a British force of 130,000 six months to put
down a widespread rebellion, at a cost of 2,500 casualties. Determined to establish
firm authority in their mandates, Britain called a conference of Arab representatives in Cairo in March 1921 at which the dethroned Feisal was offered the throne
of Iraq, and his older brother, Abdullah, who had originally been considered for
Iraq, was offered the emirship of a new territory east of Palestine, to be called
Transjordan. Thus Britain imposed monarchies upon a restless Iraq and a largely
bedouin Transjordan.

Conscious of Iraqi nationalism, Britain did not formally establish a mandate
but negotiated a treaty in 1922 that gave the United Kingdom the right to appoint advisers in finance and foreign affairs, assist the army, and protect foreigners.
Largely with support from traditional tribes, the treaty was ratified by Iraq in 1924.
Dissatisfaction with the degree of British control remained. A new treaty with Britain in 1930 proclaimed Iraq's full independence and obligated Britain to support
Baghdad's membership in the League of Nations. Britain, however, retained the
right to consult on foreign affairs, the right to use Iraqi facilities in time of war,
and the right to retain military bases. Iraq was formally admitted to the League of
Nations on October 3, 1932.

This arrangement may have been considered by the British to represent independence for Iraq, yet twenty years later, when I served in Iraq, the Iraqi feeling of
being an appendage of Britain was still strong.

As public affairs officer in the U.S. Embassy, I was constantly reminded by

Iraqis that theirs was an "imposed" monarchy and that the country was run largely by the British. When the cabinet changed—as it frequently did—bazaar talk speculated on whether the list had been drawn up in the British or American embassies. An Iraqi journalist, writing of new dam construction in the north of the country, insisted that no dams were being built; the construction was for barracks for British soldiers who would return to take over the country. When I offered to arrange a visit to the site of the new dam, he refused. He told me, "I don't care what is happening up there. My job is to embarrass the government." In Iraq at that time, to attack the British or the Americans was the same thing as attacking the government—but safer for the attacker.

The Iraqi structure that was established and, in large part, maintained by the British was swept away in a revolution in July 1958. Some Iraqis may say that the coup brought about true independence, but given what followed in Iraq, such independence provided little freedom.

The French Connection

The history of France in neighboring Syria and Lebanon, not unlike the history of France in East Asia, was one of continual resistance to any lessening of imperial control. France gained power in Syria and Lebanon not only as a result of the San Remo treaty but also from a long-standing, although not officially conferred, French protection of Lebanese Christians.

Efforts by Syria and Lebanon to replace the mandate regime with treaties, as Britain and Iraq had done, came to naught. A Franco-Syrian treaty was signed in September 1936 and a similar Franco-Lebanese agreement was signed in November of that year. Paris, claiming concern over a coming European war, delayed signing and then ultimately refused.

During World War II, the Free French supplanted the Vichy French in the Levant and proclaimed Syrian and Lebanese independence, but then it refused to transfer authority. In 1943, when the Lebanese parliament voted to drop all reference to the French mandatory power from the constitution, the French delegate general placed the president and many members of the cabinet under arrest. Finally, on June 21, 1945, Syria and Lebanon dismissed all French citizens from their services. On July 7, France agreed to terminate the relationship. The last foreign soldiers left Syria and Lebanon in December 1946.

Jordan

In that same year, 1946, Britain signed a treaty with Transjordan (the name was changed in 1949 to the Hashemite Kingdom of Jordan) that recognized the country as an independent state. Britain retained strong influence in Amman, however, until 1956. Late in the previous year efforts were made by the British and King Hussein to effect Jordanian adherence to the Baghdad Pact (a Northern Tier security arrangement to be discussed in a later chapter), but Arab nationalist opposition led to serious riots. In March 1956, in recognition of the growing power of the nationalists, King Hussein suddenly dismissed General Sir John Glubb, who had commanded Jordan's armed forces and had been a symbol of the British presence in the country. Jordan also wished to abrogate its treaty with Britain but was reluctant to lose the subsidy that went with it. Only when Jordan gained the assurance of Egypt, Syria, and Saudi Arabia that they would replace the subsidy did Amman proceed to negotiate the abrogation, which was finalized on February 13, 1957.

As George Lenczowski asks in his book *The Middle East in World Affairs,* "Thus the final act of Jordan's emancipation was consummated. But was it real emancipation? More appropriately one could call it a change of allegiance."[6]

Palestine

For Britain, the most traumatic departure from the empire was that of Palestine. The determination of the Jewish diaspora to establish a national home, a determination magnified by the Holocaust and supported by political pressures in both London and Washington, clashed with the expectations of the Arabs, hopes supported by various treaties that the post-Ottoman period would bring independent Arab states, including Palestine. Britain was caught in the middle and, in the end, departed, leaving others to resolve the deep differences.

As noted above, the Sykes-Picot agreement called for an "internationalized" Palestine. Nevertheless, the Palestinian Arabs and their neighbors insisted that Britain had committed itself to independence for the territory. At the same time, the Balfour declaration committed Britain to support a Jewish homeland—albeit without damaging the interests of other populations in Palestine. The British thought they had reason, in 1917, to believe that the Arabs would accept a Jewish homeland. In his book *End of Empire,* Brian Lapping quotes Philip Noel-Baker, who was a young member of the British delegation to the Versailles conference:

> I did not believe the Arabs would accept a Jewish national home in Palestine, but one of my colleagues took me to see the Emir Feisal in Geneva. T. E. Lawrence, the great friend of the Arab leaders, was with him and Feisal said that the arrival of European Jews with their energy and enterprise and modern scientific skills would be good for Palestine and good for the Arabs. It was that conversation which converted me to Zionism.[7]

Lapping should have added that Feisal's comments were based on his assumption that he would be king of an Arab nation that included Palestine.

When the British League of Nations mandate was established in 1922, London adopted the policy of permitting Jewish immigration so long as the numbers did not exceed the absorptive capacity of the country. In 1918, 70,000 Jews lived in Palestine. Between 1922 and 1926, after the mandate was established, an additional 75,000 arrived.

Whatever Emir Feisal's view may have been, increased Jewish immigration stirred resentment and fears among Palestinian Arabs. In April 1920, when news of the mandate scheme began to appear, in one of the first outbreaks of violence, anti-Jewish disturbances broke out in Jerusalem and Jaffa; forty-seven Jews were killed. Agitation grew as Jews purchased land from absentee Arab landlords and then expelled the Arab tenants.

Palestinian leadership under the Mufti of Jerusalem, al-Haj Amin al-Husseini (whose name eventually became anathema to both Jews and British because of his pro-German sympathies) refused to acknowledge the mandate.

In the immediate post–World War II period, as the Arabs became increasingly resentful, Britain sought to limit immigration, intercepting ships bound with illegal immigrants, but reaction to Hitler's extermination of the Jews made it more and more difficult to carry out such measures in the face of opinion in Britain and America. British efforts were undermined not only by external pressures but also by the increasingly violent acts of the Jewish underground, represented by the Irgun and the Stern Gang. On October 31, 1945, the combined efforts of the Jewish underground took the form of several hundred coordinated explosions throughout Palestine, causing damage to railways and police equipment. The campaign continued against bridges and military camps; several British soldiers and civilians were killed. The most spectacular was the bombing by the Irgun of the King David Hotel in Jerusalem on July 22, 1946; ninety-one people were killed, including seventeen Jews. When the British hanged three Irgun members, the organization captured two unarmed British soldiers and hanged them in retaliation. Pressure grew in London for the British to leave.

British efforts to resolve the problems by negotiation bore little fruit, complicated not only by Jewish intransigence but also by the refusal of the Palestinians to talk with Jewish leaders. In February 1947, Britain referred the question of Palestine's future to the United Nations. A special commission was set up (The UN Special Commission on Palestine—UNSCOP); in September 1947, UNSCOP recommended the ending of the British mandate and the partitioning of Palestine into Jewish and Arab states. Britain saw the proposals as both unfair to the majority Arabs and, under existing circumstances, impossible to implement.

The partition plan was put to a UN General Assembly vote on November 29, 1947—strongly supported by the United States. The plan was approved, but Britain's decision to leave without trying to implement the plan left Jews and Arabs face to face in a political vacuum. Arabs and Jews attacked each other. In a particularly brutal event, the Stern Gang and Irgun participated in the massacre of Arab villagers in Deir Yassin near Jerusalem on April 9, 1948. Even before the end of the mandate and other pressures, this event spurred a flight of frightened Arabs.

The British set May 15, 1948, as the end of the mandate. On that day a well-organized Zionist movement declared the establishment of the State of Israel. Rejecting the partition plan, poorly coordinated Arabs made an abortive effort to destroy the Jewish state. Only the Arab League's success in holding the area west of the Jordan prevented a complete Jewish victory.

The British high commissioner departed from the docks in Haifa with minimal ceremony, leaving problems for the inhabitants of Palestine, the citizens of the

new state of Israel, the Arab countries, the Muslim world, and the Western powers
that would preoccupy them into the twenty-first century.

Egypt

In the unsuccessful Egyptian effort against Israel in 1948, a young Egyptian army
officer was part of a battalion in a group of Arab villages called the Faluja Pocket,
which was surrounded by Israelis. That officer was to have a profound effect on the
ultimate departure of the British from the Middle East. His name was Gamal Abdul
Nasser.

Embittered against the British from his school days, Nasser, while serving
with the Egyptian army in Sudan in 1947, set up a secret society with three fellow
officers—the Free Officers. They dedicated themselves to ousting the British and
the Egyptian royal family.

On July 23, 1952, they succeeded in toppling the monarchy of King Farouk in
a bloodless coup. Within two years Nasser and his Free Officers would accomplish
their other mission: the ouster of the British.

Egypt had obtained formal independence in the Anglo-Egyptian treaty of
August 26, 1936. To many Egyptians, however, the continued presence of British
troops in the Suez Canal zone denied the country full independence. When World
War II came with threats to Egypt from Germany and Italy, Britain exercised its
rights under the treaty and substantially expanded its presence. Cairo became the
principal British and, ultimately, Allied base in the Middle East. British subjects
were in key positions in the police force, in the courts, and in border security agencies. More than half a million Allied troops passed through Egypt in the course of
the war. Egypt, however, declined to declare war until February 1945, and even then,
Prime Minister Ahmed Maher Pasha was assassinated as he read the declaration.

The end of World War II saw the renewal of Egyptian political activity, including the rise of an Egyptian Communist Party and, on the other side of the
spectrum, the fundamentalist Muslim Brotherhood. The latter was dedicated to
terrorism against all who had collaborated with the British during the war. Pressure
resurfaced to revise the treaty with Britain, especially those portions relating to the
presence of British troops and the Anglo-Egyptian condominium over the Sudan.
Egyptians wanted the troops removed and Sudan reunited with Egypt. Both issues
were raised, without Egyptian success, in the UN Security Council in July 1947.

Treaty revision talks resumed in 1950, but with the Soviet Union threatening
invasions in Europe, neither London (nor Washington) believed the time was appropriate for a withdrawal of British troops. At the same time, British and American identification with the establishment of Israel increased agitation against any
Western presence.

On October 15, 1951, the Egyptian parliament approved decrees abrogating the
1926 Anglo-Egyptian treaty. Rioting occurred in Cairo when Britain refused to
accept the decision. Britain, France, Turkey and the United States then presented
to Egypt a proposal for a Middle East defense pact in which Allied troops would

replace the British in the canal zone. Egypt rejected the proposal. (The proposal was the opening salvo of a Western effort that led to the controversial Baghdad Pact, a subject for Chapter 15.)

In January 1952, continuing attacks on British forces led to the British occupation of the city of Ismailia in the Suez Canal zone. That sparked one of the most serious riots of the entire period. George Lenczowski describes it in his book *The Middle East in World Affairs:*

> The mobs . . . attacked and put to fire seven hundred commercial, social, and cultural establishments, mostly foreign-owned but including also a number of Egyptian-owned firms and institutions. Such well-known landmarks as the Shepheard Hotel, Barclay's Bank, the Turf Club, Groppi restaurants, and the Cirucel and Chemla department stores were either partly or totally destroyed with attendant loss of life. The toll was 522 wounded and 26 killed after a day of rioting.[8]

Six months later, on July 23, the Free Officers staged their coup. General Mohammad Naguib appeared as the leader; Nasser was to stay in the background for some time. Internal reforms of what they considered a corrupt regime was their primary objective. King Farouk abdicated and left for Italy. They also moved to fulfill their objectives regarding the troops and Sudan. A third objective, to build a high dam at Aswan on the Nile, was to lead ultimately to convulsive events.

The troop issue was relatively easy. On October 19, 1954, a new agreement abrogating the treaty of 1936 called for evacuation of British troops within twenty months (the last troops actually departed in June 1956), the retention of British technicians in the canal, and the right of Britain to deploy troops in the event of an armed attack by an outside power against Egypt. Britain still had a foot in the door, but that was to change over the following two years.

The Sudan problem was resolved on December 19, 1955, when Sudan declared its independence. Egypt and Britain accepted the declaration. More serious problems for both Egypt and the West lay ahead.

In February 1955, retaliating against infiltrators from the Gaza Strip, the Israelis attacked the Gaza garrison of the Egyptian army, killing 38 and wounding 31. The Egyptian regime felt the need to enhance its security and requested arms from the United States. The United States offered the Egyptians a package of $20,000,000 with credit and an option to buy $20 million more. The terms of the agreement, however, limited the type of arms the Egyptians could purchase and insisted on a U.S. military team to monitor their use. The Egyptians considered this an unsatisfactory response and thereafter referred to it as a "refusal." In September of the same year, Cairo announced that an agreement to purchase Soviet-bloc arms had been negotiated with the Czechs. The Western monopoly on arms supply in the Middle East had been broken. The discussion with Soviet-bloc representatives on arms led also to discussions about the third objective, building the high dam. In October 1955 the Russians expressed their willingness to finance the dam.

Concerned at this further possible advance of Soviet influence, the Western countries made an offer to finance the first stage of the dam in December 1955. The

United States would lend $56 million, Britain would lend $14 million, and the World Bank would lend $200 million. All would be conditioned on Egypt's refusal of Soviet aid.

The Western offer came at a time when President Nasser was unhappy over the Baghdad Pact, U.S. and British objections to the Czech arms deal, and what he saw as the partiality of both countries toward Israel. He delayed responding, possibly hoping for a better offer from Moscow.

On July 17, when a further Soviet offer did not materialize, the Egyptian ambassador to Washington was instructed to inform the U.S. government that Egypt accepted the Western offer. Two days later, Secretary of State John Foster Dulles informed the Egyptians that the U.S. offer had been withdrawn.

The withdrawal of the high dam offer certainly ranks as one of the most fateful decisions in the story of the modern Middle East. At the time the reasons for and the wisdom of that decision were widely debated. In the short term it led to an accelerated reduction of Western influence in Egypt. Looked at from the longer perspective, however, it may only have speeded up trends already in motion. A further look from the perspective of 1999 also suggests that predictions of permanent damage to Western interests proved premature.

Lenczowski gives some of the reasons for the decision:

> The official explanation of the American decision was that (1) Egypt had failed to reach a Nile waters agreement with Sudan and (2) Egypt's ability to devote adequate resources to the project had become more uncertain "than at the time the offer was made." In reality Egypt was rebuffed for a number of reasons such as opposition of southern senators fearful of the competition of Egyptian cotton should the dam be constructed and by a few western senators anxious to secure funds for similar projects in their own states; the general criticism in the Senate of foreign aid programs, especially if given to neutralist countries; and, above all, Dulles' resolve to call the Soviet bluff on this particular issue and to teach Nasser, whose fresh recognition of Red China still rankled, that sustained hostility toward the West did not pay.[9]

I was in the Office of Near Eastern Affairs in the State Department at the time. I recall Secretary Dulles explaining to us another reason: he was almost certain that the Senate would reject the proposed offer, and he did not wish to set a precedent of Senate rejection of an aid offer that might affect other offers that he was pursuing—particularly at that time one with Yugoslavia.

Roger Kirk who, as the officer in the State Department's executive secretariat responsible for the issue, sat in on the meetings at which Secretary Dulles discussed the decision. He writes:

> In the discussion about the denial, as I remember, Soviet arms were also important because it was felt they would absorb so much local currency that Nasser would not be able to meet his obligations to us in that area. A very important factor was ... the congressional opposition. If I remember correctly, Dulles in one of the

final meetings read out a letter from Senator George stating that it was highly unlikely that the Congress would approve the funds for Aswan. To some extent then Dulles was simply making the best of a choice almost forced upon him.[10]

Events moved swiftly. On July 26, one week after the withdrawal of the offer, Nasser announced the nationalization of the Suez Canal Company. Although he promised compensation to the stockholders, the reaction in Britain and France was volcanic. They feared not only the loss of valuable assets but also interference in a vital world waterway. A conference of interested powers, convened in London on August 16, decided to establish an international authority to administer the canal and appointed a five-nation (Australia, Sweden, Iran, Ethiopia, and the United States) committee to negotiate with Egypt. When Nasser insisted on establishing the principle of full Egyptian sovereignty over the canal, the negotiations collapsed. The Suez Canal Company pulled out its pilots. Western commentators at the time insisted that Egypt could not operate the canal without these experienced pilots. To the surprise and frustration of many, particularly of Britain and France, Egypt was able to recruit alternate pilots and to demonstrate that it could manage the canal.

For both Britain and France, the nationalization of the Suez Canal Company was the last straw. Nasser, with his strident (and effective) pan-Arab rhetoric, was already seen to be undermining the interests of the two powers throughout the Mediterranean and Middle East.

King Hussein's dismissal in March 1956 of John Glubb, the British commander of Jordan's Arab Legion, was blamed on nationalist pressures stimulated by Nasser. The French were engaged in a bitter war with Algerian nationalists and accused Egypt of supporting the rebels both politically and materially. France was in no mood for further challenges to its prestige in the region.

The canal was but one issue; Britain and France believed that if Nasser could be removed, their influence throughout the area could be more easily preserved.

Much has been written on the efforts of Britain and France, in collusion with Israel, to capture the Suez Canal and, hopefully, to topple Nasser by military action in October 1956. What was seen, unrealistically, as a blow to reassert imperial control, turned out, in the end, to be one of the final nails in the imperial coffin in the Middle East. Nasser survived and remained in power until his death fourteen years later, in 1970.

The Maghreb

By the end of 1956, the southern shore of the Mediterranean was independent, with one notable exception: Algeria.

At the end of World War II, the former Italian colony of Libya had come under British and French military administration. After four years of deliberation, the UN General Assembly in November 1949 voted that Libya should become a united and independent kingdom. With strong British encouragement, the head of a North African religious order, the Senussi brotherhood, was chosen as King Idris I. He proclaimed independence on December 24, 1951. Britain and the United States provided financial help and retained military bases until Idris was overthrown by Muammar Qadhaffi in September 1969.

In neighboring Tunisia, a French protectorate, nationalists under Habib Bourguiba, in alliance with the traditional ruler, the Bey of Tunis, looked to the Free French to grant them greater autonomy after World War II. They were disappointed; in 1945 the Bey was overthrown and Bourguiba forced to flee in disguise to Egypt. Even after Bourguiba was permitted to return in 1951, the French still resisted nationalist efforts. Finally in June 1955, they granted limited autonomy, to be followed on March 20, 1956, by a new treaty which replaced the protectorate and granted independence but permitted France to retain troops at Bizerte, a French naval base.

In Morocco, nationalists had the support of the popular king, Mohammad V, but, in a familiar pattern, the French believed that they could bypass the king and the nationalists and maintain the protectorate by collaborating with the Pasha of Marrakesh, Tihami al Glaoui. In February 1953, after violent anti-French demonstrations, Mohammad V was sent into exile in Madagascar, and his uncle, Mohammad ben Arafa, was placed on the throne. In the face of strong protests in Morocco and, after granting autonomy to Tunisia, the French changed course to bring back Muhammad V and concede independence on March 2, 1956.

The French apparently hoped that by granting independence to Tunisia and Morocco, France's power could concentrate on retaining "French Algeria," where an open revolt against Paris's rule was already raging.

In French eyes, Algeria was different from Tunisia and Morocco. Algeria had French settlers. The coastal strip across from France had been settled for over a century by more than a million émigrés from southern France and Malta, referred to as *colons*. In 1900, the region was made a part of metropolitan France. Algerian nationalists faced not only the resistance of the settlers but the political power the settlers wielded in France. The *colons* were determined to stay and to exercise their full influence in Paris. But that was not to be.

On October 31, 1954, a group of Algerians in the name of the National Liberation Front (FLN from the French initials) issued a pamphlet calling for the restoration of a sovereign Algerian state. Guerilla warfare broke out in 1955. A cycle of killings of Europeans and Muslims began; the French sent an army of 500,000 to quell the disturbances.

The French expectation that the independence of Tunisia and Morocco in 1956 would lessen their burdens in North Africa proved unfounded. The new countries now provided havens for the FLN on both sides of Algeria. More and more the war was receiving support from other Arab states; leaders of the FLN had established headquarters of an Algerian government-in-exile (GPRA) in Cairo. The French belief that if they could eliminate Nasser they could end the war in Algeria was one of their motives in joining the British and Israelis in the Suez attack of 1956.

In October 1956, on the eve of Suez, Habib Bourguiba invited the FLN leaders to come to Tunisia from Rabat, where they were visiting the king of Morocco. French intelligence diverted the plane; Ahmed Ben Bella, leader of the FLN, and five others were arrested and imprisoned for all the six remaining years of bitter warfare between France and the Algerians. The French action resulted in further attacks on French settlers and the embitterment of Muhammed V of Morocco, whose guests the FLN leaders had been.

To isolate the country from the independent neighbors that were harboring some 30,000 Algerian fighters, the French erected barbed-wire fences along both frontiers. In February 1958 the French Air Force bombed the Tunisian frontier village of Saqiyat Sidi Yusuf. Algerian Muslims and *colons* both resorted to terrorist tactics, and French settlers sought alliances with military officers in Paris who might be prepared to overthrow French leaders friendly to Algerian independence. A settler organization, the Secret Army Organization (OAS), began a campaign of violence against French installations in Algeria.

The end finally came under the presidency of Charles de Gaulle. On June 4, 1958, he visited Algiers and, speaking to the French settlers, he made one of the great equivocal statements of all time. In French, he said, "Je vous ai compris." (I understand you.) His statement suggested to the *colons* that he was on their side; to de Gaulle, the utterance provided him with the flexibility to do what he wanted. In September 1959, he stated publicly that the Algerians had the right to determine their own future, sparking renewed settler efforts to sabotage any likely negotiations with the GPRA. Such negotiations did open in May 1961 at Evian in France. After interruptions, agreement was finally reached on March 8, 1962, that a referendum would be held on independence. Despite violent opposition from the OAS, the referendum was held on July 1, 1962, bringing 6 million votes in favor of independence and only 16,000 votes against it. Algeria became independent on July 3.

Cyprus

While the French were dealing with their North African issues, the British were facing another complex Mediterranean problem: the island of Cyprus.

In Cyprus, as in Palestine, the British encountered two antagonistic communities, a majority Greek and a minority Turkish, locked in the same space. They faced deeply emotional issues, a determined and wily leadership supported by sympathetic populations abroad, and a campaign of terror. This time the problem unfolded against the backdrop of tensions between two NATO members, Greece and Turkey. And they responded as the French had responded in North Africa by exiling the key figure—and with the same degree of success.

In 1878, the British seized the island and subsequently signed a lease with the Ottoman sultan. But the Greek population, which represented a majority of 80 percent, had always preferred *enosis,* union with Greece, rather than alliance with Britain. The hope was supported by a strong pan-Hellenic campaign led by the Greek Orthodox Church. When the Ottoman empire took Germany's side in World War I, the British assured the Cypriots that if Britain won the war it would cede Cyprus to an independent Greece. In fact, the offer was made to King Constantine of Greece in 1915, but he rejected it, fearful of appearing to take sides in the European war. The Greek hope for *enosis* remained alive until 1925 when the British, desiring a secure base in the eastern Mediterranean, annexed the island. After pro-*enosis* rioting in 1931, Britain terminated institutions of self-government and instituted governor's rule. The display of Greek flags and the pealing of church bells were banned. But the hope for *enosis* did not fade. It was kept alive in schools where, with British agreement, teachers used textbooks imported from Greece emphasizing *enosis*.

Greek-British cooperation in World War II again raised hopes for *enosis*. When the British proposed a consultative assembly on the island at the end of the war but excluded self-determination, Greek Cypriots turned down the proposal. In 1947, Britain was moving its forces from Palestine to bases on the island and was under attack in Egypt. Cyprus suddenly became more important to London just as two men who would change the course of the island's history came on the scene: Archbishop Makarios III and George Grivas.

From 1950, Makarios had attracted British attention as a determined and skillful advocate of *enosis*. In that year, the World Council of Churches sent him to Boston to study for two years; he took advantage of his presence in the United States and at the United Nations to bring the cause of *enosis* to the attention of American Greeks. Upon his return to Cyprus in 1952, he organized a revolutionary committee and appointed Grivas, a decorated but brutal officer, as military organizer. Both were determined to press for *enosis*.

Categorical statements have a way of affecting history; so it was in Cyprus. In September 1953, Britain's Foreign Secretary Anthony Eden visited Greece. When Greek officials raised the future of Cyprus, Eden reportedly replied that there was no Cyprus question, that there never would be, and that he would not discuss it.[11] The Greek prime minister, General Alexandros Papagos, declared, "He told me *never*."[12] Eden made this response in part because Cyprus continued to be important to Britain, in part because he believed the Turks would never let Greece have Cyprus. The following July, as British troops were being evacuated from Egypt to a new headquarters in Cyprus, a junior minister, Henry Hopkinson, was asked about Cyprus in a parliamentary debate. He replied:

> It has always been understood and agreed that there are certain territories in the Commonwealth which, owing to their particular circumstances, can never expect to be fully independent. (Hon Members: "Oh!") . . . I am not going as far as that this afternoon, but I have said that the question of the abrogation of British sovereignty cannot arise—that British sovereignty will remain.[13]

Britain sought to recover by inviting the Greek and Turkish foreign ministers to London for a conference. Because no Cypriot was invited, the calling of the conference only worsened the situation on the island.

Angered by the two British "nevers" the Greek government asked in August

1954 that Cyprus' right to self-determination be put on the agenda of the UN General Assembly. The Cyprus problem became an international problem. On the island, it became a war of terrorism.

Under the acronym of EOKA (Greek initials for National Organization of Cypriot Fighters), Grivas's group began a campaign of bombing and attacks on police stations in April 1955.

To seek a cease-fire and a more permanent solution, the British began a series of negotiations between the governor, Field Marshall Sir John Harding, and Makarios. In the archbishop, however, Harding faced an interlocutor who pocketed each British concession and then asked for more. The effort ended when the British government, alarmed by setbacks in Jordan and Egypt, deported Makarios to the Seychelles in March 1956.

The archbishop's deportation was followed by a major military effort to eliminate EOKA. Thirty-six thousand British soldiers faced a few hundred EOKA fighters. The British campaign put Grivas and his men on the run after several months; in August 1956, EOKA called for a truce.

In the hopes of renewing negotiations the British released Makarios in August 1956 and permitted him to return to Athens. A new governor, Sir Hugh Foot, released detainees and lifted restrictions. But these measures angered the Turkish Cypriots, who launched demonstrations of their own. Civil strife spread across the island. The Turkish government entered the picture, demanding partition and a military base on Cyprus.

Prime Minister Harold Macmillan described the problem:

> It is really one of the most baffling . . . which I can ever remember . . . like one of those children's puzzles where the effort to get three or more balls into their right position is continually frustrated; two would fall into place but then the third would immediately escape. To whatever Turkey might agree Greece would object. To whatever Greece might demand Turkey would be obstructive. What Makarios might be inclined to accept, EOKA under General Grivas would refuse.[14]

The issue ultimately came to a head in December 1958, when Foreign Ministers Evangelos Averoff of Greece and Fatim Zorlu of Turkey met at the United Nations. The anti-Communist Greek government was increasingly concerned that its position in the United Nations depended mainly on Communist-bloc votes. Because of these votes, Greece was more and more regarded as damaging NATO and was ready for compromise.

The two ministers continued negotiations in secret. Their efforts ultimately led to meetings in Zurich, during which they agreed on a formula for independence for Cyprus in February 1959. This understanding was confirmed by a London conference that same year. A reluctant Makarios and a protesting Grivas ultimately agreed under pressure from the Greek government. Cyprus became independent in August 1960—but independence did not end the Cyprus question. Lapping sums up Britain's departure:

So eager were the British to put an end to the horrors of Cyprus that they left the island with an independence constitution of doubtful validity. Its main purpose was to avoid war between Greece and Turkey. To this end the sovereignty of Cyprus was restricted: it could not form part of a political or economic union with any other state and the forty-eight basic articles of the constitution could never be changed. The three guaranteeing powers, Britain, Greece, and Turkey, were given the right to intervene, together if possible, otherwise individually, to restore the constitutional arrangements should they be upset. The UN Charter requires every member state to have full and equal sovereignty. Cyprus was given a Supreme Constitutional Court whose President could be neither Cypriot nor Greek, neither Turkish nor British. The first President, Professor Forsthoff, a German, concluded in 1963: "I consider it wrong to regard Cyprus under the present agreement and constitution as an independent state." By then the British, to their relief, and amid an unexpected show of friendliness on all sides, had got away.[15]

SIX

The Gulf and the Peninsula

In 1968, the British Labour government made a fateful decision—to withdraw officially from east of Suez. This meant changes and greater independence for the principalities of the Persian Gulf.

Changes had begun even before the British decision. In any changes, however, the British endeavored to preserve their special relationships and commercial access. The old order in which the British Resident of the Gulf ruled over semi-autonomous principalities was clearly on its way out. The protection of the route to India was no longer a British priority; access to the oil and gas reserves of the region became far more important.

The Gulf States

The sheikhly mini-states of the Gulf and their relations with Britain were under pressure from many quarters: Iraq, Iran, Saudi Arabia, Egypt, and the United States.

Even under the Iraqi monarchy Baghdad had been equivocal about renouncing its traditional claim to Kuwait, based on the organization of the Ottoman empire in which Kuwait had been part of the wilayet (district) of Basra. After the Iraqi revolution of 1958, the new leader, Abdul Karim Qassim, formally asserted Iraq's claim to the sheikhdom. Britain, obligated by its earlier treaty, responded with troops. The incident opened the way to modernizing the relationship and, in June 1961, London substituted for the 1899 "date-garden" agreement[1] a new treaty that recognized Kuwait's independence but continued Britain's obligation to come to the aid of Kuwait if such aid were requested. The new treaty was put to the test in the Iraqi invasion of 1990.

Iran had long claimed Bahrein. When a British-Saudi treaty in 1927 referred to Bahrein as under British protection, Iran protested to the League of Nations.

Teheran continued to press its claims and in 1957 proclaimed the island an integral part of Iran and assigned it seats in the Majlis. To resolve the question of the island's future, the United Nations conducted a plebiscite in 1970; Bahreini voters chose independence over union with Iran. In May 1970, Iran accepted the results and renounced its claim, provided Bahrein would not enter into any alliances, unions, or federations and that Britain would accept Iranian occupation of the three islands at the mouth of the Gulf: Abu Musa and the two Tunbs.[2] Following this, on August 14, 1970, Britain signed a new treaty terminating the several earlier treaties and acknowledging the island's independence.

Two weeks later, on September 1, 1971, Britain signed a similar agreement terminating past arrangements and recognizing the independence of Qatar. To complete the changes in the Gulf, Britain negotiated a federation among the Trucial States—Abu Dhabi, Dubai, Sharja, Ajman, Umm-el-Qaiwain, Fujaira, and Ras-el-Khaima. They became independent as the United Arab Emirates on December 2, 1971. The same day, London formally relinquished British power in the Gulf.

Oil

The full story of the diminution of the British presence in the Gulf cannot be understood without reference to oil. Throughout the period of its relinquishment of power, Britain was concerned with two presences in the Gulf, those of Saudi Arabia and the United States. London considered that both challenged British political dominance and UK access to the resources. The revised agreements granting independence to the sheikhdoms carried the proviso that oil concessions would be granted only to British companies. But as the extent of petroleum reserves and the needs for capital and markets became apparent, the British government was reluctantly forced to agree to the admission of non-British companies. These were American companies.

In the summer of 1931, the Standard Oil Company of California (Socal) tanker *Scofield* left my home town of Richmond, California, for a distant place called Bahrein. On board was a crew to drill for oil. The manager of the Richmond Socal refinery, Max Thornberg, had been among those who negotiated a concession with the Sheikh of Bahrein. The negotiators had encountered unforeseen problems; they had not realized the British interest. Only when they satisfied British concerns by registering their new company, the Bahrein Petroleum Company (Bapco), in a member country of the British Commonwealth, Canada, were they permitted to go forward.

That same problem did not arise when Socal geologists looked across the straits at promising salt domes in the Eastern Province of Saudi Arabia.

From World War I, Britain had supported the Hashemite rivals of the Saudis. A form of understanding was reached in the Saudi-British treaty of May 20, 1927 which reaffirmed the "complete and absolute independence" of Ibn Saud; in turn, the Saudis acknowledged the special British position in Bahrein and the Gulf sheikhdoms and accepted the border with Hashemite Transjordan. Nevertheless, Britain's trust of Saudi Arabia was never complete. With the death of King Abdul Aziz Ibn Saud in 1953 and the accession of his son, Saud bin Abdul Aziz, to the throne, his next son, Faisal, became crown prince. Faisal, a strong Saudi and Arab nationalist, was considered by the British to be too close to Gemal Abdul Nasser and therefore a threat to British interests in the Peninsula and Gulf. U.S. efforts to persuade the British otherwise were unavailing. U.S.-British relations also became intertwined with London's discomfort at the growing role of the United States in the oil development of the region.

Socal's approaches to Saudi Arabia were successful after King Ibn Saud learned that Socal discovered oil in Bahrein on May 31, 1932. A concession agreement was signed with Socal on May 29, 1933. Ultimately, the Socal concession was expanded to include Texaco, Standard Oil of New Jersey, and Socony Mobil to form the Arabian American Oil Company (ARAMCO).

Negotiations with British interests were necessary for the third major U.S. petroleum concession in Kuwait. Under pressure from the U.S. government and the personal intervention of Andrew Mellon, at the time U.S. ambassador to London, Britain reluctantly agreed to Kuwait's granting one-half of a concession to U.S. Gulf Oil. Combined with a 50 percent share of Anglo-Persian, the enterprise became the Kuwait Oil Company.

Other major concessions in the Gulf were given to the Iraq Petroleum Company (IPC), consisting of British Petroleum, Compagnie Française de Petrol, Standard Oil of New Jersey, Socony Mobil, and five percent was granted to the Armenian discoverer of Iraq's oil, Calouste Gulbenkian. The two American participants in IPC were also partners in ARAMCO, a relationship that was to involve them, unwillingly, in the politics of the Gulf.

Buraimi

Boundaries in the Arabian desert were seldom defined. Territorial claims rested on traditional rights to oases or on to whom nomadic tribes paid taxes. Among these undemarcated boundaries was that between Saudi Arabia and Abu Dhabi. At a point where the claims of the two countries intersected with that of the neighboring independent Sultanate of Muscat and Oman lay a cluster of nine villages around the oasis of Buraimi. In 1952, a small Saudi Arabian force entered the oasis and claimed it for the Saudi kingdom on the basis that the tribes of the villages paid their *zakat*, or taxes, to Saudi tribes. The British, responding to Sheikh Zaid, the ruler of Abu Dhabi, protested the Saudi move. The dispute went to international arbitration.

ARAMCO, which by then had assembled an impressive staff of Arabists, undertook to prepare the memorial, the submission to the arbitration panel, on behalf of Saudi Arabia. The moving spirits in the preparation were James Terry Duce, vice president for government relations, and George Rentz, an Arabic scholar. The activism of ARAMCO placed the company's two IPC partners in an embarrassing position.

I was the officer in charge of Arabian Peninsula affairs at that time. Once, after I had had a long session with Duce and Rentz, I received a call from a senior official of Standard Oil of New Jersey.

"Has Terry Duce been in to see you?

"Yes."

"We want to make clear that he does not represent the position of this company."

The arbitration panel ultimately broke down amid charges of bribery. In October 1955, the British-led Trucial Oman Scouts entered the oasis and expelled the Saudis. The incident remains as one of the signal examples of the inimical intersection of British, Saudi, and American interests.

Muscat and Oman

The third party to the Buraimi dispute, the Sultanate of Muscat and Oman, which had close ties with the British, had nevertheless preserved its independence over several centuries by careful diplomacy—although Saudi Arabia made periodic claims of hegemony. In the nineteenth century, the Sultan's domain had extended down the East African coast; for a time its capital was in Zanzibar. It was to Zanzibar that a roving American consul and trader, Edmund Roberts, came in 1833 to negotiate a treaty of friendship with the sultan on behalf of the United States, predating by six years a similar treaty between Muscat and Britain.

The U.S.-Muscat treaty became relevant in the early 1950s, when Cities Service Oil Company gained a concession in the Omani province of Dhofar. The 1833 treaty exempted U.S. citizens from local law. Because this extra-territorial exemption was no longer acceptable policy for the United States, it became necessary to renegotiate the treaty. To assuage Saudi sensitivity over U.S. relations with Oman, the U.S. negotiators had to refer back to Consul Roberts's original reports to be sure that the form of address used for the sultan had not changed since 1833.

Aden

At the time of the Oman discovery the Dhofar province was the target of insurgents from another British colony, Aden and the East Aden Protectorate. In one of the more unlikely twists of the decolonization story, the Aden colony became the only Marxist state in the Middle East after independence in 1968.

Aden lay at the southwest corner of the Arabian Peninsula, buffered against Yemen to the north by a series of traditional Arab principalities. Yemen, in 1960, was the world's most isolated kingdom; no one entered except by the personal permission of the Imam or his agent. I went in in 1956 to negotiate the opening of a resident U.S. legation. My "visa" was a handwritten note written on a page torn from a spiral notebook and signed by the Imam's agent in Aden.[3]

Seized originally as a coaling station on the way to India, Aden became increasingly important with the establishment of a major British Petroleum refinery in 1954 and the British Middle East Command in 1960. The economic boom fueled by these developments and a port made busy by the closing of the Suez Canal in 1956 brought thousands of job-seekers from the hinterland of Aden and Yemen to the north. The new arrivals were ripe for the message of the growing Aden Trade Unions Congress (ATUC), which espoused Nasser's call for Arab unity and called for an independent socialist state and for the overthrow of the Imam of Yemen. But in May 1956, the British were not thinking of independence. As in Cyprus, they said, "Never." Lord Loyd, undersecretary of state for colonies, told the four elected and twelve appointed members of the Aden Legislative Council:

> Many of you have a perfectly legitimate desire to take a greater part in the affairs of government and there is no reason that desire should not be realized. But I should like you to understand that for the foreseeable future it would not be reasonable or sensible, or indeed in the interests of the Colony's inhabitants, for them to aspire to any aim beyond that of a considerable degree of internal self-government. . . . Her Majesty's Government wish to make it clear that the importance of Aden, both strategically and economically, within the Commonwealth is such that they cannot foresee the possibility of any fundamental relaxation of their responsibilities for the Colony. I feel confident that this assurance will be welcome to you and to the vast majority of the inhabitants of the Colony.[4]

To bolster their position against the ATUC and any threat from Yemen, the British used promises of financial aid and some force to pressure the majority of the tribal rulers in the hinterland to join in a Federation of Arab Amirates of the South in February 1959. The Federation immediately became the target of armed attacks from Yemen and protests from the ATUC in Aden itself. To respond, the British used the promise of ultimate independence to engineer the incorporation of the Aden Colony into the Federation in September 1962.

The day after the new union was formed, however, Imam Ahmed was overthrown by pro-Nasser republicans. This development had the effect in Aden of changing the objectives of the ATUC and its allies. Where once they had no interest in seeing Aden absorbed into an anachronistic monarchy, they now saw in the republicans a chance for unity with Yemen. Many of the ATUC members were Yemeni. Their hopes were bolstered by the deployment of what became 20,000 Egyptian troops to Yemen by 1967.

The republican campaign in Yemen initially held only key cities. A pro-monarchy force under Badr, the son of the late imam, began resistance. A debate over policy ensued within the British government, where the Foreign Office, wary of being identified with reactionary forces in the area, favored recognition of the republican regime. Washington agreed with this assessment, but others in the British government put their faith in its Federation tribal partners and began to back the monarchists. Nevertheless, the United States proceeded with recognition of the republican regime.

Britain immediately came under attack in the United Nations as well as in Aden. Under this pressure, the governor, Sir Kennedy Trevaskis, proposed that the colony and the Federation be granted independence with a target date of 1968.

The proposal was short-lived. Very shortly after Trevaskis's proposal, a Labour government was voted in in Britain. The new government, initially inclined to come to terms with the ATUC and move toward independence, reversed course, in part under pressure from the U.S. government. President Lyndon Johnson, immersed in the Vietnam war, did not wish to see a diminution of the British military role in the Middle East. To encourage the British to hold on, Johnson offered help to avert a devaluation of the pound.

But the British immediately faced a new threat. In June 1963, a group of Yemenis and Adenis organized the National Liberation Front (NLF). The republican government, now solidly in power in Sanaa, reacted to Britain's denial of recognition and British support for the royalists by supporting the new group, whose members were drawn from "those who had hurried to Yemen to welcome the new regime: tribal leaders, army officers who had been serving as mercenaries in Saudi Arabia and the Gulf, workers from Aden, young men from the federal states who had gone to Aden to study and had been inspired by Arab nationalism."[5] Adeni newspapers reported the establishment of the NLF, but it made no impact on British officials inured to the many organizations dedicated to overthrowing imperialism. Ironically, Egypt, which was later to oppose the NLF, assisted in its early organization. Lapping quotes Egyptian Foreign Minister Mahmoud Riad: "We helped in two ways, by sending arms directly to groups who were asking for them and by establishing a centre for training in Taiz."[6]

The NLF was a new form of adversary. The British did not know its leaders. It resorted to terrorism and surprise. When the British called for a constitutional conference, the NLF, already responsible for several murders, threatened to kill anyone who attended. The conference was suspended.

The ATUC, faced with the challenge of the NLF, adopted similar tactics. Under the reorganized name of the Front for the Liberation of Occupied South Yemen (FLOSY) it began its own campaign of violence and intimidation. Aden descended into civil war; the two sides, now anticipating independence, were fighting to determine who would be on top. The Federation tribal leaders still looked to the British to protect them. But the British, despite harsh measures, were unable to crush the NLF; British intelligence agents who gained knowledge of the organization were promptly assassinated.

Under these circumstances, the British government decided in February 1966 to close its base and quit the colony. A bitter and disenchanted group of tribal leaders was so informed. Ideally, London hoped that it might make an orderly turn over of power to the Federation leaders in league with the ATUC, but this was not to be. The increasingly powerful NLF, now openly calling for a Marxist-Leninist state, dubbed the tribal leaders British stooges and the ATUC tools of Egyptian imperialism.

Britain tried to improve relations with Nasser, which were broken over the unilateral declaration of independence in Rhodesia in 1965, but to little avail. Just as their efforts were progressing, the June 1967 Arab-Israeli war devastated Egypt, and Nasser withdrew his troops from Yemen and his support from FLOSY.

Neither side in the internal conflict was prepared to assist the British to an orderly departure. The British did send a representative, Sir Sam Falle, to meet with members of the NLF. Falle describes the encounter in *End of Empire:*

> I explained that the British Government wanted to negotiate independence and to involve all parties concerned so that the government that emerged would be acceptable to the people of Aden. I said that the NLF were a very important party to this and that if we could start talking with them we would of course consider releasing their detainees and taking the ban off their party so that we could discuss things in a reasonable and relaxed atmosphere. But there was one minor condition that we'd like to make. If it were possible we would be very grateful if they would stop killing us. And the two representatives roared with laughter. And one of them said, "Very sorry, Abu Sami, this is quite impossible." Being young, naive, and foolish I said, "But why? We come with peace and we want to talk to you. It would be rational if you'd stop killing us." He said, "No, you must understand. FLOSY constantly accuse us of being the running dogs of the imperialists. If we at this moment were seen to be talking to you this would simply give credence to their story. And so, Abu Sami, we are very sorry, but we have got to drive you out of Aden. And we have to be seen to drive you out."[7]

The British turned to FLOSY, but FLOSY, motivated by the same desire to be seen to drive the British out, refused to talk. The last support for Britain's presence, the Federation, collapsed when its military forces began fighting over who would be the commander after independence. They, too, turned on the British. Twenty-two British soldiers were killed by mutinous federal forces in the last days of the colony. In the final days, NLF prevailed over FLOSY and took power when the British left. The British indeed were driven out. As Elizabeth Monroe notes in *Britain's Moment in the Middle East,* "On November 29, 1967, the last helicopter flew out to a naval task force assembled in the harbor, and Aden was handed over unconditionally to jubilant Adenis of the National Liberation Front."[8]

Lapping gives a final assessment:

> The NLF took Aden and the Protectorates further to the left than most citizens can have expected. The new state was before long named the People's Democratic Republic of Yemen and soon proved itself a whole-heartedly Marxist, Soviet satellite. Ships of the Russian Navy became regular visitors to Aden harbor, Bulgarian and East German advisers helped develop new industries. The journalists who, until 1967, had been freely reporting on the failures of the British in Aden were now firmly kept out. By 1984 the concept of editorial freedom had become totally baffling, if not unintelligible, even to sophisticated Government officials. Not only was the PDRY unique in the aftermath of the British Empire in turning to Soviet Marxism, it was also unique in the Middle East. The departure of the British from Aden was certainly the worst shambles in the End of Empire, the successor regime the most completely opposed to all Britain had stood for.[9]

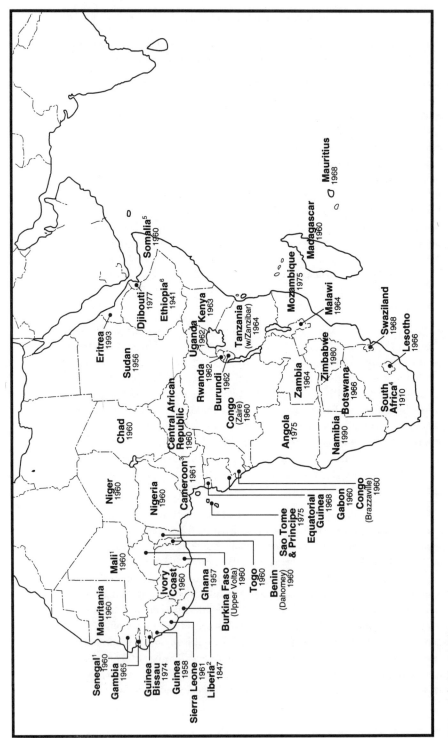

Map 4. Sub-Saharan Africa

1. Senegal and the Soudanese Republic became independent as the Mali Federation in June 1960. Senegal withdrew in August, and the two countries became separately independent as Senegal and Mali.

2. Founded by freed slaves from the United States.

3. The Republic of the Cameroon brought together British and French Cameroonian colonies.

4. The Union of South Africa was created as part of the British Commonwealth in 1910. In 1961 the country became the Republic of South Africa and withdrew from the Commonwealth.

5. Somalia was created by a union of Italian Somaliland and British Somaliland.

6. Ethiopia was liberated from Italy in 1941. Ethiopia had been, for centuries, an independent nation prior to the Italian invasion in 1936.

SEVEN

Africa I: Where Blacks Prevailed

Across the strait of Bab al Mandab, the gate to the Red Sea, lies Africa, the second largest continent, with more than fifty separate political entities. As the drama was unfolding in Aden in the 1960s, so, too, were independence stories taking place in the vast continent to the west.

Relations in Africa in colonial times were largely in straight lines to imperial capitals in Europe, whether for travel, education, trade, or defense. The dissolution of these empires is most easily understood by relating the experience of each European power and its colonies—Italy, Britain, France, Belgium, and Portugal. Germany was not a player in the final acts; its colonies of Tanganyika, Togo, and the Cameroons were made mandates of Britain and France after World War I.

No easy way exists to divide a discussion of Africa—whether by geography, European metropole, or ethnic and linguistic categories. I have chosen to separate the discussion of independence between those countries on the continent in which the indigenous black populations are clearly dominant and those with the complications of large white settler populations. We start with the Horn of Africa.

The Horn of Africa

The eastward protrusion of Africa comprised of Ethiopia, Somalia, Eritrea, and Djibouti—known as the Horn—was (and remains) a region of conflicting claims of clans and nations.

Despite setbacks already recounted, Italy retained a foothold on the Somali coast and in Eritrea until 1935, when the Italians used the pretext of a minor border incident to invade once more, this time to occupy Ethiopia. Their stay, however, was short-lived. In 1941, British forces retook all of Italian East Africa: Ethiopia, Somalia, and Eritrea.

At the heart of post–World War II efforts to create a stable region in the Horn was the question of the future of the divided Somali people, spread in an arc from Northern Kenya to Djibouti. As in the Arabian Peninsula, borders were not easily established in regions that had for decades been roamed by nomadic peoples.

The northern corner of the Somali territory had been administered as a protectorate, British Somaliland, since 1844. Somali areas that were not incorporated in the British colony of Kenya or the Ogaden region of Ethiopia had, before World War II, been Italian Somaliland. After the war, a UN decision placed the Italian colony under Italian trusteeship for ten years. Independence came in 1960 when British Somaliland was joined to the former Italian territory to create the Somali Republic.

After World War II the Italian colony of Eritrea was placed under British administration until 1952, when a UN decision made it autonomous as a part of a federated Ethiopia. In a staged maneuver, Ethiopia abolished the federation and declared Eritrea part of the empire in 1962. The move in Addis Ababa led Eritreans to armed resistance to Ethiopian rule and a prolonged war. Eritrea gained its independence in 1993, but fighting with Ethiopia again broke out in 1997.

The small territory of Djibouti to the north voted in 1967 to continue as an overseas territory of the French Union, but, in 1977, with the French departure, the territory became independent as the Republic of Djibouti.

Sudan

To the west of Djibouti and Ethiopia lay Africa's largest country in territory, Sudan.

A line across Africa on the edge of the Sahara divides Arab Africans from non-Arabs and, often, Muslims from Christians and animists. This line has affected the unity and stability of every country from Sudan to Mauritania—but nowhere more tragically than in Sudan. Three southern provinces that account for approximately 30 percent of the population, Bahr-al-Ghazal, Upper Nile, and Equatoria, are predominantly non-Arab and non-Muslim. They feel more affinity to the five bordering African countries—Ethiopia, Kenya, Uganda, Congo, and the Central African Republic—than to Egypt and the Muslim north. Egypt's life, however, depends on the Nile, and the two branches of the Nile come together and flow through Sudan. In the late nineteenth century, Britain believed control of the Nile was essential to its rule in Egypt. Britain's occupation of Uganda to the south and all of Sudan were designed to prevent any other power—and particularly the French—from gaining a foothold in the Nile basins.

After the battle of Omdurman in 1898, when British and Egyptian forces defeated the Sudanese Mahdi, London created the Anglo-Egyptian condominium—always more Anglo than Egyptian. Egypt promoted the idea of the unity of the Nile valley, but growing Sudanese nationalism resisted not only the British presence but that of Egypt as well. The deep division in Sudan between north and south remained.

In 1946, the British convened a conference to discuss the future of the country but included no southerners. Miffed at the exclusion, southerners in a subsequent conference in 1947 asked for separation from the north or a federation with guarantees.

At the same time, in discussions with Egypt, Britain insisted on Sudan's right to determine its future and, in 1948, introduced a constitution for self-government without Egyptian concurrence. In 1951, Egypt's King Farouk protested the rapid British moves toward Sudanese self-government by abrogating the condominium agreement of 1899 and the Anglo-Egyptian treaty of 1936. The actions, however, were of little effect; a few months later Farouk was overthrown in the coup of July 23, 1952.

The ostensible leader of the coup was General Mohammad Naguib, who was half-Sudanese. He accepted the self-government statute produced by the British, and a new Anglo-Egyptian agreement was signed in February 1953, giving January 1961 as the date for Sudanese independence. But again Egyptian politics had its impact in Sudan.

At the end of 1954, Gemal Abdul Nasser, the real power behind the coup, ousted Naguib. In the next year, Sudanese leaders in Khartoum, after suppressing a revolt in the south, repudiated both the British and the Egyptian efforts and proclaimed independence on January 1956. An uneasy and divided country was born.

Ghana

Fifteen months later, on March 6, 1957, across the continent, Ghana, the former Gold Coast, became the first fully sub-Saharan black African country to achieve independence.

The Ghana story deserves to be told at some length because it includes so many elements that, in one form or another, were present in nearly every colonial transition. What happened in the Gold Coast affected British policy in every colonial transition thereafter. The coming to independence of Ghana created alarm in areas of white-dominated southern Africa, where the idea of a black-ruled country had been considered inconceivable. Further, Ghana under Nkrumah was the cradle from which sprang the principal forces of pan-Africanism.

The story is once more a repetition of the cycle of the rise of nationalism: protest, arrest, release, and negotiation. The spark in this case was a British- and American-educated pan-Africanist named Kwame Nkrumah.

The colonial Gold Coast was typical of much of West Africa, where a division existed between the coastal people, who had first encountered and been influenced by the Europeans, and the interior population, dominated by traditional chiefs. Colonial powers often found their strongest support from the chiefs. Their political challenges came from the coast. The careful balance of coast and interior, however, was upset after World War II.

In 1938, even before the war, Britain had foreseen the need for political evolution. A retired Indian civil servant, Lord Hailey, was asked to survey the continent of Africa and assess whether it was properly governed. He recommended that Africans be appointed to the colonial administrative service and suggested the Gold

Coast as the place to start. The colonial secretary at the time, Malcolm MacDonald, began the implementation of Lord Hailey's recommendations. A new governor of the Gold Coast, Sir Alan Burns, appointed Africans to his administrative service and to the Legislative Council. In 1945, he brought a new constitution into effect which created a majority of Africans in a Gold Coast legislature. The careful pace of political development, however, was soon upset by several developments—the return of Gold Coast veterans who had fought for the British in East Africa, deteriorating economic conditions, and rivalries among Gold Coast political figures.

One of the nominees to the new legislature was Dr. Joseph Danquah, a Ph.D., member of a chiefly family, and organizer of the Gold Coast Youth Conference, an organization of educated Africans. He recalled that Clement Attlee, who was then Britain's prime minister, had reminded a meeting of African students in London that self-determination applied to all races. Danquah pressed for greater autonomy for the state he now called Ghana. Dissatisfied with the new constitution, he set up a new party, the United Gold Coast Convention (UGCC). He chose as the secretary a student in London, Kwame Nkrumah.

The two had their chance to broaden their protests on February 28, 1948. Serious riots by veterans broke out when British-led police prevented them from marching on the governor's residence. In three days of rioting, 29 people were killed, 237 people were injured, and the business district of Accra was destroyed. Danquah and Nkrumah sent telegrams of protest to the Colonial Office, to the United Nations, and to newspapers in London, New York, and Moscow.

A new governor, Sir Gerald Creasy, was unprepared for the riots. Advisers convinced him that Danquah and Nkrumah and other leading members of the UGCC had planned the riots and had links with Communist organizations. Danquah, Nkrumah, and four other members of the UGCC were banished to the Northern Territories of the Gold Coast. The governor called for more troops and declared a state of emergency.

The Accra events brought about a re-examination of colonial policy in London. Arthur Creech-Jones, the colonial secretary, had experience in Africa in the 1930s as an official of the Transport and General Workers' Union. The head of the Africa division of the Colonial Office was a young Cambridge classicist and anti-colonialist named Andrew Cohen. Lapping describes the approach of Creech-Jones and Cohen:

> Their argument for change was simple. Post-war Britain was desperately hard-up and needed the colonies to raise their profits by modernization and investment. This meant getting some Africans to do the growing, packing, manufacturing, transporting, and clerking that were required and others to co-operate in assigning land, planning roads and clearing administrative blockages. All this called for Africans to run the local government and public services in an innovative, energetic spirit. The urban, educated African could help . . . the traditional chiefs could not. A new system of government would therefore have to be introduced

throughout the African empire. It involved nation-building hand in hand with educated Africans.[1]

When Creech-Jones and Cohen presented their ideas to a conference of colonial governors, they were rebuffed. The governors objected that the Africans were not ready, that the introduction of democracy would undermine imperial authority, and that loyal Africans would be driven into the arms of irresponsible and radical nationalists. Creech-Jones and Cohen, however, convinced that Britain would lose friendship in the colonies if the pace of self-government were too slow, bided their time. They waited until the incumbent governors retired and then called for a judicial inquiry into the Accra riots. Judge Aiken Watson, who led the inquiry, came to radical and controversial conclusions:

> The concession of an African elected majority in the legislature, in the absence of any real political power, provided no outlet for a people eagerly emerging into political consciousness. . . . The constitution and government must be so reshaped as to give every African of ability an opportunity to help govern the country. . . . In all appointments or promotions in the public services the first question to be asked is "Is there an African capable of filling the appointment?"[2]

Despite objections to the Watson report, Cohen moved ahead. Recalling how Winston Churchill had undermined efforts to create self-government in India, he wanted to move as far as possible before another Conservative government was elected. Becoming more and more concerned about the ambitions and left-wing views of Nkrumah, Cohen sought to create a new government with Danquah as leader, sidelining Nkrumah. This ploy did not work.

In June 1949, Nkrumah launched a new party, the Convention People's Party (CPP) and took many of the members of the UGCC with him. With the slogan "Self-Government NOW" Nkrumah carried his message to stall-keepers, drivers, clerks, primary school teachers—a grassroots approach new to Africa.

When the governor presented a new constitution, Nkrumah called it "bogus and fraudulent" and threatened to institute civil disobedience. The deputy governor, Reginald Saloway, met with Nkrumah to persuade him that new elections would be fairly held and that the CPP could put up candidates. But, facing taunts from Danquah and conscious of an aroused public, Nkrumah felt that if he were to maintain the political initiative, he must reject the governor's plea and begin "Positive Action" with a general strike and boycott of British goods.

Nkrumah was promptly arrested, found guilty of fomenting an illegal strike and sedition, and sentenced to three years in prison. The governor then proceeded with the election, the first general election with an adult franchise ever held in black Africa. With Nkrumah locked up, both Danquah and the government believed the UGCC would win. But just as Nkrumah was entering prison, one of his associates, Komla Gbedema, was coming out. He took up Nkrumah's campaign. He also invented the distinction of "prison graduate," proposing that CPP followers gather at prison gates to greet each member released and that they wear distinctive dress indicating their status as a former prisoner. Of the thirty-eight elected seats in the new parliament, Nkrumah's CPP won thirty-four. Governor Charles Arden-Clarke felt he had no choice. He released Nkrumah and appointed him "leader of government business." Nkrumah took office and immediately pressed for the removal of the three British civil servant ministers and the rapid promotion of Africans in government jobs. He coined the phrase—soon known throughout Africa—"Seek ye first the political kingdom."

In 1951, a Conservative government was elected in London and Winston Churchill returned as prime minister. The new government sought to slow the pace in the Gold Coast, but the momentum was too great. Reluctantly, the new government agreed that Gold Coast should have an all-African government responsible to an assembly elected by universal adult suffrage. Lapping comments, "Conservative ministers who did not like the idea consoled themselves with the thought that this was only West Africa, a steamy unhealthy place where no whites had settled permanently and no strategic interest was affected."[3]

The rise of Nkrumah caused opposition to the CPP to form in the interior Ashanti territory, where conservative chiefs grew concerned about their fate under the "verandah boys" of Accra. They formed the National Liberation Movement (NLM) to contest a critical election in July 1956. But, although they won majorities in the interior, the CPP still retained 40 percent of that vote and won overwhelming majorities on the coast. Governor Arden-Clarke appointed a CPP cabinet under Nkrumah that led to Ghana's independence on March 6, 1957. In the succeeding years, Nkrumah pursued his pan-African dreams while becoming increasingly repressive at home. He introduced measures to hold individuals without trial and detained not only opposition figures but members of his own party as well. In 1963, J. B. Danquah, who had brought Nkrumah into politics, died in leg irons in prison after being held three years without trial.

The independence of Ghana accelerated the march to decolonize the remainder of Britain's African empire. So did the appointment in 1957 of Harold Macmillan as Conservative prime minister and his appointment of a new colonial secretary, Iain Macleod. Macleod is quoted in Lapping as having written:

> It has been said that after I became Colonial Secretary, there was a deliberate speeding-up of the movement toward independence. I agree. There was. In my view any other policy would have led to terrible bloodshed in Africa. This is the heart of the argument.[4]

Nigeria

After Ghana came Nigeria, Africa's most populous country, in October 1960. With its many language and ethnic groups, Nigeria was more of a sub-continent than a nation. But, as Immanuel Wallerstein writes in *The Horizon History of Africa*, "In nearby Nigeria political leaders of the three regions, West, East, and North, into which the country was divided buried their differences the following month [April 1957] and agreed to work together to achieve independence."[5]

Although the later history of Nigeria was to be marred by a civil war, the immediate path to independence was less troubled than that in Ghana. From 1922, African representatives from Lagos and Calabar had been elected to the legislative council of Southern Nigeria. In 1947, the British government promulgated a constitution giving traditional chiefs a greater voice in national affairs, sparking immediate protests from the increasingly active group of educated Nigerians. New arrangements in 1951 provided for elected representatives on a regional basis. This proved unworkable and, in 1954, the colony was divided into three regions: the north (largely Muslim), the West (largely Yoruba), the East (largely Ibo), and a federal district of Lagos. The east and west regions were given internal self-government in 1956, the north in 1959. Nationwide elections were held in 1959; independence came on October 1, 1960. Abubakr Tafawa Balewa of the north became prime minister and Nnamdi Azikiwe of the east became governor general. Three years later, when Nigeria became a republic, Azikiwe became its first president.

Nigeria had become independent, but its subsequent history was to be plagued by differences among the three main regions and the ambitions of its military— problems that the path to independence not only did not solve but exacerbated.

The independence of Sierra Leone in 1961 and of The Gambia in 1965 completed the transition of the British empire in West Africa. Across the Atlantic, Britain's principal West Indian colonies, Jamaica and Trinidad and Tobago, became independent in 1962, further accelerating the pressure for independence in other colonies.

Francophone Africa

Surrounding the British territories of West Africa were the fourteen territories which, with Madagascar and the Comoro Islands, constituted French Africa. Three more, the Congo, Rwanda, and Burundi, were under French-speaking Belgium; the latter two had been German colonies given to Brussels as protectorates as part of the post-war peace settlement after World War I.

Francophone and Anglophone Africa might almost have been on different continents. Although joined in some places by tribal affiliations, they were otherwise separated by language, education, and the differences in colonial rule. Belgian Francophone and French Francophone represented still a further division.

With the French colonies in Africa, independence was a matter of degree. For most, full freedom from the bonds of Paris came only through a lengthy process— one that was still continuing as the twentieth century ended.

The French African empire was based on a five-pronged relationship. Individual territories were ruled as colonies through Paris-appointed governors. They were closely tied economically and financially through French aid and through currency links to the French franc. French troops, many of them recruited in Africa, were stationed in key capitals, backed up by a standby intervention force in France;

the purpose was to defend countries as well as regimes. Maintenance of the French language was essential to preserving the network of interests. And Paris paid close personal and paternal attention to the leaders by providing villas on the Riviera and special privileges in France. The relationships benefited both France and the favored elite. As France moved toward some form of independence for the African empire, Paris sought to retain as many of these ties as possible.

At the beginning of World War II, French Africa was divided into two federations: Afrique Occidentale Française (AOF, French West Africa), and Afrique Equatoriale Française (AEF, French Equatorial Africa). The former consisted of Senegal, Soudan (Mali), Guinea, the Ivory Coast, Upper Volta, Dahomey (Benin), Mauritania, Niger, and Togo. The latter was comprised of Chad, Central African Republic, Cameroon, Gabon, and French Congo. The island of Madagascar (later the Malagasy Republic) was separately administered.

With the French defeat in 1940, the federations went their separate ways. The AOF remained loyal to Vichy and the AEF joined an obscure brigadier general, Charles de Gaulle, in continuing hostilities. As allied armies gained control of North Africa, de Gaulle felt he could look to the future. He called a conference of governors and governors general in Brazzaville in January 1944. In the face of pressures for decolonization in the Atlantic Charter and the principles of the new United Nations, de Gaulle wished to make it clear that France would proceed at its own pace. The Free French, in fact, used France's African territories as the base from which they sought to re-conquer metropolitan France.

Speaking of the French empire, de Gaulle said, "It belongs to the French nation, and only to her, to proceed, when the time is opportune, to make reforms in the imperial structure which she [France] will decide upon in the context of her sovereignty."[6] The conference spoke of "the incorporation of the African mass into the French world." Rene Plevin, the chairman, told delegates:

> We read from time to time that this war must end with what is called an enfranchisement of colonial peoples. In colonial France, there are neither people to enfranchise, nor racial discrimination to abolish. There are people who feel themselves French, and who wish to take, and to whom France wishes to give, an increasingly large role in the democratic institutions of the French community. These are people whom it is intended will move step by step towards the purest form of political enfranchisement. But it is not intended that they gain any form of independence other than French independence.[7]

The thrust of this conference of colonial governors was clearly not independence but the incorporation of the African countries into the political body of France—in other words, continuing the empire through a federation. The governors recommended the establishment of assemblies of Europeans and Africans within each territory to be elected on the basis of universal suffrage. The power of these assemblies, however, would be limited. The Brazzaville conference started the move toward independence, but the process would take sixteen years. Business and pro-colonial forces in France pressed to retain economic and political ties, but the momentum toward greater autonomy for the territories had started.

A French constituent assembly organized under the Fourth Republic in 1946 decreed that black African deputies would sit as full and equal members representing French African territories in the French National Assembly.

Francis McNamara, a U.S. foreign service officer who has written on France in black Africa, comments:

> Whatever the shortcomings of the new constitution, no other 20th century colonial power—the British, the Americans, the Belgians, the Dutch, the Portuguese, or any other—would make such a gesture. Its generosity of spirit surely created an abiding sentiment that has helped bind Francophone Africans to France long after the French empire has formally ceased to exist.[8]

The Fourth Republic administration created a pyramid of assemblies in the territories and the federations—forming a sizeable African political elite of 800 legislators at various levels of government. And in 1956, one French African, Felix Houphouet-Boigny of the Ivory Coast, became a minister without portfolio in a French cabinet.

As the process moved forward, differences arose over whether independence should come to the two federations or to the individual territories. Houphouet-Boigny, tribal chief, planter, and politician, pushed for the individual identity of the territories. When the Fourth Republic, shaken by the defeat at Dien Bien Phu in Vietnam and determined not to repeat the mistakes of Indochina, decided to bring constitutional reform to black Africa, they called on Houphouet as adviser. The result was the Loi-Cadre of June 23, 1956. The principle of territorial autonomy was accepted and the way cleared for independence of the individual components of the federations.

A further adjustment occurred when a new constitution, adopted in Paris in 1957, established the French Community as a framework under which independent African states could continue their association with France. Under his plan, the president of France would retain substantial powers over such matters as unified defense, external affairs, currency, economic policy, and strategic minerals. Unless excluded by agreement, France would also retain authority over courts, higher education, external transportation, and telecommunications.

The new constitution was put to a referendum in 1958; territories were to vote "yes" to join or "no" to stay out. It was made clear that French aid would continue to flow to those that voted "yes" and would be abruptly terminated for those that voted "no." All but Guinea, under a mercurial leader, Sekou Toure, voted "yes." De Gaulle, now France's president, showed his displeasure by terminating all assistance to Guinea and withdrawing all French personnel.

In 1971 I visited Toure in Guinea. He regaled me, as he did all visitors, with the evils of the "colonialists" and the "feudalists" and told tales of how the departing French ripped out telephones and took away toilets.

Guinea became independent. The thirteen other countries chose independence within the French Community. Even though the countries varied greatly in their readiness to exist as independent nations and even though many were artificial creations of colonial borders, none wished to forgo the pride of its own flag and identity.

But the community was short-lived. By 1960, African leaders were demanding greater freedom of action. The French replied imaginatively through a series of economic, cultural, and defense cooperation agreements that tied most countries to France more closely than was the case for any other country's former colonies.

The course of France's possessions took somewhat different forms off the southeast coast of Africa. As early as the eighteenth century, France had colonized the Mascarene Islands of Réunion and Mauritius, and, from these islands, undertook a gradual occupation of Madagascar. In 1896, the French Parliament voted the formal annexation of Madagascar, and, after suppressing an insurrection, sent Queen Ranavalona III into exile. Under the French Constitution of 1946, which created the French Union, Madagascar was made an overseas territory of the French Republic with representatives in the French Parliament. This arrangement did not quiet agitation for independence, and in 1947, a full-scale insurrection began in eastern Madagascar. The French responded brutally; an estimated 11,000 died. In 1958, when France agreed to let the overseas territories decide their fate, Madagascar voted for autonomy within the French Community. On October 14, 1958, the Malagasy Republic was proclaimed.

Two other remnants of the French empire in the southern Indian Ocean went different ways. Mauritius was taken by the British in the Napoleonic Wars and subsequently became independent in 1968, but only after the British (with American cooperation) took the island of Diego Garcia as a major naval base. Réunion became the most distant department of metropolitan France.

France's African relationships have been held together through the continuity of French financial support for their resource-poor nations, resulting in a mercantilist system that obviously benefits France. Francis McNamara describes the system in his book *France in Black Africa:*

> The preferences France enjoyed in trade and investment would not last long without generous French aid or, in some countries, without France honoring her security guarantees. The cost to France is high, but the return has been extraordinary. No other middle-sized power in the world enjoys similar status and international influence. To a large degree, this influence and position result from the special position France occupies at the center of a family of Francophone African nations.[9]

After independence, cooperation agreements maintained quotas, exemptions from customs duties, guaranteed commodity prices, and unrestricted movement of goods between Africa and France. To compensate, France paid higher than world-market prices for African imports and extracted higher than world-market prices for the manufactured and processed goods. As the European Community has developed, France has shifted part of the burden of this subsidized trade to the Community through earlier trade arrangements between Africa and the European Common Market, the Yaounde and Lome Conventions. Even Guinea ultimately saw the benefit of this relationship and, shortly before he died in 1984, Sékou Touré restored relations with France.

As of 1989, most French African countries remained part of the Franc Zone, using Communauté Financière Africaine francs (CFA) as their currency. Upon the independence of the individual countries, two central banks, representing countries of the previous federations, were formed that had headquarters in Paris and a close relationship to the Bank of France. Participating countries accepted limitations on their sovereignty, but in return the French guaranteed them virtually unlimited convertibility of the CFA.

Changes were bound to come and, in 1994, they did.

On January 12, 1994, thirteen countries in the Franc Zone announced a major devaluation of the CFA that was designed to increase domestic production and investment. As William Drozdiak reported in *The Washington Post* on January 22, 1994, "It was the first time the parity of the franc zone was ever altered, and the magnitude of the devaluation demonstrated how out of whack the economic relationship between France and its colonies had become."[10]

According to Drozdiak, Prime Minister Edouard Balladur announced that France would limit its aid to Africa to those countries that subscribed to terms set by the International Monetary Fund: "In France, young technocrats . . . are insisting that Paris can no longer afford the moral and financial luxury of propping up autocrats willing to do France's bidding as long as they can loot the treasuries."[11]

He added this description of the French system:

> Behind the guise of paternalistic care lies an ugly image that France has treated black Africa like a cash cow, exploiting its resources and markets, protecting dictators that do Paris' bidding and even using those countries as conduits to channel funds to French political parties.[12]

Even after declared independence, France continued to maintain both troops in selected African countries and the standby intervention force in France. The forces were generally welcomed by rulers in the French Community, who saw them as protection for regimes as well as countries. In 1988, the French had 6,500 troops in six countries: Cameroon, Central African Republic, Gabon, Ivory Coast, and Senegal. The latter three countries were considered the core of French interests. French military policy served the former colonies in another way as well. French citizens could substitute service in Francophone Africa for their military duty, working as teachers, engineers, and medical personnel.

Until the 1990s, the French had been prepared to intervene not only to protect French citizens and interests but regimes as well. Between 1956 and 1988, the French intervened ten times in former colonies: Cameroon, Chad, Gabon, Mauritania, and the Central African Republic. France also intervened twice in the former Belgian

Congo, Zaire, once in cooperation with Moroccan forces and once with the Belgians.[13]

As internal turmoil has become more frequent in Francophone countries and France has concentrated more and more on European issues, Paris's interest in intervention and troop deployments has declined. In 1997, French Prime Minister Lionel Jospin announced a cutback in troop deployments and a full review of financial assistance.

No reference to French Africa is complete without mention of Jacques Foccart. Throughout the presidencies of de Gaulle and Georges Pompidou, Foccart was the secretary general in the presidency of the republic for the French Community and African and Malagasy Affairs. He maintained links with the African leaders, saw to their needs when they visited France, and made certain that both French interests and the political interests of the president were fully maintained.

Foccart represented a personal aspect of the relationship to Africans that I have not seen duplicated in any other European power. I stood beside him at the celebration of the tenth anniversary of Malagasy independence in 1970. He had arrived only the day before and had not visited the capital city, Tannanarive, for some time, yet, as each Malagasy passed, he knew their names, asked about their relatives, and demonstrated an astonishing familiarity with their personal affairs. He was a French Jim Farley.[14]

In French eyes, the French language played a role in cementing relations with Africa that was as important as economics and security. When I was assistant secretary of state for African affairs in the early 1970s, we introduced the Peace Corps into several Francophone countries. The one condition the French considered fundamental was that, contrary to Peace Corps policies in other countries, volunteers would not teach in the local language. It was to be French—or nothing. This did not prevent the Peace Corps from providing the volunteers with training in indigenous languages.

McNamara comments on the importance Paris attached to language:

> In Francophone Africa the educational system has been the main instrument used to spread French culture. Since World War II a determined effort has been mounted to create a black African elite whose language, modes of thought, professional orientation, and tastes were French. Although the French educated elite was a small part of the total population, the French reinforced its importance in later years of colonial rule by placing its members in positions of increasing power in the administration and by expanding their role in politics. . . . To maintain linguistic and cultural ties, cooperation agreements were signed with all the new states ensuring French support in the vital area of education.[15]

France's former African colonies are seen today by the world as independent nations, but the ties to Paris remain strong. At least for the present generation, those ties are likely to outlast other political changes. McNamara predicts a long life for French influence:

The tastes and professional orientation of a French-speaking African elite have out-lived France's official departure. Thus France continues to gain long-term benefits from her assimilationist efforts. Whether these attitudes can be passed on to fu-ture post independence generations is moot. Much will depend on the continuing of a major French cultural and educational effort in these Francophone countries and on the attitudes of future leaders. For most of these African countries, French is the only viable lingua franca and is likely to remain their official language and the principal medium of modern education. Given these linguistic and cultural advantages, France should continue to enjoy a special privileged position in the commercial life of Francophone Africa long after the last ministerial adviser has departed.[16]

Belgian Africa

The decolonization of those French-speaking African territories under Belgian control left Africa and the world with problems that were to make headlines until the end of the century. Once the pressure for independence became clear, Belgium was much less determined than France to find ways to perpetuate the relationships. The abrupt departure of the Brussels government from African responsibilities compounded the problems of transition in Congo, Rwanda, and Burundi.

The Belgian Congo, equivalent in size to the United States west of the Missis-sippi River and bordered by nine other African countries, was the second largest colony in Africa. From 1884, this huge, rich, varied territory was in effect the private estate of Belgian King Leopold II.[17] No political activity was tolerated, and educa-tion above the elementary level was reserved for a favored few. At the time of in-dependence, the Congo had only eight university graduates. The possibility of an ultimate transfer of power to the Africans was not considered. In the 1950s, as Brit-ish and French territories began to move toward independence, Belgian attitudes started to change. Tribal unrest led the Belgian government to assemble a confer-ence of Congo Africans in Brussels in January 1960. To the surprise of the Belgians, the Africans unanimously asked for independence. It was decided that indepen-dence was to be given; the dates were set for elections in May and independence on June 30—six months away!

In the elections that followed, most votes were cast for the principal non-tribal political organization, the Mouvement Congolais National. The movement had been founded in 1958 and its leader, Patrice Lumumba, was already in touch with other newly independent African leaders. Although he had at one time been im-prisoned by the Belgians, he remained on good terms with Brussels. He became the Congo's first prime minister when independence was declared on June 30, 1960. Forty-eight hours later, the Congolese army, the Force Publique, mutinied, de-manding the dismissal of Belgian officers.

On July 11, Moise Tshombe, the charismatic leader of the rich Katanga prov-ince in the south, declared the independence of the province. These events led to a serious breakdown of order and to international intervention. Congolese independence was born into circumstances that ultimately involved the United Nations, the major powers, and the complications of the Cold War. The immediate post-independence consequences will be considered in Chapter 14.

On the Congo's eastern border were Rwanda and Burundi, two former German colonies awarded to a Belgian mandate after World War II. The peoples of the two territories, Hutu and Tutsi, are alike in appearance, but during eighty years of colonial rule they acquired separate occupational identities. The Hutu remained primarily agriculturists, but the Tutsi were treated by the colonial masters as a superior administrative cast. In 1959 the Hutu of Rwanda revolted; the Tutsi king was deposed and fled to Uganda. Rwanda declared a republic under a Hutu, Gregoire Kayibanda; Burundi remained a Tutsi monarchy. In 1962, the Belgian mandate was terminated, leaving two divided, independent, but unstable states that were in future years to shock the world with their brutality.

But, if the transition to independence was far from smooth in parts of Francophone Africa, it was to be even less so in the Portuguese territories and the British colonies that bordered South Africa. Like the Congo (later Zaire), their transitions would become international issues involving the United Nations and, particularly, the United States.

EIGHT

Africa II: The Settler Countries

In east and southern Africa, dismantling the empire required dealing with white settlers—a factor not present in areas found unsuitable for European settlement.

From the time the Dutch landed at Cape Town in 1652, the high veld of the south and the plains and highlands to the north and east represented tempting territory for Europeans. The Africans were driven from their lands but ultimately reclaimed their rights after centuries of struggle.

In 1999, the southern cone of Africa consisted of eight black-ruled countries. Forty years before, such a situation would have been inconceivable to most observers.

As the official told the visiting U.S. National War College group in Luanda in 1960, the Portuguese expected to be in Africa "for another 500 years." Apartheid seemed firmly planted in South Africa. The South-West African mandate was clearly under Pretoria's power. And Southern Rhodesia's controlling white minority looked forward to a comfortable future.

But change was already in the air, dramatized particularly by the "wind of change" speech of British Prime Minister Harold Macmillan. Speaking in Cape Town in February, 1960, he said:

> Ever since the break-up of the Roman Empire one of the constant facts of political life in Europe has been the emergence of independent nations. They have come into existence over the centuries in different forms, with different kinds of government, but all have been inspired by a deep, keen feeling of nationalism, which has grown as the nations have grown. In the twentieth century, and especially since the end of the war, the processes which gave birth to the nation states of Europe have been repeated all over the world. We have seen the awakening of national consciousness in peoples who have for centuries lived in dependence upon

some other power. Fifteen years ago this movement spread through Asia. Many countries there of different races and civilizations pressed their claim to an independent national life. Today the same thing is happening in Africa, and the most striking of all the impressions I have formed since leaving London a month ago is of the strength of this African national consciousness. In different places, it takes different forms, but it is happening everywhere. The wind of change is blowing through this continent, and, whether we like it or not, this growth of national consciousness is a political fact. We must all accept it as a fact and our national policies must take account of it.[1]

South Africa

South Africa, itself, was nominally independent. The Union of South Africa had been formed as part of the British Commonwealth in 1910; in May, 1961, the Union withdrew from the Commonwealth and became an independent republic. But, because of policies of racial separation embodied in apartheid, most of the world did not accept South Africa as a member of the family of nations.

I visited South Africa three times. In 1940, the wartime tension between the British and the Boers was palpable. On one occasion, two English-speaking soldiers left the train compartment when two Afrikaaners entered. Twenty years later, in 1960, my visit coincided with the killing of 83 Africans and the wounding of many more who were protesting apartheid pass laws outside a police station in Sharpeville. The African National Congress (ANC), founded in 1912, was increasingly active. In 1963, the government in Pretoria cracked down on the organization and sent its leaders, including Nelson Mandela, to jail for long terms.

In 1970, as the U.S. assistant secretary for Africa, I visited South Africa with a State Department colleague who was African American, Beverly Carter. We found a white population increasingly defensive and pleading to be understood. But it would be still twenty years before the dramatic developments of the early 1990s. In 1990, a new South African prime minister, F. W. de Klerk, took the courageous step of opening discussions with Mandela and releasing him from prison. The two men negotiated a new constitution which, after an election won by the ANC in 1994, went into effect with Mandela as president and de Klerk as vice president. Apartheid was ended and South Africa joined the world as an honored member.

Namibia

Next door in South-West Africa, pressure for an end to the South African mandate and independence was growing. The South West African Peoples' Organization (SWAPO) had been formed under the leadership of Samuel Nujomo in 1960. Ultimately, in 1990, in a complex negotiation involving the United Nations and the United States that was linked to neighboring Angola and the withdrawal of Cuban troops, South-West Africa gained its independence as Namibia.

The Portuguese Territories

The decolonization of the principal Portuguese territories of southern Africa, Angola, Mozambique, and Guinea-Bissau, came only after prolonged armed struggles with liberation movements. The struggles involved indigenous resistance to Portuguese rule as well as interaction with the separate conflicts in neighboring Rhodesia, South Africa, and the Congo. Settlers from Portugal and the multiplicity of tribes in the territories immensely complicated the transition. Lisbon, coveting the national prestige of a 400-year-old empire, tried to hang on, but its efforts to improve conditions in the colonies proved insufficient and came too late. Independence came eventually, but the largest of the territories, Angola, remained deeply divided and at war at the end of the century.

Serious resistance to Portuguese rule first erupted in Angola in 1961, stimulated in part by the independence of neighboring Congo. Internally, insurrection was driven by forced labor practices and increased white settlement that diminished employment opportunities for Africans. In response, Portugal deployed large numbers of troops, set up strategic hamlets, and encouraged even greater settlement. By 1974, Angola had 300,000 non-African settlers.

From the beginning, the anti-colonial resistance in Angola was divided. The first of three principal liberation movements, the Movimento Popular de Libertação de Angola (MPLA), was founded in 1956 with Portuguese Communist Party help; it represented those from the Luanda area most exposed to Portuguese influence. Initially based in Brazzaville, the MPLA moved to Zaire in 1965; Agostinho Neto, a poet, became its leader in 1967. It was basically non-tribal. Holden Roberto, leader of the Bakongo peoples of northern Angola, based in Zaire, founded the Frente Nacional de Libertação de Angola (FNLA) in 1957. In 1966, a third movement, the União Nacional para a Independência Total de Angola (UNITA), was founded by Jonas Savimbi of the Ovimbundu group of central Angola. The rivalry and occasional conflict between and among the three groups enabled the Portuguese to gain the upper hand, but at a heavy cost.

At the same time as rebel activity increased in Angola, the Portuguese faced insurrections in Mozambique and Guinea-Bissau. By 1970, Portugal had 130,000 troops in the three African territories and was forced to spend half of its budget and 6 percent of its gross national product on its colonial wars.

Organized efforts against Portuguese rule in Mozambique began in 1964 with an armed uprising led by the Frente da Libertação de Moçambique (FRELIMO), founded by exiles in Tanzania under the leadership of Dr. Eduardo Mondlane. The Portuguese, resisting, determined to remain and began a large-scale development program designed to increase opportunities for white settlement. The plan centered on a major hydro-electric project at Caboro Bassa in the north of the territory. But when the project's link to resisting independence became clear, it was strongly opposed by other black African countries and by those sympathetic to African aspirations in the world community.

The end of Portuguese resistance to black rule began in the smallest of the three territories, Guinea-Bissau, where the African Party for the Independence of Guinea and the Cape Verde Islands (PAIGC) was holding down 30,000 Portuguese troops. The Portuguese governor, General Antonio de Spinola, convinced of the hopelessness of their cause, resigned and returned to Lisbon to campaign against colonial rule. His writings helped stimulate a coup on April 25, 1974, in which young military officers came to power, members of the Armed Forces Movement, who were determined to bring independence to Portugal's African colonies.

Independence for the smaller colonies followed rapidly. Guinea-Bissau became independent on September 10, 1974, followed by Cape Verde, Sao Tome, and Principe in 1975.

Mozambique became officially free in June 1975, but the country's trials were not over. To prevent the government of the new country from supporting resistance groups aimed at the Federation of Rhodesia and Nyasaland and at South Africa, Rhodesian and South African troops raided Mozambique in 1979. These raids were followed by the organization of an insurgency group, Resistencia Nacional Mocambicana (RENAMO), supported by Rhodesian intelligence. It was not until 1992 that a peace accord was signed between FRELIMO and RENAMO. In an election that followed, FRELIMO won a clear victory and the internal conflict largely ended.

Angola was not so fortunate. When the Portuguese left in November 1975 without managing any transfer of power, the MPLA seized the capital, Luanda. The MPLA declared itself the provincial government of Angola and was recognized as such by many African countries.

With the Portuguese departure, each of the liberation movements jockeyed for power with outside support. UNITA turned to South Africa. The FNLA looked to western Europe and the United States. The MPLA had close ties with the Soviet Union and Cuba. With Soviet help, the MPLA repulsed an FNLA raid on Luanda in March 1975 only to face an incursion by South African forces and a UNITA attack in October. The MPLA in Luanda called on Cuba for immediate assistance and Havana responded. In *World Politics since 1975*, Peter Calvocoressi describes the Cuban response:

> Castro and Neto had become personal friends. Cuban aid had helped to fill the gap when Moscow turned cold on Neto in 1973–74. Several hundred Cuban advisers arrived in MPLA camps in April and September 1975[,] and when Neto appealed to Castro early in November for combat troops to fight the South Africans he did not appeal in vain. The first unit arrived by air two days later. It consisted of eighty-two men in civilian disguise, the forerunner of what was to become an army of 20–30,000. The first seaborne reinforcements arrived at the end of November and this first ocean crossing of nearly 10,000 km was followed by forty-one more during the ensuing six months of active hostilities. At one point no fewer than fifteen ships were simultaneously at sea on an eastward course, the biggest procession of men and materiel across the Atlantic since the Americans had sailed to North Africa and Europe to make war on Hitler.[2]

The Cuban forces remained until they departed in mid-1991 as part of a U.S.-brokered deal that brought independence to Namibia. Negotiations began between MPLA and UNITA that led to elections in 1992. However, when Jonas Savimbi failed to win the presidency as he had expected, he began the war once more. At the end of 1999, Angola remains an independent, rich, but deeply divided country with 10 million land mines still strewn across the country.

Rhodesia and Nyasaland

As changes were taking place elsewhere in southern Africa, world attention was also focused on the future of the Federation of Rhodesia and Nyasaland. Because the fate of this federation was a central preoccupation in the final days of the British empire, it is treated here at some length. Established in 1953, it was clear as the years passed that the Federation would not withstand its internal contradictions.

Southern Rhodesia, although it escaped the formal establishment of South African–style apartheid, remained dominated by a white minority that represented 3 percent of the population.[3] They resisted efforts to bring educated Africans into the political process and opposed any official contact with leaders of the emerging nationalist organizations.

Northern Rhodesia and Nyasaland, by contrast, which were under the rule of Britain's Colonial Office, looked forward to ultimate rule by Africans.

When the Federation was formed in 1953, elections were held for three provincial and the federal assemblies under an elaborate formula designed to preserve white rule. In 1957, a new formula was proposed that increased the number of African representatives but still maintained the dominant white position. A refusal by London to reverse the proposed law sparked serious reactions in Nyasaland and Northern Rhodesia. In both countries, Africans increasingly saw in the Federation concept the threat of extending the white rule of Southern Rhodesia to the whole Federation.

In 1960, London called for a review of the federal structure. At that point, a new figure, Hastings Banda of Nyasaland, entered the picture. A British- and American-trained doctor, he had returned to his native territory in 1958 after an absence of forty years. In his absence he had worked actively for Nyasaland independence and had become to his people a symbol of the struggle. He had reinforced his nationalist credential by spending three years in Kwame Nkrumah's Ghana before returning to Nyasaland.

Upon his return, Banda became president of the Nyasaland Congress. Although he did not encourage violence against whites, he believed, after he surveyed the scene and had felt the intensity of youth feelings, that pressure on the British government was necessary if Nyasaland was to escape control of the Rhodesian whites. He believed that the arrest of Congress leaders, including himself, would bring attention to their cause in London. To that end, he encouraged unauthorized open-air meetings. In visits to Salisbury, he encouraged Southern Rhodesian Africans to "seek freedom."

Under the federal constitution, law and order were the province of each governor. Federal troops from Southern Rhodesia could be introduced in other territories only at the request of the governor. The Federal Prime Minister, Roy Welensky, alarmed at what he saw as the growing violence in Nyasaland, pressed the governor, Sir Robert Armitage, to call federal troops. The governor obliged and, on March 3, 1959, federal troops and police arrested 1,322 people, including Banda. Ninety-eight Africans were killed in the ensuing violence.

As Banda had hoped, the action caught London's attention. An appointed commission of inquiry determined that the governor's actions had been justified but exonerated Banda and noted that no one in Nyasaland was in favor of continuing the federation.

With the Nyasaland riots occurring at the same time as the Hola Camp murders in Kenya (see p. 119), Prime Minister Harold Macmillan decided the time had come to review colonial policy. He became convinced that Banda should be released and that Nyasaland as well as Northern Rhodesia should be permitted to leave the Federation if they so chose. His conclusions were implemented when a new colonial secretary, Iain McLeod, was appointed in November 1959.

On April 1, 1960, Banda was released. He met with McLeod and, in a radio address, urged calm on the basis that he was opening talks with the governor and McLeod on constitutional reform. Two outcomes were clear: the end of the Federation and independence for Nyasaland and Northern Rhodesia. Nyasaland became independent as Malawi, with Banda as president in July 1964; Northern Rhodesia became Zambia, with Kenneth Kaunda as president in October 1964.

Southern Rhodesia, left behind, also demanded independence—but with minority rule and restrictions against Africans. At this point a new factor entered British thinking: the Commonwealth. By 1964, newly independent Ghana and Nigeria, as well as former British colonies in Asia, were prominent in the Commonwealth. These former colonies made it clear they would oppose the admission of any country with a white minority government. Their position won the support of the older Commonwealth members of Canada, Australia, and New Zealand.

Lapping characterizes the mood of the time in Southern Rhodesia:

> The Rhodesian electorate was by now thoroughly confused. They [the voters] had supported the party of Huggins, Todd, and Welensky, [former governors], dutifully voting for what they considered liberal measures, in the belief that this was the way to secure both the Federation and full independence. By 1961, they had neither. Why, they asked, did Britain now want to impose black rule and chaos? Did they want to subject Rhodesia to Congo-type rape and murder? To Kenya-type savagery? To the corruption and Marxism of a black dictatorship like Ghana? The whites of Southern Rhodesia were convinced that they could run what they considered their own country better than the British or the Africans. They had no more patience with Britain.[4]

In this mood, the whites of Southern Rhodesia were ready for a unilateral declaration of independence (UDI). They found their champion in a new Southern

Rhodesia prime minister, Ian Smith, a Rhodesian-born farmer. After nearly two years of efforts to negotiate with the British, Smith declared UDI on November 11, 1965, invoking phrases from the American Declaration of Independence in his proclamation.

British Prime Minister Harold Wilson made it clear that while Britain did not accept UDI, it would not use force to reverse it. Britain had balance of payments problems, and the use of force against whites in Africa would have been damaging politically; a basic sympathy for the whites existed in Britain and many British had relatives among the Rhodesian settlers. Wilson and the international community turned to economic sanctions, but with regimes in Portuguese Mozambique and South Africa sympathetic to UDI, this was a weak weapon.

Wilson made efforts to negotiate with Smith on board *HMS Tiger* in December 1966 and *HMS Fearless* in August 1968. Smith would not accept reforms that sought black rule, and with sanctions making little impact, he saw no need to compromise. He raised the stakes in June 1969 when the white minority voted a new republican constitution that was "non-racist." Africans were not excluded from the vote, but voter registration depended on income and few Africans could qualify.

In 1970, the British government under Lord Home made a further effort, and on November 24, 1971, Home and Smith signed "Proposals for a Settlement." Under this agreement, popular opinion was to be tested by a royal commission. Smith saw no problem, convinced that his Africans "were the happiest in the world."[5] The commission, under a senior British judge, Lord Pearce, found otherwise. The commission concluded that whites, colored, and Asians favored the settlement by fourteen to one, but added, "We are equally satisfied, after considering all our evidence, including that on intimidation, that the majority of Africans—thirty six to one—rejected the proposals."[6] After the Pearce findings, the British government withdrew its proposals.

Until that point, the Rhodesian Africans had made small and unsuccessful attempts to use force against the Smith regime. Rival nationalist groups—the Zimbabwe African National Union (ZANU) under Joshua Nkomo and the Zimbabwe African Peoples' Union (ZAPU) under Robert Mugabe—fought each other. After UDI most of the leaders of both groups were locked up. Some leading members of ZANU, however, escaped to Tanzania and, after training in Communist China, were able to mount attacks on Rhodesia from areas in northern Mozambique freed from Portuguese surveillance.

In the face of stepped-up guerilla activity, Smith's military leaders urged reforms that might win greater loyalty from the Africans. Smith disagreed and, instead, imposed apartheid-type restrictions. But Smith, too, was beginning to have his doubts when even the traditional chiefs, Smith's allies, opposed the new measures.

On April 25, 1974, circumstances suddenly changed. A coup in Lisbon led to independence in Portuguese Mozambique, bringing to power FRELIMO under Samora Machel and opening the way for ZAPU and ZANU to have wider base areas for attacks on Rhodesia.

The greater opportunities provided to the Rhodesian guerrillas now worried the South Africans, who did not want effective black forces on their borders. The South African prime minister, John Vorster, reached out to Hastings Banda and Kenneth Kaunda to seek their help in resolving the Rhodesian problem. Vorster persuaded Smith to let ZANU and ZAPU leaders out of jail to meet with Kaunda and two other African leaders, Julius Nyerere of Tanzania and Seretse Khama of Botswana. The conference was held, but it foundered when ZANU and ZAPU leaders, divided by personalities, ambition, and tribal affiliations, failed to present a united front. Vorster, alarmed by what he had seen of the liberation movement rivalries in Angola, did not want similar problems in Rhodesia.

When this initiative failed, Smith turned to Nkomo, the leader of ZAPU, but, given the failure of the last conference, Smith saw no need to make the concessions necessary to open a genuine negotiation with Nkomo.

South Africa then created new pressures for Smith. When Rhodesian troops entered Mozambique in August 1976 and killed 1,200 ZANU supporters, Vorster cut off vital supplies to Rhodesia, and a new player entered the scene, the U.S. secretary of state, Henry Kissinger. Kissinger, alarmed by the introduction of Cuban troops into Angola, flew to South Africa late in 1976 and met Smith in Pretoria. Under Kissinger's pressure, Smith appeared to agree to move toward majority rule and establish a black administration. He turned to a black bishop, Adel Muzorewa. In February 1978, Smith worked out an agreement with Muzorewa that increased black representation, although on close examination the agreement showed that the hands of real power continued to rest with the whites. Nevertheless, a black electorate, tiring of war, was prepared to accept the agreement. In an ensuing election, Muzorewa won 67 percent of the votes cast. Meanwhile, however, ZANU and ZAPU, united in the Patriotic Front, stepped up their attacks on whites and blacks who were cooperating with the regime. Muzorewa's government not only failed to stop the violence, it also gained little support from other African countries.

At this point, Margaret Thatcher, Britain's new prime minister, was scheduled to attend a Commonwealth prime ministers' conference with Queen Elizabeth in Lusaka. Contrary to expectations that Mrs. Thatcher would press to recognize the Muzorewa government, she listened to other Africans and, under the skillful guidance of her foreign secretary, Lord Carrington, became convinced that other steps were necessary before Britain could be freed of the Rhodesian question. The result was the Lancaster House Conference of December 1979 which brought together all parties. After six weeks of intense negotiation, an agreement was reached. The front-line states, Tanzania, Zambia, Malawi, and Botswana, tired of the war's effect on their countries, played a leading role by convincing ZAPU and ZANU to cooperate.

Under the agreement, a British governor would take office for an interim period to supervise an election to a 100-seat parliament with 20 seats reserved for whites. A cease-fire would go into effect.

An election was held on February 25, 1980, under the new arrangement. The British hoped that it would result in a victory of Muzorewa, Nkomo, and Smith, but this was not to be. Robert Mugabe's ZANU captured 57 seats, ZAPU, 20, and Muzorewa, 3. And on April 17, 1980, Mugabe became prime minister of an independent Zimbabwe. The maldistribution of land between the majority black population and the remaining whites continued to plague the new republic and, in 2000, resulted in efforts by blacks, especially veterans of the liberation war encouraged by President Mugabe, to occupy white lands.

Kenya

The fates of three East African countries, Kenya, Uganda, and Tanzania, were closely linked. Their history—particularly that of Kenya—also involved white settlement.

London wanted to encourage settlement along the right of way to pay for the railroad to Uganda that was built in 1901 in order to ensure British control of the headwaters of the Nile. In 1902, the land was offered to Zionists as a home for the Jews, but they had their hearts set on Palestine. In their place, white settlers from Britain and the Commonwealth were encouraged to buy land in the highlands along the rail route in what had been tribal lands. Disease and, in some cases, massacres of the Africans had made land available. In 1908, Undersecretary of the Colonies Winston Churchill wrote of one punitive expedition in Kenya: "It looks like butchery, and if the House of Commons gets hold of it all our plans in the East African Protectorate will be under a cloud. Surely it cannot be necessary to go on killing these defenseless people on such an enormous scale."[7]

The political influence in London of the growing white settler colony forced through the establishment of the King's colony of Kenya in 1920. Making the former protectorate a colony meant abrogating earlier treaties with the Africans and giving the crown legal authority to dispose of land as it wished. The British government insisted that it recognized Kenya as an African territory and that the interests of the African must be paramount. As a gesture in this direction, in 1923 a white missionary was appointed to the Legislative Council to represent the Africans. White settlers, nevertheless, successfully resisted proposals to let Africans grow cotton and coffee, to publish laws in the Kikuyu language, and to add an African to the Legislative Council.

The balance of power began to shift in the late 1930s as the Kikuyu, the predominant people, organized, and the requirements of World War II brought opportunities for black farmers as well as white. Although Britain proscribed the principal African organization, the Kikuyu Central Association (KLA), in 1940 and interned its leaders, it failed to intern one leader, Jomo Kenyatta, who in 1929 had been sent by the KLA to London. Kenyatta married in England and wrote *Facing Mount Kenya*, described by anthropologist Bronislav Malinowski as "one of the first really competent and instructive contributions by a scholar of pure African parentage."[8] He refused to return to Kenya, where he felt he would be treated as an inferior, and from his exile kept up the pressure for African rights. In 1946 he returned to Kenya and within a year was chosen president of the new moderate

Kenyan African Union and emerged as the acknowledged spokesman for Kenyan nationalism. He toured the colony, urging Africans to obtain independence by peaceful means and protect other races living in Kenya. He also told his fellow Kenyans that to get freedom they must abandon laziness, theft, and crime.[9]

Driving the Africans from the land had not affected the Kikuyu chiefs who still held valuable land. But those Kenyans, especially young men who had been driven from the lands and had seen the luxuries of Nairobi, became increasingly frustrated. They saw their way to freedom through using tribal traditions to organize and enforce loyalty in a secret society designed to drive the white settlers from their land. In 1946, Mau Mau (a term with no known meaning) began. Its first violence was against Africans who refused to swear the Mau Mau oath and were suspected as possible informants. The movement began to kill chiefs and attack white interests by crippling their cattle. Kenyatta at first spoke out against the movement, but he became more equivocal when he was threatened by its leaders. The governor, Sir Evelyn Baring, declared a state of emergency in October 1952 and arrested leaders of the Kenya African Union, including Kenyatta. Settlers and many Africans were convinced Kenyatta was a leader of the movement.

Kenyatta and the others were tried before a retired justice of the Kenyan Supreme Court, Ransley Thacker QC, who had close ties with the settlers and stayed in a club exclusively for Europeans during the trial. The judge placed great store by the testimony of one man, Rawson Macharia, who swore that Kenyatta had tried to administer the Mau Mau oath to him.

At the conclusion of the trial, the defense counsel said, "It is the most childishly weak case made against any man in any important trial in the history of the British empire."[10]

Thacker adjourned the trial to consider the verdict just as the Mau Mau began to attack settlers. In March 1953, he found all defendants guilty and gave the maximum sentence of seven years for "managing an unlawful society." An appeal to the Privy Council was rejected. Kenyatta was not only sentenced to serve seven years but, after completing his sentence, he was to be restricted indefinitely to a remote place. Five years later his original accuser, Macharia, testified that his evidence had been false.

Lapping compares Mau Mau to other violent anti-colonial movements and finds it does not compare:

> Mau Mau affected only one tribe and a limited area of Kenya. In both Malaya and Cyprus a senior British soldier was brought out as Governor to turn the entire resources of the country against the terrorist challenges. In Kenya this was not necessary. The Governor, Sir Evelyn Baring, a notably unmilitary figure who was repeatedly ill and could therefore easily have been relieved, stayed in charge throughout. The number of European civilians killed by Mau Mau was thirty-two—each case horrifying but the total fewer than the number of Europeans killed in traffic accidents in Nairobi in 1952–6, when Mau Mau was active. The number of African civilians killed by Mau Mau was officially recorded as 1,819.

Mau Mau caused an emotional shock to the British and created panic among many of them, but the danger was more psychological than military.[11]

The strength of Mau Mau was broken by mid-1954. Nearly 80,000 Kikuyu, almost a third of the tribe's adult population, had been removed to detention camps. At the same time, Governor Baring told the settlers bluntly that the only protection against a renewal of Mau Mau was to share power with the Africans.

At that point, another African, Tom Mboya, arrived on the scene. Young and personable, he gained the confidence of the settlers. A political rival, Odinga Odinga, breached a taboo and began to propose the release of Kenyatta. Odinga at first was shouted down, but, as sentiment around the country was expressed, it was clear he had judged correctly. Kenyatta was still popular.

Then, in March 1959, it was revealed that at Hola, a remote detention camp, eighty-eight of the remaining Kikuyu detainees had been beaten to death by wardens. Macmillan's colonial secretary, Iain Macleod, decided that Britain must address Kenyan independence. MacLeod moved gradually to release Kenyatta and at the same time reward the settlers who remained important to Kenya's economy. Kenyatta was finally released in October 1961. With his lion's-mane fly whisk, he dominated a constitutional conference held in London in 1963 and, after an election in May, became prime minister and president of an independent Kenya in December 1963. He spoke to the white settlers:

> There is no society of angels, whether it is white, brown, or black. We are all human beings, and as such we are bound to make mistakes. If I have done a wrong to you, it is for you to forgive me; and if you have done something wrong to me, it is for me to forgive you. The Africans cannot say the Europeans have done all the wrong; and the Europeans cannot say the Africans have done all the wrong [speaking of his imprisonment]. This has been worrying many of you; but let me tell you Jomo Kenyatta has no intention of retaliating or looking backwards. We are going to forget the past and look forward to the future. I have suffered imprisonment and detention; but that is gone and I am not going to remember it. . . . Many of you are Kenyan as myself. . . . Let us join hands and work for the benefit of Kenya, not for the benefit of one particular community.[12]

Independence in Kenya's two East African neighbors, Tanganyika and Uganda, had already been established—Tanganyika in December 1961 and Uganda in October 1962. The circumstances in each varied.

Tanzania

Tanganyika, a former German colony, had been allotted to Britain as a League of Nations mandate after World War I. Early British governors sought to build up governments on the basis of traditional authorities. A Legislative Council was formed as early as 1926, but the first two African members were not named until 1945. An effort was made to establish a non-racial government in 1955 when

Europeans, Asians, and Africans were given equal numbers of seats in the Legislative Council. This experiment ended, however, in 1959, when a constitutional committee recommended that after elections in 1960, the majority of members of the council should be Africans. In September 1960 a government led by the Tanganyika African National Union (TANU) took office and led the country to independence. Its leader, Julius Nyerere, became president at independence on December 9, 1961. In 1977, Tanganyika was joined to the neighboring islands of Zanzibar and Pemba to form Tanzania.

Uganda

In Uganda, the British faced the unusual problem of reconciling independence with the claims of substantial monarchical entities within the colony. The largest was Buganda, which had its own king, or *kabaka*, Frederick Mutesa II. He became alarmed in 1953 over rumors of efforts to create an East African Federation; he feared the incorporation of Buganda into an entity dominated by white settlers. He quarreled with the governor, Sir Andrew Cohen, and was sent into exile in London. In 1955, however, new constitutional arrangements were worked out by which Buganda became a constitutional monarchy within Uganda, and Mutesa was returned.

As early as 1950, a legislative council was formed in Uganda. The settler problem did not exist, but a substantial Asian minority, descendants of those brought in to work on the railroad, demanded a share of representation. The original legislative council consisted of eight Africans, four Asians, and four Europeans. In 1961, Uganda was given self-government. Independence, delayed by the need to reconcile with the *kabaka* and resolve a dispute between Buganda and Bunyoro, another kingdom, came finally in October 1962.

The three East African colonies came into independence with common services, a common currency, and a common market. They made efforts to expand these cooperative efforts into a political federation, but many elements stood in the way: differences over the choice of a capital and a president, the relationship of the kingdom of Buganda to the federation, conflicting philosophies and policies, the constitutional division of powers, and opposition of other African countries, especially Ghana, to federations that were not clearly pan-African. The efforts ultimately collapsed in 1977 and the countries went their separate ways.

The settler territories of Africa represented the final battleground of imperial rule, but the effect of decolonization lasted well beyond the last lowering of a colonial flag.

Part 3

THE THIRD
WORLD
AND THE
UNITED STATES

Question: How would you describe your attitude toward the United States?
Answer (Indian graduate student): It is the new East India Company.
Conversation at author's home, April 30, 1999

We ourselves are the first colony in modern times to have won independence. We have a natural sympathy with those who would follow our example.
John Foster Dulles, 1954

NINE

The Legacy of the Twentieth Century

Whatever the history of individual nations or regions, past Western domination has, in varying degrees, left a legacy of issues, sensitivities, attitudes, recollections, and myths that still affects the views of Third World citizens and plays significant roles in their politics.

Three and four generations may have passed since independence and the end of mandates, but the deprivations of the colonial period remain alive through texts and oral traditions. Indians remember the Amritsar massacre of 1919 and the resultant praise in Britain for the actions of Brigadier General Reginald Dyer. Citizens of the Malagasy Republic remember the French massacres of 1947. Filipinos still recount the U.S. atrocities against Aguinaldo's revolutionary forces in 1901. South African blacks remember Sharpeville. Muslims talk of the Crusades.

The Heritage of Attitudes

The catalogue of attitudes still powerful in the Third World is long, but, like all generalizations, the list does not apply in equal measure in each country or region. "Imperialism" and unresolved issues such as Palestine, Kashmir, and Cyprus remain popular rallying cries in some regions. Manifestations of xenophobia or pride may be expressed in extreme forms in the megalomania of a Saddam Hussein or a Kim Il Sung or in the bizarre policies of a Muammar Qadhafi. Certainly the passage of time has modified many attitudes toward the West, but resentments of the past still lie dormant within the populace in many countries, ready for exploitation by demagogic leaders. They appear frequently in the declarations of the several Third World–dominated organizations formed to reflect the solidarity of previous colonial peoples.

Diplomats serving in these areas are often criticized for paying too much attention to the idle rhetoric of "the street," but nevertheless, attitudes are political realities. When broadcast by modern technologies, they reach millions quickly. Widely held among a people, they may frequently limit a leader's foreign affairs choices.

Restoration of Pride. For many, and particularly for educated elites, the colonial period was humiliating, both personally and nationally. Memories of past discrimination led to demands for respect and dignity. Nationally, whether in India, West Africa, or the Arab Middle East, recollections of past glories heightened the humiliation of colonial rule and created demands for pride and status to be restored. Indians, reflecting on their past empires, considered their exclusion from the nuclear club a form of national humiliation. Arabs speak of being humiliated by the establishment of Israel in lands they consider theirs.

This was brought home to me in Libya in 1967. The Libyans had not been combatants in the Israeli-Egyptian war, but they felt the Egyptian defeat deeply. Belief that the United States had provided air cover for the Israeli attack on Egypt—the so-called big lie—was widespread. Libyans avoided U.S. diplomats except for necessary official business.

One afternoon I passed a senior Libyan official on the street. I greeted him and asked whether I might call on him.

"No," he said, "but I will come to your house this evening."

He did, and we sat in the embassy garden. He said to me, "In my head I know that you did not help Israel in its attack on Egypt, but in my heart I must accept it. Otherwise, it means that two million people whom we always considered second-class citizens have defeated eighty million Arabs. I cannot accept the humiliation."

Race was a major factor in forming Third World attitudes. Discrimination against the indigenous peoples took many forms. Much of it was manifested through sheer brutality; in every empire massacres, enslavement, and physical humiliation were common. In its less brutal forms discrimination was social and economic. Clubs in British territory excluded even prominent and well-educated "natives." In French and Portuguese territories, where greater mixing of races took place, the mulatto suffered subtle discrimination. The Dutch gave economic benefits to the Chinese minority in the East Indies, creating tensions that remain to this day in Indonesia.

Reaction to past humiliation is often expressed in ambitions to match the West or in rationalizations for opulent lifestyles. In an advertisement in *The Washington Post* on October 6, 1998, Prime Minister Atal Bihari Vajpayee of India asserts that "the task of the next millennium is to place India among the world's most advanced economies to forge it into an economic super power."[1] In 1999, Muammar Qadhafi unveiled a new automobile to be manufactured in Libya. Imelda Marcos, wife of former Philippine President Ferdinand Marcos, railed against critics of her lavish lifestyle by claiming that such criticism was merely part of the desire of Westerners to keep her in a humble state.

The Sacredness of Sovereignty. At a time when concepts of sovereignty are eroding in Europe, peoples of the Third World attach particular importance to sovereignty and to the principle of non-intervention in internal affairs incorporated in the UN Charter in 1949. Even though many new nations are the result of the artificial boundaries of the colonial period and sometimes brutally interfere in each others' affairs, they resent involvement by major Western nations. They fear precedents that may be applied to them. Even offers of economic and humanitarian assistance have at times been rejected as violations of national sovereignty.

Sensitivity to Criticism. Closely related to the question of pride is an acute sensitivity to observation and criticism, either because of embarrassment about the facts, the political costs of admissions, or resentment at intrusive interest. Even though outside reports can sometimes stimulate improvements, foreign comments on human rights abuses, ethnic violence, and even famine breed efforts to conceal and, frequently, anger. In the 1970s, the world grew conscious of serious famine conditions in Ethiopia. The government in Addis Ababa reacted sharply to foreign reports and offers of aid—at first denying and later, reluctantly, acknowledging the facts.

With some justification, Third World countries complain that the negative aspects of their lives and culture are featured in the films and literature of outsiders and that scholars regard them more as laboratory specimens than people. Until the rise of internationally respected indigenous scholars, much of the research and writing regarded as objective was indeed done by Western academics. It has been common for many years for European and American scholars to gather to discuss Asian and African affairs without ever inviting representatives of these regions. Edward Said describes the phenomenon in his book *Orientalism.*[2]

The sensitivity toward sovereignty also inhibits Third World nations from criticizing each other. Criticism is seen not only as intervention in another's internal affairs but also as a challenge to that country's newly gained sovereignty.

Search for Identity. The colonial period also created serious problems of individual identity. Education was based largely on the history and culture of the colonial power; local traditions were denigrated or destroyed. One result has been the strong emphasis in the post-colonial period on a return to cultural and religious roots, including a revival of the power of Islam in much of the Third World. Even traditional medicine has achieved greater respectability, especially as major pharmaceutical companies have demonstrated new interest in the healing properties of indigenous plants and other substances.

Resentment against the West. Inevitably, because Western nations were identified with domination—whether through colonialism or indirect manipulation—Third World attitudes have often assumed an anti-Western character. The powerful global position of the United States means that it has, in the eyes of many, inherited the imperial mantle from Europe; some of the most violent anti-Western manifestations have been directed against U.S. citizens and interests.

The animus against North Americans has been particularly noticeable in the Western hemisphere. In the Caribbean, during the twentieth century eleven former colonies joined the Third World. Older nations of South America that became independent from Spain and Portugal in the nineteenth century also identified themselves with the newly independent nations of the twentieth. U.S. efforts to extend "manifest destiny" southward in the nineteenth century created suspicions—that still exist—about Yankee policies and intentions. Decisions such as that by Attorney General Richard Thornberg in 1989 to extend the U.S. power of arrest to the territories to the south helped perpetuate such suspicions.

Anti-democratic Tradition. Because the metropole powers were democratic, the Western world assumed that new nations would emerge in the democratic mold. A few, such as India, which had participatory traditions in the village *panchayats,* have done so, but the real lessons handed down by the colonial period were of repression and administrative dicta. Elections, where they have taken place, have often been rigged; where free, they occasionally bring results unwelcome to the leadership and, at times, to Western friends. The Algerian elections of 1991 that threatened to bring to power an Islamic party are a case in point.

At least until late in the colonial period, imperial rule was marked by intolerance toward political opposition. Few imperial powers were free of legitimate charges of harsh and brutal repression. Administrative laws and regulations dating from the colonial period designed to curb dissent are still used, even by ostensibly democratic governments, in Malaysia, Israel, Zimbabwe, and elsewhere.

Sense of Betrayal. Closely associated with anti-Western sentiments is a sense of betrayal. Arabs felt betrayed by the secret post–World War I European treaties that carved up the Eastern Mediterranean into spheres of influence. Pakistanis felt betrayed by the Radcliffe decision that facilitated India's access to Kashmir at the time of partition. Africans have been the victims of artificial boundaries created in colonial times and a prevailing mistrust of Western intentions and declarations exists to this day.

Suspicion of Manipulation. Not only did the past leave a legacy of betrayal, it also created a deep assumption of external manipulation. The firm belief that their destinies are being determined by powerful outside powers remains alive in many countries. Third World peoples continue to blame the colonial powers for their current problems; Indians still insist that the divisions between Muslim and Hindu were the result of Britain's "divide-and-rule" policy. But where once the British or the French were the culprits, the target of suspicion today is the United States. With the past in mind, the new nations are inclined to view with suspicion Western overtures that may imply a return of manipulation and domination, whether through political action or offers of aid. This view is perhaps natural among populations that have lived many years under foreign rule. Conspiracy theories involving outside manipulation are common. Reports of covert efforts by Western nations to change or influence governments such as those in Iran in 1952, in Guatemala in 1954, and in Chile in 1973 confirmed beliefs that such efforts were widespread. Indira Gandhi harbored a deep suspicion of the U.S. Central Intelligence Agency throughout her time as prime minister of India; she referred frequently to "the foreign hand."

Continuing Economic Disadvantage. Perhaps the deepest division between many of the Third World nations and the industrialized West is economic. Nations of the former empires entered independence with the view—justified in many cases—that they had been exploited for the benefit of the metropole. The transition to independence brought serious economic problems; colonial burdens persisted at the same time that subsidies fell off. Many new countries counted on major industrial nations, and particularly the United States, to provide substantial economic assistance and were bitter when that did not materialize. Many turned to the Soviet bloc or the Chinese or sought indigenous measures—such as the *ujama* villages of Tanzania[3]—to reduce dependence upon Western Europe. The failures of such experiments and of unrealistic industrialization led to even greater bitterness over poverty and underdevelopment.

Recollections of exploitation by colonial powers created strong feelings against foreign investments, especially in India. A more or less permanent atmosphere of distrust was created. Because donor nations often demanded conditions considered onerous, the search for foreign assistance—both economic and military—also awakened political opposition to the signing of agreements.

Each of these remnants of the colonial experience has appeared in decisions of Third World leaders over the past century. Although many factors helped form these attitudes, at the base of each was the desire generated in the colonial period to challenge the domination of Western powers.

The list is not meant to evoke sympathy for former colonial territories, but to further an understanding of the historical and contemporary context in which Third World politics operate. Neither should the impact of these attitudes be exaggerated. Many Third World governments have been able to move beyond an emphasis on the past. They have close relationships with the United States and Western Europe and with their former colonial power. But myths and legends remain just below the surface, ready to appear or to be stimulated in times of crisis or in confrontations with the West. And these beliefs, in their worst manifestation, lead fanatical men and women on the political fringes to terrorism, threatening the interests of both developed and developing countries.

Some Third World leaders have over the years moved their countries to policies friendly to the West, whether through endorsing peace processes or supporting external financial restructuring. But on such issues they have faced populations still affected by attitudes of the past. U.S. diplomacy has frequently urged Third World leaders to take locally unpopular actions or positions. For these leaders, self-preservation is a primary concern. Whatever their true sentiments, they either do not wish to stir up "their street" or they believe it politically beneficial to be seen to "stand up to" a big power. They weigh the risks to themselves of following a U.S. lead and decide otherwise. Even in a nation as relatively stable as Saudi Arabia, concerns over regime preservation have frequently stood in the way of full cooperation with Washington.

Third World Solidarity[4]

These frustrations, fears, suspicions, and attitudes of Third World nations have been most pointedly expressed through various conferences and organizations that developed in parallel with the demands for independence.

The roots of Third World solidarity go back into the nineteenth century, when students and exiles from colonial territories gathered in European capitals and the United States to bemoan their colonial fates and seek ways to independence. Out of such contacts grew liberation movements and conferences designed to bring the plight of colonial peoples to world attention. In the twentieth century, those who could followed closely the Paris Peace Conference of 1918 and sought in various ways to put in a word for independence.

The first moves toward broader contacts among colonial peoples in Asia and Africa took place in the decade that followed.

At the International Conference for Peace held at Bierville, France, in 1926, Asian delegates declared in a memorandum that Asia deserved a place in the considerations of world problems. Many of the Asian delegates participating in this conference expressed the belief that Europe tended to view world issues only in terms of Europe. This refrain would be heard again the following year at the Congress of Oppressed Nationalities, which was held in Belgium in February 1927. This meeting brought together 175 delegates representing 134 organizations as well as 300 observers from China, India, Syria, Arabia (Palestine and Egypt), Korea, Indonesia, Indochina, Annam, Japan, Africa, North and South America, and almost every European state. The conference produced 40 resolutions after 6 days of meetings, although its importance rests mostly with the fact that "the downtrodden of the earth came together for the first time to share their sufferings and their hopes."[5] Out of this meeting came the belief among its participants that oppressed regions of the world, particularly the regions of Asia and Africa under European imperialism, shared common problems and needed to coordinate their struggle against imperialism. Jawaharlal Nehru, one of the delegates at Belgium (and later at Bandung in 1955), claimed that the importance of the conference was in the impression that it made on its participants. For Nehru, Brussels provided him new insights into the problems of other colonial countries and the realization that his mission was a worldwide struggle.[6]

World War II not only led to the independence of many former colonial possessions, it also served to re-energize the belief that cooperation between the new nations in Asia and Africa would be vital. At the first Asian Relations Conference, held in New Delhi in March and April 1947 (which included the Central Asian Soviet republics and all the countries of Asia except Japan), participants considered the common problems that all Asian countries had to face: national movements for freedom, racial problems, the legacy of the colonial economy, industrial development, intra-Asian migration, the status of women, and cultural cooperation. Delegates first addressed the necessity of Asian cooperation in confronting these issues, an idea that grew in significance between 1946 and 1949, when Indonesia, Burma, Ceylon, India, Pakistan, and the Philippines won their independence. A second conference of newly independent Asian nations met in New Delhi in January 1949, primarily to consider the situation in Indonesia. They condemned the Dutch actions against nationalists and expressed the need for cooperation among the new countries.

The Asian countries met again in May 1950 at Baguio in the Philippines, a conference that produced the recommendation that the nations of south and southeast Asia must consult each other to further the interests of the peoples of the region and to ensure that in any consideration of Asian problems the views of the peoples of the area should be kept in mind. Although these early meetings brought together a diverse group from a variety of cultures (and thus a wide range of opinions of how common problems could best be addressed within each nation), most of the delegates agreed on the necessity of some form of cooperation among former colonial possessions. A loose confederation began to develop through these early conferences, a confederation that led directly to the Bandung conference of 1955, the formation of the Afro-Asian Group in the United Nations, and the Non-Aligned Movement.

Bandung: Burma, Ceylon, India, Indonesia, and Pakistan brought the idea of a joint Afro-Asian conference closer to realization at their first conference in April 1954 in Colombo. The proceedings were again dominated by discussions about how to tackle the number of common problems each nation faced in the region. The Colombo delegates released a statement that the answers could best be found at a conference including all the newly independent countries of Asia and Africa. The final decision to hold a joint conference came at the Bogor conference in December 1954 in Indonesia, where the five prime ministers of the Colombo countries specifically met to arrange the Bandung conference. They determined that the upcoming conference should discuss colonialism, prospects for mutual aid and cooperation, and possibilities for world peace and should be composed of all countries of Asia and Africa with independent governments. Thirty countries received invitations, although many others from Africa, Asia, and America sent observers. Congressman Adam Clayton Powell of the United States was one such observer.

The Bandung conference convened in April 1955, bringing together representatives from twenty-nine participating countries. The delegates represented 25 percent of the land mass of the world and nearly two-thirds of the world population.

When the conference commenced at Bandung, the agenda—initially left open at Bogor because of disagreement—was grouped around five subjects: economic cooperation (including the peaceful uses of atomic energy); cultural cooperation; human rights and self-determination (including discussions of Palestine and racialism); the problems of dependent peoples (with particular attention paid to Tunisia, Algeria, and Morocco); and the promotion of world peace and cooperation (with discussion centering on weapons of mass destruction and disarmament). Each topic prompted substantial discussion and disagreement, particularly the last three subjects, where two camps emerged: one believing in the necessity of military pacts like the South East Asian Treaty Organization (SEATO), the other in Panch Sheel's five principles of peaceful co-existence.[7]

In a communiqué issued after six days of deliberations, Bandung's participants universally condemned colonialism in all its forms, agreed to promote economic development within the Afro-Asian region on the basis of mutual interest and respect for national sovereignty, and agreed to develop cultural cooperation among themselves through the acquisition of knowledge of each other's country and cultural exchange programs. On the issues concerning human rights, world peace, and oppressed peoples, only general statements emerged after much disagreement about what form Afro-Asian solutions to these problems should take. The participants at Bandung merely declared that they supported the UN's declarations on human rights and self-determination, only adding that they supported the rights of the Arab peoples of Palestine and that they generally deplored the policies and practices of racial segregation and discrimination throughout the world. Finally, Bandung's delegates advocated making the United Nations more universal, particularly by admitting more of the newly independent countries of the Third World (Cambodia, Ceylon, and Laos, among others). The delegates supported universal disarmament and international control of experimentation with nuclear weapons and their production and use.

The importance of Bandung rests less with the decisions made at the meetings and more with the so-called Spirit of Bandung. Although the final communiqués that were issued expressed the solidarity of the nations of the Third World and the commonality of the issues facing them, the meetings contained numerous disagreements among its diverse nations, and the final drafts issued by the participants did not express many radically new ideas. Despite this, Bandung remains an important watershed in the history of Asian-African (and later Latin American) relations. Bandung created a powerful symbol of solidarity among former colonial possessions, a symbol that resonated for years after the participants had left the conference site. Delegates from Asia and Africa who had been separated by imperial barriers began to learn about their neighbors as they never had before.

The Non-Aligned Movement: The growing contacts among Third World nations and their desire to avoid involvement in the East-West confrontation led to the organization of the Non-Aligned Movement (NAM).

The first NAM conference came as East-West tensions grew. After the Soviets shot down a U.S. U-2 spy plane on May 1, 1960, and a scheduled US–USSR Summit Conference collapsed, the presidents of Ghana, Indonesia, the United Arab Republic, Yugoslavia, and the prime minister of India proposed at the Fifteenth UN General Assembly in 1960 a draft resolution by which the assembly would call upon the leaders of the two superpowers to resume contacts and begin disarmament.

This cooperation led to the First Conference of Heads of State or Government of Non-Aligned Countries, held in Belgrade in September 1960. The most immediate aim of the twenty-five participants was to find ways to decrease the international Cold War tension, while its long-term aims consisted of action against all colonial occupation, with particular emphasis on resisting apartheid and supporting the restoration of rights to Palestinians. In the wake of the conference, Third World countries began to coordinate international activities, especially in the United Nations, where NAM members helped to elect the first non-European secretary general, U Thant of Burma.

By the beginning of 1999, twelve non-aligned conferences had been held. Although many in Western countries—and especially the United States—considered the NAM to be irrelevant to global issues and biased toward the Soviet bloc, it has remained, even with the collapse of the Soviet Union, an important symbol of the post-colonial world. Nations such as Pakistan worked hard to gain admission despite its membership in Western defense alliances. Even in the declining years of the East-West confrontation, President Suharto of Indonesia campaigned to become president of the NAM to demonstrate his ideological succession from Sukarno.

All has not been solid within the NAM. India, for example, was deeply disappointed when NAM members failed to criticize China when it invaded India in 1962 or take India's side in the disputes with Pakistan.

The Group of 77: The initiatives that grew out of Third World gatherings have had their greatest impact in the organs of the United Nations, and especially the UN General Assembly. Blocs of nations (Africa, Asia, American republics) often vote in common. But perhaps the most effective has been the grouping concentrating on economic issues, the Group of 77 (G-77). Although membership by 1999 had reached 133, the original name has been retained.

The G-77 was established in Geneva in June 1964 by seventy-seven countries that signed a "Joint Declaration of the Seventy-Seven Countries" at the conclusion of the first session of the UN Conference on Trade and Development (UNCTAD). At the first ministerial meeting of the group in Algiers in 1967, a permanent institutional structure was developed which led to chapters in other UN organizations, the Food and Agriculture Organization (FAO), the UN Industrial and Development Organization (UNIDO), the UN Educational and Cultural Organization (UNESCO), the UN Environmental Program, and a group of 24 in Washington within the International Monetary Fund and the World Bank.

The achievements of the G-77 are expressed primarily in its various declarations and statements of principles. Its most important initiative was the New International Economic Order, to be discussed in a subsequent chapter.

The Organization of Petroleum Exporting Countries: Probably the most effective of the Third World organizations has been the Organization of Producing and Exporting Countries (OPEC) that has, since 1960, exercised significant influence over the world prices of oil and gas. The organization was founded in Baghdad in September 1960 by five countries: Venezuela, Saudi Arabia, Iraq, Iran, and Kuwait and was subsequently joined by Qatar, Libya, Indonesia, United Arab Emirates, Algeria, Nigeria, and Ecuador. The founders were moved to organize because the Standard Oil Company of New Jersey (ESSO) unilaterally reduced the posted price of Arabian crude oil. Their initiative also reflected disagreements with companies over revenue, taxation, sovereignty, and supply and demand. Through annual meetings, OPEC attempted to coordinate member policies on production, price, and marketing. Obviously, differences developed among the members and some did not adhere to agreed limitations, but, in general, this group of countries has been able to increase its revenues and influence with both governments and companies. Daniel Yergin in *The Prize* calls it "a colossus in the world economy."[8]

OPEC members consider themselves part of the Third World, and many Third World nations saw inspiration in an organization that could so effectively challenge

Western industrial giants.[9] Ironically, while many new countries praised OPEC's initiative, they suffered substantially from the resulting increases in energy prices—more, in fact, than the industrial countries that were OPEC's targets.

The Organization of the Islamic Conference: The growing communication among Third World countries also stimulated solidarity among the many Islamic countries. In September 1969, in the wake of an assault on the Al-Aqsa mosque in Jerusalem, heads of state and government of countries with substantial Muslim populations gathered in Rabat to organize the Islamic Conference. In the intervening years, there have been eight conferences, the most recent in 1997. By that year, fifty-six states and four observer states constituted the membership. Only four of the participating states—Turkey, Yemen, Afghanistan, and Thailand—had been independent before 1950. In addition to the objective of promoting Islamic solidarity, its objectives and principles parallel those of other expressions of Third World solidarity:

- to eliminate racial segregation and discrimination and to eradicate colonialism in all its forms;
- to support international peace and security founded on justice;
- to respect the right of self-determination and non-interference in the domestic affairs of member states;
- to respect the sovereignty, independence, and territorial integrity of each member state;
- to settle any conflict that may arise by peaceful means such as negotiation, mediation, reconciliation, or arbitration;
- to abstain from the threat or use of force against the territorial integrity, national unity, or political independence of any member state.

A Word about Rhetoric

At the heart of the problem of relationships between Third World countries and the West lies rhetoric. On both sides of the divide statements may represent genuine hopes and fears but they also reflect peer and political pressures on leaders. They constitute collections of words often substantially at variance with the realities of the time.

Statements issued by the various Third World organizations contain noble principles relating to fundamental freedoms, human rights, cultural and economic cooperation, disarmament, the peaceful uses of atomic energy, justice, respect for international law, and non-intervention in the internal affairs of other states. Yet, the reality is that many of the signatory countries of these organizations are gross violators of the very principles they espouse: India and Pakistan have developed nuclear weapons, the Angolan civil war has defied efforts at peace, despite a democratic revolution in 1999 Indonesia continues to have severe human rights problems, and North Korea threatens its neighbors—to name but a few. Such actions hardly lend credibility to the sincerity of their declarations.

Why this discrepancy?

From the beginning, the objective of Third World conferences was to put pressure on the Western imperial powers to agree to independence. The principles were intended to apply to those powers, not to each other. Freedom was meant to refer to independence, not to internal liberties. Self-determination was for other states, not for the ethnic minorities within their own borders. Disarmament applied to the major powers, not to the brutal wars in Africa. International law and justice were terms to apply to those they saw as oppressors, not to themselves.

As the countries became independent and the East-West struggle disappeared, the emphasis in rhetoric has become economic—the North-South divide. Many of the same words are used, but in different contexts to apply to economic imperialism and the inequities of globalization.

Their statements further reflect an aversion to criticizing other Third World countries or to calling attention to the gap between their words and their actions. One rarely finds pronouncements on conflicts between and among Third World countries.

In 1969, during one of the periodic eruptions of violence between Hutu and Tutsi in Burundi, I was assistant secretary for African affairs. The United States was, even then, being pressed to call attention to the tragedies and, possibly, to intervene. I asked the Nigerian foreign minister why African countries did not express their outrage at the atrocities. He replied, "If we call attention to them, they are seen in Europe and America as reflecting what Africans—not Burundis—do. They reflect on all of us. When you criticize events in Northern Ireland, you do not say they are typical of what Europeans do."

To point to the discrepancies does not deny that these expressions represent genuine hopes on the part of the peoples of these countries. Desires for dignity and recognition, to remain aloof from big power conflicts, to achieve peace and better lives are all sincere. Members of the political elites who attend these conferences and write the communiqués know they must reflect aspirations of their citizens, even if they are far from being achieved. They know, also, that delegates from other countries are observing each other to ensure their adherence to the general principles of the group. Peer pressure among the delegates also plays a part.

But if gaps exist between Third World rhetoric and reality, they also exist in the case of the United States and its efforts over the past half century to balance expressions of principles with the realities of policy. This is not a one-way street.

TEN

Economics

The powerful economic position of the United States at the end of World War II raised expectations among nationalists that Washington would use that power to pressure reluctant countries to grant independence and that the wealthy North American giant would be sympathetic to their financial and trade demands and share its largesse with the new countries. The new countries, believing that richer industrial nations had an obligation, in justice, to provide help were destined generally to be disappointed.

The priority given by Washington to the reconstruction of Europe tended to blunt possibilities of U.S. support at a critical moment in the moves to decolonize. Washington's aid to developing countries was considered inadequate, conditional, and complicated. The United States, with its powerful position in the international financial institutions, was identified with unpopular policies of the International Monetary Fund and the World Bank.

Economic considerations did enter into U.S. policy relating to decolonization, but, with one notable exception, they served more to inhibit than encourage support for nationalists. The break up of empires at the end of World War II came at a time when the United States was preoccupied with the success of the Marshall Plan.[1] The United States understandably did not wish to push changes in the empires that would make the economic revival of the continent more difficult. Confrontation with the Soviet Union was beginning, but the Cold War had not fully developed. Washington was, nevertheless, worried about weakening the non-Communist regimes in Europe in the face of growing Communist parties, especially in France. American European specialists, less conscious of the power of rising nationalism, were reluctant to deprive European countries of valuable colonies and access to resources. In spite of these concerns, the United States did seek to promote the independence of the new nations, although at a pace and often in a manner that did not satisfy the impatient nationalists.

The European allies did not make it easy. Minimizing the pressures of the nationalists, they insisted that their problems could be overcome with more sympathetic help from the United States. The United States, on the other hand, contended that the long-term interests of the Western European countries could only be protected by coming to terms with the nationalists. But, with one exception—the Dutch East Indies—Washington did not employ economic pressure.

Indonesia

Previous chapters have referred to the U.S. role in Indonesian independence. Details of this complex involvement might have fitted in a variety of places. They are presented here because they represent the most dramatic illustration of the use by the United States of economic pressures to bring about independence.

Although the United States had expressed its views on the need to accommodate Asian nationalists on various occasions to the British and French governments, the most direct involvement of the United States in the decolonization in Asia—outside of the Philippines—was in Indonesia. The size and location of the country, U.S. investment in its resources, evidence of Soviet overtures to the nationalists, and the importance of the Netherlands in Europe all dictated a strong American interest in a satisfactory resolution of post-war conflict between the Dutch and the nationalist Republic of Indonesia.[2] Here, too, the problems of post-war reconstruction of the Netherlands under the Marshall Plan were very much part of Washington's consideration. But it was a congressionally initiated threat to suspend Marshall Plan aid that ultimately broke the deadlock over this island nation's desire for independence.

As noted in Chapter 4, for five years Washington was involved, with increasing intensity, in the effort to resolve the Dutch-Indonesian conflict. Within the U.S. government debates included issues common to other mediation efforts. Supporters of U.S. European allies argued with regional specialists about where U.S. long-term interests lay. Assessments of European claims of Communist influence in independence movements had to be carefully evaluated. Strong efforts were made to avoid identification with either side. Reference to the UN Security Council, where the Russians had a veto was, if possible, to be avoided. At critical points, U.S. public and congressional views became important. And, until all else failed, the United States was reluctant to use its Marshall Plan aid to the Netherlands as leverage.

This changed when the Dutch launched their police action in July 1947. Secretary of State George C. Marshall had warned the Dutch government on June 17, 1947, "This government wishes again to express the view that the use of military force would not be regarded favorably by this government, would arouse serious adverse reaction of U.S. public opinion, and would be self-defeating in purpose."[3] The news of the Dutch action brought strong condemnation from the U.S. press and Congress. Despite U.S. reluctance, the Dutch military move brought the matter before the UN Security Council when India and Australia raised the issue.

Throughout the period of attempts at negotiation, the question of U.S. assistance to the Netherlands was on the table. The *New York Times* reported on December 22, 1948, that "besides $298 million in Marshall Plan aid for the Netherlands and $61 million for Indonesia [through the Dutch], the Dutch, since the war have received Export-Import Bank credits of $300 million, credits for the purchase of U.S. war surplus supplies totaling $130 million, and $190 million worth of civilian supplies as military relief."[4] The United States, on the same day, announced that authorization for the procurement of supplies to be used in Indonesia had been suspended. However, since this represented only $11.6 million from the amount originally allocated, it was but a token gesture.

The assumption was clear that the Dutch would not have been able to support their colonial war without this assistance. Until the second Dutch police action, Washington was reluctant to curtail its help to The Hague. Pressure mounted, however, from other allies and leading Third World countries. Within the United States, significant members of Congress, labor unions, and the National Association for the Advancement of Colored People (NAACP) called for a suspension of assistance.

The question of aid to the Dutch in Indonesia took a more serious turn when Senator Owen Brewster of Maine and nine other Republican Senators threatened to block extension of the legislation authorizing the Marshall Plan if the Dutch did not comply. Secretary of State Dean Acheson brought this to the attention of the Dutch government in meetings with Foreign Minister Dirk Stikker on April 2 and 5 and stated that "in the absence of an Indonesian settlement" there was no chance that the United States could authorize funds for military supplies to the Netherlands.[5] On April 14, the Dutch resumed negotiations with the Republican leaders. This resulted in a compromise proposed by the U.S. representative, Merle Cochran, that led to a roundtable conference at which independence was finally negotiated. In early July, the imprisoned Indonesian Republic leaders returned to Jogjakarta to be greeted by, among others, Ambassador Cochran.

The New International Economic Order

Dissatisfied with the response of the industrial nations and the international financial institutions to their economic needs, in 1974 the Group of 77 of the Third World nations launched a major economic offensive under the title the New International Economic Order (NIEO). The story of the NIEO and of the U.S. response illustrates the issues that Washington has faced in its economic relations with many of the new nations.

The NIEO was inspired, in part, by the formation of OPEC, which by 1974 was already making its influence felt in petroleum production and pricing. Ironically, although the developing nations applauded OPEC as an example of weaker nations challenging the dominant position of the industrial West, the increase in oil prices mandated by OPEC in 1973 wreaked more havoc on the poorer nations of the world than on the rich. As Henry Kissinger points out in *Years of Upheaval*, "The Tehran decision [to raise oil prices] also cost the developing countries more than the entire foreign aid programs extended to them by the industrial democracies."[6] Yet, so intrigued were the developing countries with the OPEC demonstration of power that few criticized the decision. Instead, they saw OPEC as a model for their own mounting of pressure.

Their list of complaints mirrored the relations with the metropoles as they saw them, supplemented by the harsh realities of the world trading system experienced since independence. Special trade arrangements with the former metropoles had shielded many colonies from these realities. In many new countries, these special arrangements had ended, along with colonial subsidies that had paid for salaries, pensions, and other expenses.

Prices for their basic commodities fluctuated; they could not pay for needed imports. Synthetics were challenging traditional agricultural products such as cotton. They found freight and insurance rates exorbitant. Many were saddled with debt. Developed countries, stressing that the new countries should build on their agricultural base, discouraged their ambitions to industrialize. Obtaining modern technology was expensive, and often the technology was unsuitable for their needs.

Although some still benefited from post-imperial relations, they found major developed countries, and especially the United States, unwilling to provide the type of aid needed without burdensome conditions. The World Bank and the International Monetary Fund, controlled by the developed countries, raised unwelcome questions about their internal policies when they sought aid.

Skeptical of private enterprise and foreign investment, the new countries looked for an unchallenged transfer of resources "without strings." They feared that multinational corporations would intervene in their internal affairs and would cause political embarrassment because they were often involved in other countries that were politically anathema, such as apartheid South Africa. Countries had little control over corporate profits. Some countries had nationalized foreign enterprises and had been penalized by a loss of aid. The United States had amendments to economic assistance legislation requiring such suspension when prompt and adequate compensation was not provided.

In all economic relations with the Third World, whether assistance, investment, or trade, the United States encountered the fundamental differences in outlook between a rich, industrial, capitalist nation and poorer nations; many of the new nations, enamored of state-directed socialist economies believed the United States, along with European nations, had exploited the colonial territories and, therefore, that assistance to compensate for the exploitation was justified. To a donor nation such as the United States that believed it knew how transferred resources should be used, that attached importance to laws and agreements, and that believed strongly that private investment contributed more to development than government aid, the Third World ideas were unacceptable.

The ideas for the New International Economic Order were incorporated in a UN General Assembly Resolution (No. 3201) on May 1, 1974. Resolution 3201 was accompanied by the "Programme of Action on the Establishment of a New International Economic Order." In a preamble, Resolution 3201 articulated the principal complaints of the developing world:

> The greatest and most significant achievement during the last decades has been the independence from colonial and alien domination of a large number of peoples and nations which has enabled them to become members of the community of free peoples. Technological progress has also been made in all spheres of economic activities in the last three decades, thus providing a solid potential for improvement of the well-being of all peoples. However, the remaining vestiges of alien and colonial domination, foreign occupation, *apartheid* and neo-colonialism in all its forms continue to be among the greatest obstacles to the full emancipation and progress of the developing countries and all the peoples involved. The benefits of technological progress are not shared equitably by all members of the international community. The developing countries which constitute 70 per cent of the world population, account for only 30 per cent of the world's income. It has proved impossible to achieve an even and balanced development of the international community under the existing international economic order. The gap between the developed and the developing countries continues to widen in a system which was established at a time when most of the developing countries did not even exist as independent States and which perpetuates inequality.[7]

The resolution then set forth a number of demands, including many direct assaults on established practices and principles of the developed world—and particularly of the United States. They presaged trade issues that were to divide developed and developing countries at the end of the century. They represented a litany of the real and imagined discriminations of the colonial period and a plea for help in the post-colonial era. The list remains virtually the same when Third World nations meet in the new century. The list included:

- arranging and promoting an increase in the net transfer of resources from the developed to the developing countries (the foreign minister of Canada, Lester Pearson, had proposed that developed nations should allocate 0.7 per cent of their GNP to help developing countries, a figure enthusiastically endorsed by the Third World);
- the extension of active assistance to developing countries by the whole international community, free of any political or military conditions, thus securing favorable conditions for the transfer of financial resources to developing countries;
- the establishment of "just and equitable" relationships between the prices of raw materials, primary products, manufactured goods, and semi-manufactured goods exported by developing countries and the primary commodities, manufactures, and capital goods imported by them, thus improving the competitiveness of natural materials facing competition from synthetic substitutes;

- facilitation of the role of producers' associations, including commodity agreements;
- reimbursement of taxes and duties on imports from developing countries or devoting them to providing additional resources for development;
- full permanent sovereignty over natural resources and all economic activity;
- promotion of foreign investment, both public and private, from developed to developing countries in accordance with the needs and requirements as determined by the recipient countries;
- reformation of the international monetary system (International Monetary Fund and the World Bank) with greater participation by the developing countries in decision-making;
- the right to adopt the economic and social system that it deems to be the most appropriate for its own development and to not be subjected to discrimination of any kind as a result;
- relief of debt burdens of developing countries through cancellation, moratorium on interest payments, or renegotiation;
- the right to restitution and full compensation for the exploitation and depletion of, and damages to, the natural and all other resources of these states, territories, and peoples;
- ending the waste of natural resources, including food products, which includes efforts by the international community to prevent ecological damage to food-producing areas;
- promotion of access to and transfer of modern science and technology and the creation of indigenous technology for the benefit of the developing countries in circumstances suited to their economies.[8]

Not unexpectedly, the United States found much of this program unacceptable but, conscious of the importance of the issues to the new nations, Washington made extraordinary efforts to respond positively.

The resolution was adopted without a vote, but the United States objected to the claim of the sponsors that the resolution represented a consensus of the General Assembly. Ambassador John Scali, the U.S. permanent representative, explained on May 1, 1974:

> Some have referred to the procedure by which these documents have been formulated as that of "consensus." My delegation believes the word "consensus" cannot be applied in this case. . . . But our objecting at the last minute would only have served to exacerbate the divisions that we have worked to the best of our ability to bridge during the past weeks.[9]

The term "order" would cause problems. Whether it be in the U.S. executive, the Congress, or the public, anti-authoritarian free-enterprise Americans do not react well to any "order." In a statement made in the Ad Hoc Committee of the Seventh Special Session of the UN General Assembly on September 16, 1975, U.S. Representative Jacob M. Myerson said, "The United States cannot and does not accept any implication that the world is now embarked on establishment of something called, "the new international economic order."[10]

Moreover, the set of demands seemed to ignore the workings of the international economic system, glossing over such issues as the patents for technology transferred, the need to create a proper climate for foreign investment, or the complexity of setting precedents in debt relief. To demands for changes in the decision-making structure of the World Bank and the IMF, the United States continually responded, "Participation in decision making must be equitable for all members and take due account of relative economic positions and contribution of resources."[11]

In American eyes, the documents, clearly intended to pressure the developed countries to provide more resources unconditionally to the developing countries, suffered also from lack of any statement of obligations on the part of the recipient countries. Referring to previous resolutions, Ambassador Scali pointed out that:

> Resolution 1803 (XVII) [establishing the NIEO] provides among other things that, where foreign property is nationalized, appropriate compensation shall be paid in accordance with national and international law; it also provides that foreign investment agreements by and between states shall be observed in good faith. By way of contrast, the present declaration does not couple the assertion of the right to nationalize with the duty to pay compensation in accordance with international law.[12]

Beyond this, Ambassador Scali raised objections to producer associations (on the OPEC model), the regulation of multinational corporations, marketing arrangements for primary products, and provisions that would place obligations for compensation on the United States.

In December 1974, the United States was one of six members that voted against a Charter of Economic Rights and Duties of States in the Economic and Financial Committee of the UN General Assembly. Senator Charles Percy, U.S. Representative to the General Assembly, explained the U.S. reservations:

> To cite a few: the treatment of foreign investment in terms which do not fully take into account respect for agreements and international obligations, and the endorsement of concepts of producer cartels and indexation of prices. . . . [T]he provisions of this charter would discourage rather than encourage the capital flow which is vital for development.[13]

Nevertheless, despite reservations and insurmountable differences in concept, over the next two years the United States made a genuine effort to put forward proposals in response to at least some of the issues raised. The result was a major bureaucratic struggle between economists—especially in the U.S. Treasury—who dismissed the initiative as unrealistic rhetoric and diplomats in the Department of State, who recognized the significance of an adequate response to relations with the Third World.

Earlier maneuvers had presaged these struggles. When I was assistant secretary of state for African affairs in 1971, the Department negotiated with the Treasury instructions for the U.S. delegation to a conference in Abidjan on coffee. Treasury had been reluctant to go along with any U.S. commitment that involved maintaining the price, but it had agreed to language recognizing the problem. In the middle of the night of the conference, I was awakened by a phone call from the Department of State representative on the delegation to tell me that the Treasury representative had received instructions from his department to ignore the previously negotiated instructions. Only by awakening my Treasury counterpart did I get our original plan back on track.

The U.S. response to the NIEO was delivered in a series of speeches at various UN sessions. With some persuasion, Secretary of State Kissinger, preoccupied with Middle East peace, détente, and other geopolitical issues, agreed to deliver a speech to the Kansas City International Relations Council on May 13, 1975. Secretary Kissinger was not enthusiastic about the NIEO initiative; his true feelings were perhaps best expressed when he wrote in his memoirs, "The developing countries had temporarily sated their yearning for center stage by an orgy of rhetoric at the Sixth Special Session of the UN General Assembly in April [1974]."[14]

In the Kansas City speech, after noting the cohesion and progress of the developed world, Kissinger recognized that "the world economic structure is under increasing challenge from many countries which believe that it does not fairly meet their needs."[15] He then said, "The United States is prepared to study these views attentively, but we are convinced that the present economic system has generally served the world well."[16] He outlined what the United States had done and was doing in the fields of energy, food, and primary commodities.

At that time I was U.S. ambassador in Indonesia. Because this was the first serious U.S. response on an issue of major importance to the Indonesians, I sent a copy immediately to the secretary general of the Foreign Ministry, Ali Alatas (later foreign minister). He called back to say the Kissinger speech represented progress, but asked, "Why did Dr. Kissinger have to say, not once, but twice, that the old economic order has served well? That is the heart of the issue; we do not agree." When I returned to Washington on consultation, I asked Assistant Secretary for Economic Affairs Tom Enders, who had drafted the speech, why he had inserted these phrases. "That," he replied, "was the price of getting Treasury to clear the speech."[17]

On September 1, 1975, at the opening of the Seventh Special Session of the General Assembly, U.S. Ambassador Patrick Moynihan read a speech by Secretary Kissinger. This was a more complete response, containing both critical comments on Third World initiatives, realistic assessments of U.S. assistance, and proposals designed to respond as positively as possible to the demands of the NIEO.

Recognizing the mounting confrontation with the developing countries, the secretary urged proceeding in a spirit of cooperation. He was critical of both the non-aligned movement and OPEC:

> It is also ironic that a philosophy of non-alignment, designed to allow new nations
> to make their national choices free from the pressures of competing blocs, now

has produced a bloc of its own. Nations with radically different political concerns are combined in a kind of solidarity that often clearly sacrifices practical interests. And it is ironic also that the most devastating blow to economic development in this decade came not from "imperialist rapacity" but from an arbitrary, monopolistic price increase by the cartel of oil exporters.[18]

He emphasized the need to turn to private capital. Speaking of concessional assistance from the developed countries, he said, "To put it frankly, the political climate for bilateral aid has deteriorated. In the industrial countries, support for aid has been eroded by domestic economic slowdown, compounded by energy problems in the developing countries."[19]

The speech contained a number of proposals for specific initiatives:

- a development security facility in the IMF to stabilize export earnings;
- expansion of the International Finance Corporation (IFC) in the World Bank to support private enterprise;
- formation of an International Investment Trust in the IFC;
- improved ways, through the World Bank, to provide access to capital;
- encouragement of increased technical assistance and improved access to technology, especially in the energy field;
- codes of conduct for both transnational corporations and governments;
- improvements in the world trading system to better serve development goals;
- establishment of food reserves;
- discussions of commodity issues on a state-by-state basis;
- establishment of an International Fund for Agricultural Development;
- priority in development assistance to the poorest countries.

The results of the Seventh Special Session were deemed a success. Fifteen of the specific proposals advanced in Secretary Kissinger's speech were adopted. A *New York Times* editorial commented that "it is too early to be sure that the corner will stay turned; but this sixteen-day session at least brought a dramatic turnaround of the Assembly—from incendiary rhetoric and confrontation to reality and genuine negotiation."[20] The editorial continued:

Among the factors contributing to the improved climate over Turtle Bay, two stand out. The United States shifted from stonewalling third-world demands as unrealistic and fanciful to a policy of presenting comprehensive proposals for coping with the chronic problems of poorer nations. And inside the group of developing nations, the moderates—weary of sterile confrontation, eager for negotiation and for as wide an area of agreement as possible—usually prevailed over their more radical brethren.[21]

The final major Kissinger initiative came with his personal appearance and speech at the conference of the UN Committee on Trade and Development (UNCTAD) in Nairobi, Kenya, in May 1976. He could not resist an opening salvo:

"The United States, better than almost any other nation, could survive a period of economic warfare. We can resist confrontation and rhetorical attacks if other nations choose that path. And we can ignore unrealistic proposals and peremptory demands."[22]

The centerpiece of his presentation was a proposal for an international resources bank to "promote more rational, systematic, and equitable development of resources in developing nations."[23] In addition, he proposed a timetable for the study of commodity problems, an international code of conduct on export controls and a series of proposals to facilitate technology transfer. He called, further, for attention to the debt problem and to the particular needs of the poorest nations. He did not, however, endorse a Third World proposal for a common fund to finance a commodity market.

The speech was generally well received. The *New York Times* reported that a representative of the Philippine delegation told a State Department official that "with the speech the United States had moved far in advance of the other industrialized nations in facing basic issues."[24]

William Eteki, secretary general of the Organization of African Unity, expressed another view about a resources bank with private investment participation:

> The idea of a bank funded by private capital which by its nature seeks investments which are profitable does not inspire confidence. It risks the transformation of an operation of solidarity and justice into a matter of speculation and would be humiliating to the beneficiaries.[25]

The Kissinger initiatives of the late 1970s served to defuse the pressure from the developing nations, but, in the end, only a few of the major initiatives proposed became realities. In the later years of the twentieth century, the conditions of the global debate changed to some extent. The new issue of "globalization" was introduced and the more successful developing countries embraced free market principle and benefited. Nevertheless, the gap between rich and poor countries continued to grow, and fundamental differences remained between the poorer and richer nations on how to deal with the gap.

Trade

The debate over trade issues in the NIEO was largely rhetorical. Fundamental decisions on terms of trade centered in the operation of the General Agreement on Tariffs and Trade (GATT), formed in 1948 to manage global trade negotiations. The developing countries found GATT, dominated by the major world economies, an unsatisfactory forum, even though efforts were made to provide "special and differential treatment" for the poorer nations. Third World nations attempted to move trade negotiations into the UN Conference on Trade and Development (UNCTAD) in the 1960s and 1970s but were unsuccessful.

Textiles were a particular source of difficulty in trade negotiations. They were one of the most common exports of the developing countries, but they faced barriers, especially in the United States, from domestic producers in the developed world. The United States was, not unreasonably, accused of hypocrisy in its advocacy of free trade. The last successful global trade negotiation, the Uruguay Round, concluded in the 1990s, included an agreement to phase out the textile quota system by 2005.

By the end of the century, the solidarity of the developing world on trade issues had declined as major countries became more pragmatic and more conscious of the competition within the Third World. The poorer countries, for example, may be less enthusiastic about reducing textile quotas by 2005, having in mind the competition from China.

In 1995, GATT was transformed into the World Trade Organization. As described by Calvocoressi, "The Uruguay Round marked a shift away from tariffs and quotas to financial and other services and rights in intellectual properties. Its conclusion coincided with attempts to integrate ex-Soviet and satellite economies with western capitalist economies and for the latter to find a modus vivendi with surviving command economies, in particular China's."[26]

Trade represented the lifeblood of Third World economies. Decolonization brought a painful adjustment to participation in world trade arrangements, which are less protected by colonial patterns. In the latter half of the twentieth century, those adjustments became even more painful with the advent of globalization and an increasingly complex agenda of trade items. And more and more, developing countries were urged to wean themselves from official development assistance through trade.

U.S. Economic Assistance

Perhaps few aspects of U.S. policies toward the developing world have been as disappointing to the Third World as U.S. economic assistance. Expectations were raised after World War II that the United States would be generous in its support for new nations. But that support never materialized to the degree hoped for by these nations. By the 1970s and 1980s, U.S. assistance became almost entirely related to two political objectives: maintenance of Middle East peace and the pursuit of the Cold War (the subject of the next chapter). Little was left to meet the levels and conditions sought by most of the Third World nations.[27]

Within the U.S. government, including the Congress, differences existed over the proper function of aid—whether its success was to be judged primarily on its social and economic results or whether political objectives should prevail. Neither side, however, suggested that the basic criteria of sound and honest implementation should be eroded.

Third World countries looked at the billions of dollars provided under the Marshall Plan and hoped that they might be similarly blessed. Few would accept the differences between reconstructing industrial societies with strong existing institutions and infrastructures and assisting countries that lacked these advantages.

The United States recognized the needs and responded initially through a program of technical assistance, the Point Four program of President Harry Truman.[28] In the 1950s, more substantial programs of development aid were started, but from the beginning, U.S. economic assistance to the developing countries faced serious obstacles. Congress was never enthusiastic and increasingly attached conditions to the provision of aid. Initially these conditions related to the responsibilities of the recipient country in the implementation of the assistance. Over the years conditions were attached relating to U.S. foreign policy goals such as human rights, the environment, and democracy. As worthy as these objectives were, they struck sensitive nerves in many societies. The mandatory reports on human rights required after 1974 of the State Department on all aid recipients led to the rejection of assistance by one major country, Brazil.

The U.S. aid program has suffered from serious public misunderstandings about the extent of resources devoted to overseas assistance. Public opinion polls have shown that Americans believe about 15 percent of GNP goes to foreign assistance and that 5 per cent would be an appropriate figure. In 1997, the United States spent less than one-tenth of 1 per cent of its GNP on foreign aid.

In the 1970s, the United States withdrew from expensive infrastructure projects, leaving them to the World Bank and regional development banks. Bilateral economic aid levels to developing countries reached a peak in 1985 but began a decline in 1990. Total U.S. economic aid outside of Europe in 1985 was $11,802 million; by 1990, the figure had dropped to $5,197 million.

International Financial Institutions

The two major international financial institutions, the International Bank for Reconstruction and Development (World Bank) and the International Monetary Fund (IMF), together with regional development banks in Asia and Latin America, became the centerpieces of the various U.S. proposals to meet the needs of the developing countries. The United States was a major contributor and effectively held a veto over actions of the World Bank and the IMF. The United States was thus closely identified with their policies, many of which were unpopular with developing nations. One of the principal demands of the New International Economic Order was a change in the decision making of the World Bank and the IMF, moving away from the dominant position of the largest contributors. The United States remains firmly opposed to such reforms.

A further effort was made by the G-77 in 1980 to bypass the decision-making system of the banks when they introduced into the UN General Assembly a proposal for global economic negotiations in a single body. The special session of the Assembly devoted to economic issues in 1980 broke down when the United States, Britain, and Germany refused to endorse the global negotiations concept.

Developing nations also object to what they consider excessively demanding conditions in World Bank lending. This concern has only been partly assuaged by the organization of the International Development Association (IDA), a concessional lending arm of the bank. But the IDA has proven to be unpopular in the U.S.

Congress, and each administration in recent years has had difficulty obtaining authorization for IDA contributions.

Further U.S. identification with World Bank actions came through the vetoing of loans to individual countries, including Vietnam and Cuba. The demand in the NIEO that countries be allowed to adopt whatever system they pleased and not be subject to discrimination as a result is directly related to these U.S. actions.

The IMF has become even more unpopular. Responsible in the international community for resolving balance of payments and budget problems, it has taken harsh measures necessary to achieve results. Such measures include requiring countries to cut back on civil service rolls, end food subsidies, and trim military budgets, all politically unpopular acts in the Third World.

The story of this chapter is essentially the story of the last half of the twentieth century. As the new century dawns, even though the United States may still not exhibit the level of untrammeled generosity hoped for by the Third World, many of the nations of that world are, themselves, adapting more to the global economy as it is. The friction between the industrial north and the developing south will not end, but perhaps the relations may develop on a more realistic basis.

ELEVEN

The Cold War

The impression of the United States as an imperial power was heightened by the Cold War and by alliances that reinforced the positions of the former colonial powers. Confrontation between the United States and its allies and the Communist-bloc nations dominated U.S. policy toward the Third World for almost forty-five years.

This global confrontation became the primary rationale for U.S. military and economic assistance. It resulted in security commitments and a network of bases in an arc from the Mediterranean to Japan that inevitably involved the United States in the internal affairs of states. It drew the United States into direct conflict in Vietnam and surrogate conflicts in the Horn of Africa, Angola, and Afghanistan; each would become involved in Washington's domestic politics. And to the frustration of many in America, few Third World nations shared the concept of a "free world" matched against an "evil empire." U.S. actions, both covert and overt, and the inclusion of former colonial powers in regional security pacts were more likely to be seen as efforts to preserve a Western imperial structure. The concept of non-alignment first enunciated at the Bandung conference of emerging nations in 1955 became solid doctrine in most Third World countries.

It is easy, from the perspective of the end of the century, to conclude that the United States overreacted to what it saw as the Soviet threat in the Third World, to the detriment of its position within many of the newly independent nations. Recently released Russian documents suggest that Moscow's Third World initiatives were often in response to requests from the developing nations and in reaction to Western moves. No doubt they seized on opportunities to weaken and embarrass the West wherever they could. But whether or not the believed threat of a global Communist plan was real, to understand U.S. policies of the time, one must recognize that national leaders from both parties considered that the threat was real and reacted accordingly. What was done in the Third World must be seen against the backdrop of the deep disillusionment and fear created in America by the Soviet takeover of Eastern Europe and the threat of their growing nuclear arsenal. In retrospect, the fact that subsequent U.S. reverses in Asian countries bordering the Soviet Union, such as Iraq and Iran, did not result in Communist advances, as feared, is perhaps further evidence that the flimsy security structures of the time and the resulting reactions in the Third World were not needed. And among the most flimsy of structures was the Baghdad Pact.

The Baghdad Pact

In January 1953, when President Dwight D. Eisenhower and his secretary of state, John Foster Dulles, took office, the new administration was determined to strengthen the U.S. position in Asia through extending the encirclement of the Soviet Union. Washington efforts to form a Middle East Defense Organization (MEDO) had foundered on the resistance of Arab states, especially Egypt under Nasser. Instead, Dulles envisioned filling the gap between the Truman Doctrine obligations to Greece and Turkey and the U.S. position in East Asia by a "northern tier" pact.

Following a trip to the Middle East in May 1953, Dulles presented his idea to the nation on television on June 9:

> A Middle East Organization is a future rather than an immediate possibility. Many of the Arab League countries are so engrossed with their quarrels with Israel or with Great Britain or France that they pay little heed to the menace of Soviet communism. However, there is more concern where the Soviet Union is near. In general, the northern tier of nations shows awareness of this danger.
>
> There is a vague desire to have a collective security system. But no such system can be imposed from without. It should be desired and grow from within out of a sense of common destiny and common danger.[1]

The Eisenhower administration then set out to develop a northern tier alliance. The first concentration was on Iraq. In 1954, the Iraqi monarchy that had been imposed on the country after World War I ruled over a population that saw the creation of Israel as a humiliating slap at the Arabs. Iraqis were attracted by the Arab nationalism of Gamal Abdul Nasser. The ruling elite, however, was still closely tied to Britain, the former mandate power, and was friendly to the West.

As public affairs officer in the U.S. embassy at the time, I sensed the unrest beneath the surface in Baghdad. In November 1952, a mob, demonstrating against Iraq's treaty with Britain, burned the offices of the U.S. Information Service. They would have burned the British embassy, but it was on the other side of the Tigris River and they could not reach it. Donald Maitland (now Sir), Oriental Secretary of the British Embassy at the time, told me that U.S. Information Agency literature, projected skyward by the fire, drifted down into the garden of the British Embassy. He jokingly said, "You Americans will go to any lengths to distribute your propaganda."

On April 21, 1954, the prime minister of Iraq, Fadhil Jamali, signed a military assistance agreement with the United States and immediately resigned, probably to give the signal that he had signed under pressure. In a meeting with Secretary Dulles in Washington in 1955, General Nuri al Said, the strongman of Iraq at the time, argued that to make Iraqi cooperation with the West possible, the United States should make some positive gesture toward the Palestinians. As the signs mounted that Washington was pressing Baghdad to sign a northern tier pact, I was not sanguine about the future.

In the face of strong opposition from Nasser, the creation of a Western-backed security alliance proceeded. Turkey and Pakistan signed a mutual defense treaty in April 1954. Then, in February 1955, in a visit to Baghdad, Turkish prime minister Adnan Menderes signed a pact with Iraq under Nuri. Britain followed, signing in April. Pakistan adhered in September and Iran in October, and the pact was formed. Its principal provision was set forth in Article I:

> Consistent with article 51 of the United Nations Charter the High Contracting Parties will co-operate for their security and defense. Such measures as they agree to take to give effect to this cooperation may form the subject of special agreements with each other.[2]

The terms of the pact did not place any precise obligations upon any party. It was the symbolism of the pact, more than its provisions, that became the center of controversy.

The pact was doomed from the start. Each signatory joined for a different reason. Turkey, directly confronting Russia, undoubtedly wished to strengthen its regional security position. Pakistan was interested in getting Western support in its conflict with India. Iran saw the pact as a means of strengthening its regional position with U.S. help. Iraq believed that by agreeing to join a U.S.-sponsored pact, it could open the doors to U.S. military assistance and could press Washington to a more favorable attitude toward the Palestinian cause. And Britain saw the new treaty as a feasible way of gaining a new agreement with Iraq, substituting for one that would expire in 1957. Britain's signing created even more strongly the impression in the region that this was a "Western imperial alliance." With the region concentrating on local concerns over Israel and each other, little support existed for the need to defend against the Soviet Union.

Efforts to expand the treaty to include other Arab states, especially Jordan, did not succeed. And the United States never formally joined. Secretary Dulles gave as his reason that if the United States adhered to a pact with an Arab country requiring U.S. Senate ratification, the United States would almost certainly have had to sign a similar treaty with Israel because of domestic pressure. He did not believe this would be in the U.S. interest in the region.

The result was an anomaly. Each year, as annual Baghdad Pact meetings approached, the United States would be required not only to explain why it was not joining the pact, but also manifest its support in some specific way. The need for an alternative resulted, in 1957, in the Eisenhower Doctrine.

The Eisenhower Doctrine

Foreign policy in the United States is constantly subject to the vagaries of domestic politics. And initiatives with a sound policy premise often have unintended consequences. Such was the case with the Middle East Resolution of March 9, 1957.

After the tumultuous events of 1956, including the abortive French and British efforts to topple Nasser in the Suez invasion, the Eisenhower administration believed that a new initiative for the region was in order. At the same time, Washington sought to demonstrate support for friendly governments short of joining the Baghdad Pact and to gain from Congress flexibility in the dispersal of aid. Under normal aid procedures, administrations had to request congressional authorization for any changes in initially legislated appropriations—often a time-consuming and sometimes controversial proceeding.

To meet the desired objectives, the administration proposed a joint resolution of Congress and, under authority of the resolution, the appropriation of a sum of money that could be disbursed by the administration to meet the aims of the resolution.

Accordingly, on January 5, 1957, President Eisenhower sent a special message to Congress on "The Situation in the Middle East" requesting such a resolution. As was necessary to achieve congressional approval of any foreign policy issue in that era, the message stressed the menace of communism and the designs of the Soviet Union in these words:

Thus we have these simple and indisputable facts:

1. The Middle East, which has always been coveted by Russia, would today be more prized than ever by international communism.
2. The Soviet rulers continue to show that they do not scruple to use any means to gain their ends.
3. The free nations of the Middle East need, and for the most part, want added strength to insure their continued independence.[3]

The message explained that the resolution would:

- authorize cooperation "with any nation or group of nations in the general area of the Middle East in the development of economic strength dedicated to the maintenance of national independence";
- authorize programs of military assistance and cooperation "with any nation or group of nations which desires such aid";
- include "the employment of the armed forces of the United States to secure and protect the territorial integrity and national independence of such nations, requesting such aid, against overt armed aggression from any nation controlled by international communism";
- authorize the President to employ "sums available under the Mutual Security Act of 1954, as amended, without regard to existing limitations."[4]

The Joint Resolution was passed as Public Law 7 of the 85th Congress and signed by the president on March 9, 1957. The sum of $200 million was appropriated under the special authority.

Upon passage, it was decided that James P. Richards, a retired congressman to whom the administration felt indebted, would be appointed to visit Middle Eastern countries, seek countries' endorsement of the doctrine, and apportion out the money.

In the mood of the time, to get nations publicly to identify themselves with such a U.S. initiative was a challenge. The Richards mission was not a success, and the demand that nations stand up and be counted by publicly accepting the doctrine served to widen the gap between the United States and Arab nationalists even more and put pressure on pro-Western countries. Of the countries visited, only Pakistan and Lebanon formally endorsed the doctrine. Mr. Richards encountered a particularly difficult client in the Imam Ahmed of Yemen. At the outset of the meeting, the imam asked Richards how many countries he was visiting:

"Fourteen," said the congressman.

"And how much money are you distributing?," asked the imam.

"Two hundred million."

"And how much are you prepared to offer Yemen?"

"Two million dollars," was the reply.

"Fourteen into two hundred million is more than two million," said the imam and left the room.[5]

Although it was continued for a few more years as the Central Treaty Organization, the Baghdad Pact effectively ended when a revolution in Baghdad on July 14, 1958, overthrew the monarchy.

Dissatisfaction with Iraq's pro-West and pro-U.S. orientation, easily discernible in the prior years but suppressed, finally exploded. And, as would be the case in other Third World countries forced into an embrace with America, U.S. interests went down the drain.

Vietnam

On the other side of Asia, another pact, the Southeast Asia Treaty Organization (SEATO), also known as the Manila Pact, was signed in May 1955. Its membership ultimately included the Philippines, Thailand, Pakistan, Australia, New Zealand, Britain, and France. The United States, unhampered in this part of Asia by the Israeli connection, also joined.

Unlike the Baghdad Pact, the SEATO treaty obligated the parties to act. Article IV stated:

Each party recognizes that aggression by means of armed attack in the treaty area against any of the Parties or against any State or territory which the Parties by unanimous agreement may hereafter designate, would endanger its own peace and safety, and agrees that it will in that event act to meet the common danger in accordance with its constitutional processes.[6]

The United States subsequently issued an "understanding" that its agreement applied "only to Communist aggression," but it agreed to consult in the event of other aggression in the region.[7]

The SEATO treaty was to become a basis for the U.S. entry into its longest war, the war in Vietnam. And although it was joined by other nations in Asia,[8] it was seen throughout the Third World not only as America's war but, because of its repudiation of Vietnam nationalists, also as an effort to perpetuate an imperial presence in place of the French.

The story of Vietnam has been extensively told; I will not repeat it here. In a book designed to explain why the United States has a negative image in much of the Third World, however, it is relevant to look at Washington's dilemma at the beginning of the Vietnam involvement.

When it became apparent that the Allies would emerge triumphant in World War II in 1945, the French immediately began to turn their attention back to their colonial possessions, seeking acceptance of the pre-war status quo from their American allies in the process. The American ambassador in France at the time, Jefferson Caffrey, recounted a conversation he had with General Charles de Gaulle in March 1945, who claimed that he did not understand the American decision taken by President Franklin Roosevelt not to get involved in Indochina. In addition to claiming that the French presence in the Far East was founded upon agreements consistent with international law, de Gaulle began to play upon growing U.S. fears of Soviet expansionism, asking Caffrey "Do you want us to become, for example, one of the federated states under the Russian aegis?" while claiming that "we do not want to become Communist; we do not want to fall into the Russian orbit, but I hope that you do not push us into it."[9] Despite these warnings, American officials remained hesitant to get involved in the Far East, particularly in support of oppressive colonial systems. Secretary of State Dean Acheson summed up American feelings at the time in an October letter to a U.S. diplomat in China, stating:

> The U.S. has no thought of opposing the reestablishment of French control in Indochina and no official statement by U.S. Government has questioned even by implication French sovereignty over Indochina. However, it is not the policy of this government to assist the French to reestablish their control over Indochina by force and the willingness of the U.S. to see French control reestablished assumes that the French claim to have the support of the population of Indochina is borne out by future events."[10]

As the Cold War heated up in Europe and events in China began to look more ominous in 1948, official attitudes toward Ho Chi Minh and his party began to stiffen in the United States. Secretary of State George Marshall illustrated this change in attitude when he wrote to the U.S. Embassy in China in July 1948, stating firmly that "Dept info [*sic*] indicates that Ho Chi Minh is Communist," and cited his Comintern record of the 1920s and 1930s as well as evidence from French and Soviet newspapers. Although Marshall believed that Ho was a puppet of Moscow, a Department of State message admitted that "Dept has no evidence of direct link between Ho and Moscow, but assumes it exists, nor is it able to evaluate amount pressure or guidance Moscow exerting."[11] Such statements signaled a change in attitude toward the Viet Minh, who were now branded as Communists first, thus eliminating them from the minds of American officials as a legitimate political option in the region.

Throughout 1949 the Chinese situation, and the eventual victory of Mao's forces, dominated American foreign policy directives, particularly in Indochina. Prior to the Communist victory in China, French interest in restoring Bao Dai to power in Vietnam was met with considerable skepticism by Washington. After Mao had taken power, the Americans, while retaining a healthy cynicism about the chances for success, began to rethink their position on the former Vietnamese emperor. Caffrey, writing from Paris in March 1949, stated "as Bao Dai represents only foreseeable opportunity for anti-Communist nationalist solution Indochina, I recommend that Department in light our declared policy preventing spread of communism in SEA and of supporting truly nationalist movements in that area, study agreement when received with view to possibly extending to Bao Dai solution as calculated risk moral and perhaps some economic support."[12] Caffrey concluded that the "only alternative to Bao Dai solution would involve dealing with Ho Chi Minh (to whom I assume we remain unalterably opposed)."[13]

Throughout 1949 and 1950, American policymakers discussed the possibilities for the success of Bao Dai's regime and concluded that support from other Asian nations, in particular India, Thailand, Burma, and the Philippines, would greatly enhance Bao Dai's chances. State Department officials turned to their British counterparts for advice on how best to proceed in obtaining this support but received no concrete suggestions. Lewis Douglas, the U.S. ambassador in London, stated that approaching India about Bao Dai "might in the present circumstances do more harm than good, fearing a Nehru blast on colonialism," for the Indian leader had stated that "he does not consider Ho Chi Minh a Kremlin tool but rather a nationalist and does not approve of March 8 agreement," for it appeared to reinstate a colonial system in Indochina.[14] The United States Ambassador to India, Loy Henderson, also responded in June 1949 to State Department requests on how best to obtain Indian support for Bao Dai and wrote "as was manifest last session of the UN General Assembly, the GOI is still more interested in combating colonialism and racial discrimination than in actively opposing Communism outside of India."[15]

American policymakers pressured the French to make more concessions toward giving the Southeast Asian countries within the French Union greater sovereignty. Commenting on the feasibility of the French granting greater autonomy in Indochina, the newly appointed U.S. ambassador to France, David K. E. Bruce, summed up French attitudes:

> No French government would remain in power that advocated complete indepen-
> dence either now or in the future for Indochina. . . . They [the French] do not feel
> any consciousness of having on balance grievously oppressed the native popula-
> tion or exploited it for their own exclusive benefit; on the contrary they take pride
> in having by their own account led with a vast expenditure of effort, blood, and
> treasure a congeries of backward and ignorant peoples towards a state of enlight-
> enment where they are sensible of nationhood and are demanding the rights of
> self-government. Bigoted as many foreigners may think this attitude to be, never-
> theless it exists and is an element in the situation which must not be disregarded.[16]

Faced with the choice of angering a recalcitrant French ally or the Third World
nations calling for an end to colonialism, the United States chose to side with its
wartime partner.

Armed with the knowledge that he would be acting against the wishes of other
Asian nations, Secretary of State Acheson stated that the Department would go
ahead with de facto recognition of Vietnam (under Bao Dai) despite the reactions of India, Burma, Thailand, and the Philippines.[17] The State Department then
cabled the U.S. Embassy in Thailand:

> Dept concerned by apparent lack of understanding on part of Thai Foreign Min-
> ister that Ho Chi Minh is not patriotic nationalist but Commie Party member
> with all the sinister implications involved in the relationship. . . . [A]pparently
> this point of view is common among South Asian nations, including India, Burma,
> Indonesia, and the Philippines. . . . This general indifference or lack of under-
> standing may prove to be disastrous for those nations as Communism relentlessly
> advances. It is impossible for the U.S. to help them resist Communism if they are
> not prepared to help themselves.[18]

After recognition, the United States hoped that other Asian nations, including
those they regarded as allies, would in turn recognize Bao Dai, but diplomatic si-
lence followed. Some years later, when I was ambassador to Indonesia, I asked the
Indonesians whether the U.S. actions in Vietnam had not saved them from a Communist thrust. Their response was, in effect, "Yes, perhaps, but our new republic
under Sukarno could not have been seen as supporting a French puppet."

Despite the negative attitudes evident among most Asian states toward Bao
Dai, the United States began to send military and economic aid to Vietnam soon
after recognizing Vietnam in February 1950, aid that became more than token after
North Korea invaded South Korea in June. Throughout the early 1950s, U.S. aid to
Vietnam continued to increase, and by the end of French involvement in Indochina
in 1954, the United States was footing most of the bill for the military conflict.[19]

In the wake of American decisions to become more involved in Vietnam, Ambassador Henderson in India sent a memorandum to Acheson explaining the growing feelings of unfriendliness toward the United States in India:

> The criticism expressed in press or orally has been aimed at those weaknesses or
> faults, fancied or real, of US Government or people upon which Indians when

irritated with US are accustomed to dwell, including our treatment of American negroes, our tendency to support colonialism and to strive for continued world supremacy of white peoples, our economic imperialism, superficiality of our culture, our lack of emotional balance evidenced by our present hysteria in combating Communism and our cynical use of 'witch hunting method' in promoting domestic political ends, our practice of giving economic and other assistance to foreign peoples only when we believe such assistance will aid our struggle against Communism, our assumption of superiority merely because we have higher standards of living, our hypocrisy, etc.[20]

Despite the aid to Bao Dai, the United States in 1954 decided not to intervene militarily to support the French. With the fall of Dien Bien Phu on May 7, 1954, the French presence was effectively ended. The international conference on Korea and Indochina then going on at Geneva resulted in a partition of Vietnam. The United States, concerned that other "dominoes" in Asia would fall, supported the organization of SEATO and determined to maintain the independence of the non-Communist regime in South Vietnam. As the threat grew, so did U.S. support and, in 1964, that support escalated into a massive deployment of U.S. forces. The rest is history.

Vietnam is seen generally as an American tragedy, perhaps made inevitable by the insurmountable dilemma of helping an ally while at the same time trying to deal with decolonization. There are those in Southeast Asia today who will say they welcomed the U.S. effort, but they are still outnumbered by those who considered American intervention another form of imperialism.

Military Cooperation

In 1950, U.S. military bases in developing countries in Asia and Africa included those in the Philippines, Thailand, Saudi Arabia, Ethiopia, Libya, and Morocco. At various times during the post-war period, military assistance programs and accompanying military missions existed in the base countries and Indonesia, Pakistan, Iran, Iraq, and Somalia.

In the post-colonial world, the presence of foreign troops and bases was politically unpopular, awakening recollections of imperial deployments. Such cooperation, in most cases, was only possible with authoritarian rulers who could suppress opposition to a foreign presence. During these years, the United States, as the world's leading democracy, was in the ironic position of allying itself with kings and authoritarian rulers who, it was hoped, could keep the lid on internal opposition to the U.S. presence. Washington found it far more difficult to understand and relate to the world's largest democracy, India. As the pressure for the consideration of human rights in foreign policy grew in the United States, these relationships became more and more difficult to defend.

Security cooperation raised a series of questions that preoccupied U.S. diplomacy in these countries for many years.

Security arrangements: Regimes where bases were present insisted that the bases (whatever their nature) increased the threat to the country and requested some form of security guarantee. In the case of the Philippines this was embodied in a security treaty signed in 1951. The United States had a commitment to Thailand under SEATO. In other countries where treaties, requiring Senate ratification, were not deemed possible, presidential letters asserting U.S. "interest in the independence and territorial integrity"—an unratified executive commitment—were intended to suffice.

A certain amount of smoke and mirrors was involved in the retention of bases. The public conception of a base was of an installation with armed troops prepared to defend themselves and the country. Such a presence implied both a willingness and a capacity to assist in a country's defense. Except in the case of the Philippines, and, possibly, Saudi Arabia, it was not realistic to anticipate that the United States would send forces to defend the nation, yet Washington was generally reluctant to clarify too precisely its obligations to a cooperating country.

When I was ambassador to Libya in 1967, after the Suez crisis, King Idris raised with me the question of U.S. defense obligations toward Libya.[21] I could only tell him that, although we considered Libya's independence important, we had no formal obligation to come to his defense or that of the country. The Wheelus Air Base in Tripoli was solely for the purpose of training U.S. air forces in Europe; it had no independent military capacity. When Idris was overthrown by Muammar Qadhafi in 1969, the king requested no help from Washington.

Compensation: Even where formal security guarantees were not present, the U.S. government insisted that its military presence in a country was for mutual benefit and that no compensation was required. Washington attempted to argue that the economic benefits—from the employment of local people and ancillary local purchases—were sufficient compensation. No government accepted this; all insisted that the political risks incurred by the presence of foreign forces required a greater public demonstration of benefits. At the same time, the foreign countries did not like the concept of "renting" their sovereign territory. Negotiations over compensation, therefore, became negotiations over packages of economic and military assistance, in which the public dollar figures became tests of the importance the United States attached to the relationship.

Inevitably, one country compared what the United States was providing with what was being provided elsewhere. The Philippines, for example, paid close attention to what the United States was paying Spain for bases in that country and demanded comparable compensation. In the case of Arab countries, the comparison was with Israel, which was receiving not only far more weapons but more modern and sophisticated weapons than were being provided to Arab countries.

Military Assistance: Military assistance programs raised other issues. Recipient country militaries wanted showy and often expensive equipment. The United States, seeking to limit arms races and reduce budget support costs, resisted such ambitions. In the case of Iraq, in order to maintain compatibility with equipment it already had, the United States purchased British equipment, to the disappointment of the Iraqis. In some instances, the United States, to the unhappiness of recipients, incorporated used equipment into a military assistance program. I can recall being present at the arrival of a shipment of U.S. equipment in Iraq and noting, to my dismay, that the U.S. Army markings had only been thinly painted over.

Arms Use: The question of the use of arms was always an issue. The U.S. intent was that arms be used for defense and internal security, yet at the same time Washington did not want U.S. equipment conspicuously used to quell political dissent. Military assistance agreements also provided that arms could not be used across borders without U.S. consent. In the case of Iraq, this would have prevented the Iraqi army under the monarchy from going to the defense of Jordan. The problem in Arab countries was made more acute by the fact that the United States seemed to turn a blind eye to Israel's use of U.S. military equipment in actions against neighboring Arab states, particularly after 1967 when the United States became a major arms supplier to Israel.

Status of Forces: The presence of U.S. forces in a country, even if only a small military advisory mission, raised "status of forces" questions: who would have jurisdiction over U.S. military personnel in the event of their involvement in a crime? Sensitivity over sovereignty often made the negotiation of such agreements difficult, yet in the U.S. Congress, protection of U.S. servicemen and women against local laws was mandatory. Disputes over jurisdiction were constant during the life of military assistance programs; it was the Ayatollah Khomeini's strong opposition in 1964 to a bill in the Iranian parliament that would have conferred immunity on U.S. military personnel that first brought him to prominence.

In the atmosphere of the Cold War, when the United States was seeking to bolster friendly governments in competition with others that were receiving help from the Soviet Union, military assistance programs were considered justified. But the United States could never fully satisfy recipients. Moreover, the programs were constantly vulnerable to strong feelings against foreign military presences left over from the imperial period. It was, therefore, perhaps not surprising that in at least four Third World countries—Iran, Iraq, Ethiopia, and Libya—in which the United States had such programs, revolutions turned out friendly rulers and U.S. arms became the arsenal of unfriendly regimes. Ambassador Waldemar Gallman, influential in the formation of the Baghdad Pact and the U.S. programs that followed, had little praise for the military assistance to Iraq: "My final appraisal of the program is that it did not help Nuri [al-Said] appreciably within or without Iraq, nor did it enhance our prestige perceptibly among Iraqis or their neighbors."[22]

The debate over U.S. Cold War programs in Third World countries continued in the 1960s and 1970s, particularly as Washington moved to covert action.

Covert Action

Clandestine actions in support of anti-Communist political and guerilla movements organized by the CIA were part of the U.S. arsenal of the Cold War. These included such relatively uncontroversial actions as planting articles in foreign newspapers, providing money and non-lethal equipment to political movements, and gathering intelligence. But the actions also included the provision of arms and advice to paramilitary groups and direct involvement in efforts to overthrow unfriendly regimes. They were based on the premise that open U.S. interventions would be unacceptable in Third World regions; significant objectives could be accomplished by deniable involvement.

In Asia, admitted CIA operations have taken place in Laos, Iraq, Iran, Indonesia, and Afghanistan. Perhaps only the major effort against the Soviets in Afghanistan could be considered a success—although many of those trained for that effort resurfaced after the war as militant anti-U.S. terrorists.

Whatever the justification for these covert action operations, they have created a CIA myth in a Third World that is sensitive, if not paranoid, about external interventions. Indira Gandhi, late prime minister of India, never stopped believing that the United States was manipulating Indian and regional politics through the CIA. The myth has provided choice material for a region prone to seeing conspiracies and an easy basis for Soviet disinformation during the Cold War. In his book *Estranged Democracies,* Dennis Kux describes Indian reactions to the revelations in U.S. congressional hearings that the CIA had funded a number of cultural and educational groups:

> Indian intellectuals were greatly offended to learn that prestigious organizations, like the Asia Foundation, were secretly receiving funds from the CIA. Feeling tricked and betrayed, some Indian intellectuals led an anti-U.S. crusade, alleging academic imperialism. The Soviets and their local Communist allies and fellow-travelers took full advantage of the exposures to further tarnish the U.S. image in India.[23]

Much could be said about the openness of the American society that brought such matters to light, but the predisposition of many in the Third World to see the United States as an imperialist successor was not in the U.S. favor. Reports of CIA activities in Latin America further fed this impression.

To what extent this may have damaged U.S. interests is hard to say, but there is little doubt that it is one more element in the suspicion of Washington's actions and motives that exists in many of the newer nations. And if it exists with some basis in Asia, it exists with even stronger foundations in Africa.

TWELVE

Africa, Race, and Politics

The image of the United States in Africa suffered for most of four decades from the perception that Washington policies were designed to preserve European and white minority positions in the African continent. It is not surprising that this impression existed. Although official policy sought to reform rather than preserve minority regimes, many Americans and non-Americans in this period attempted to use the Washington political process to do just that. As a consequence, the United States sent mixed signals. People abroad read them as they wished and many in the Third World, inherently suspicious of big powers, read them negatively.

As the nations of Asia and Africa became independent, race became an inescapable issue. Early anti-colonial gatherings described themselves as unions of "the colored races." Independence leaders—as students and visitors—had encountered discrimination in America as well as Europe. Even with remarkable advances in civil rights in the 1960s, many still saw the United States as a racist nation. Until the full implementation of the civil rights legislation of the mid-1960s, the State Department was required to make special arrangements for the travel by car of new African diplomats between Washington and New York to avoid Jim Crow discrimination.

In the United States, the substantial African American population itself was emerging from the Jim Crow era. With African decolonization coming as it did at the height of America's struggle with civil rights, American blacks took pride in their African identity and saw in Africa, and particularly in southern Africa, struggles similar to their own. They wanted U.S. policy toward Africa to foster the ending of discrimination and to support the integrity and viability of the new African nations.

Elliott Skinner, noted African American scholar, writes of this in the foreword to a bibliography on African Americans and Africa. He referred to the immediate post–Civil War period as the first Reconstruction:

As during the first Reconstruction, Afro-Americans heralded the 1960s with great hopes for making significant strides toward freedom and equality in America. . . . The Second Reconstruction is occurring at a very different period in the world's history; the end of the Western Era. While few blacks during the First Reconstruction saw their future linked to that of Africa, the Afro-Americans during the Second Reconstruction recognize a definite connection between their Sit-Ins and Civil Rights marches and the lowering of foreign flags at midnight in many an African state.[1]

For many decades the principal U.S. link with sub-Saharan Africa was Liberia, founded by ex-slaves from the United States in 1820. In the nineteenth century, the United States helped Liberia fend off British and French encroachments but did little more to assist the new country. Despite the similarity in flag and government to those of the United States, Liberia remained a neglected remnant. As long as Liberia was the only symbol of black freedom in Africa, generations of African Americans took a special interest in its independence and vitality. But as new generations turned their interest to the other emerging states in Africa, interest in Liberia lagged. With the end of colonialism in other new countries, African American leaders expanded their horizons and their activism.

Some "went home" to Africa and stayed. In 1972, as assistant secretary for African affairs, I visited Sékou Touré, then president of Guinea. He invited me to go with him to Labe in the center of the country to meet "one of your fellow countrymen." He was Stokely Carmichael, an early civil rights leader who had gone to live in Guinea.

But an impressive group of African Americans with many white supporters remained in America and reached out to Africa through the African-American Institute, the U.S. Committee on Africa, TransAfrica, and the U.S.-African dialogues. Ted Brown, the leader of the American Negro Leadership Conference on Africa, brought together such African American notables as Martin Luther King, A. Phillips Randolph, James Farmer, Roy Wilkins, Dorothy Height, and Whitney Young.

The Carnegie Corporation initiated an Anglo-American Parliamentary Study Group on Africa, later also supported by the Ford Foundation, that met from 1964 to 1980 and introduced members of the U.S. Congress and the British parliament with experience in Africa to African issues. In the U.S. House of Representatives, the subcommittee on Africa chaired by Congressman Charles Diggs brought African issues to public attention. Diggs made frequent trips to the continent, establishing some of the earliest U.S. legislative ties with the new countries.

But those interested in U.S. policies that recognized the pressure for national independence and majority rule in Africa faced numerous obstacles.

President John F. Kennedy had a strong personal interest in Africa. He demonstrated this in his Senate speech on freedom for Algeria in 1957 and in the many visitors from Africa he received in the White House. Beginning with Kwame Nkrumah of Ghana, Kennedy met eleven African heads of state in 1961, ten in 1962, and seven in 1963. His interest was reinforced by his brother, Robert, the attorney general, who, as Arthur Schlesinger noted in *A Thousand Days,* "became a ready and effective ally for those advancing the claims of African policy."[2] Ignoring the risk of offending Portugal, Robert Kennedy met with Mozambiquan liberation leader Eduardo Mondlane in 1962. And substantial aid commitments were made to Ghana and Nigeria during the Kennedy administration.

Despite Kennedy's enthusiasm for Africa, policy toward the continent competed with preoccupation over Vietnam and the Cold War. The overriding American concern with the confrontation with the Soviet Union and its allies came at the same time as the independence of the African states and, to a large extent, shaped U.S. responses to that independence. William Roger Lewis and Ronald Robinson comment on this aspect in an article in the *Times Literary Supplement:*

> In South-East Asia and Africa, the Americans feared that the only alternative to imperial rule would be chaos or Communism. The revitalization of Western Europe depended upon the economic attachment of colonial and ex-colonial areas. To ride roughshod over European imperial pride would strain vital NATO alliances. Ideally, the United States preferred "independence" and covert influence to colonialism. In practice, the Americans gave priority to anti-Communism over anti-colonialism.[3]

Further, Washington continued to see Africa as a European responsibility and to view the continent through European eyes; responsibility for relations with the continent lay in the Bureau of European Affairs until 1959. Such leading figures as Dean Acheson, conditioned by an imperial age and by the critical relationships of World War II, showed little sympathy for the anti-colonial cause. Even Dean Rusk, Kennedy's secretary of state, did not share the president's enthusiasm for Africa. In his book *As I Saw It,* he comments:

> I always looked upon the United States as the junior partner in Africa. Yet this attitude of mine irritated some State Department colleagues and particularly our ambassadors to African countries; they believed the United States should play "Mr. Big" in every African capital. When I tried to calm them down, some in State's African Bureau concluded I was indifferent toward Africa. This was untrue. I just felt that the informal division of labor we had with our Western European allies was the right way to proceed in Africa.[4]

And the bureaucratic battles undoubtedly involved exaggerations on both sides. Arthur Schlesinger comments in *A Thousand Days* that "presidential decision making was not made easier by the tendency of both Europeanists and Africanists in the State Department to overstate the dreadful consequences which would follow from favoring the other."[5]

Over time, a growing disillusionment in Washington with foreign aid and the bizarre actions of such African leaders as Idi Amin, Jean-Bedelle Bokassa, and Sékou Touré eroded interest in the continent. Black majority rule did not necessarily mean democratic rule. The only excesses tolerated were those by anti-Communist stalwarts such as Mobutu Sese Seko of Zaire.

Kennedy's name was respected in Africa, but the expectations of support for black Africa raised by his attention could not be sustained. Dreams of giving Africa a high priority and a Marshall Plan for the continent were unrealistic. Instead, U.S. policymakers for Africa became enmeshed in a series of controversies in Africa that, with congressional involvement and competing lobbyists, became domestic as well as international issues. Occurring in the midst of the Cold War, African conflicts, even though often internal or regional in nature, tended to be seen in Washington as elements of the East-West struggle.

African Americans and their allies, reflecting a broad African consensus, did not deny the presence of Soviets and Cubans in Africa but saw their presences as legitimate responses to requests from liberation movements and new nations. Still following a general African consensus, they opposed U.S. relations not only with white minority regimes but with regimes and leaders identified with strong European—that is, imperial—support.

The preoccupation with Soviet and Cuban activities in Africa that existed among both Republicans and Democrats enabled charismatic Africans capable of plausible anti-Communist rhetoric to pursue their own paths to power with American help, both overt and covert. The efforts to promote competing approaches to the continent became intense and emotional. The question of race was ever near the surface. African Americans saw in African liberation movements parallels to their own struggles; their comments on Africa were often allegorical references to their civil rights efforts. On the other side, those who had opposed civil rights moves in the United States sympathized with white minority regimes and their allies in Africa. Networks of like-minded individuals from white-dominated regimes, including foreign intelligence and military officials, fed information and points of view to U.S. legislators and policymakers. Those black Africans who were professedly anti-Communist and emerged as sympathetic to a white minority were stage-managed by public relations firms. I could understand the views of Chester Crocker, one of my successors as assistant secretary:

> Remote from the American experience, Africa was the stuff of legends and stereotypes: it was the last remaining land of white hats and black hats, a Manichean playground for underemployed Western activists on the right and on the left. Where else was there such a pure play on racism or anti-communism? Where else was there so little need for knowledge, experience, or self-discipline? . . .
>
> Since it did not matter what one said or did, there was every incentive to view African policy as a bidding war in which you staked out "foreign policy" positions in order to "prove yourself" at home. Conservative Republicans viewed Africa as elephant country—a place to hunt for anti-Communist trophies to hang on the wall and to demonstrate doctrinal manhood in support of freedom fighters. . . . Democrats badly needed issues and causes to rally around. If the mounting violence in South African townships could be pinned on Reagan and his policies, this would open up a new "civil rights" front.[6]

Five cases will illustrate the complex interaction of these elements: the crisis in the Congo, Rhodesia's unilateral declaration of independence (UDI), conflicts in the former Portuguese territories, the Nigerian civil war, and the debate over sanctions against South Africa.

The Congo

Until very late in the 1950s, Belgians, like the Portuguese, considered independence for their African colonies only a distant possibility. George C. McGhee visited the Belgian Congo as assistant secretary of state for the Near East, South Asia, and Africa in 1950. In his book *Envoy to the Middle World,* he writes:

> Colonial Belgians were reported to suspect that we sought to accelerate the advancement of backward races, and that this was reflected in our policies toward trusteeship territories such as theirs. At that point, the Belgians were also seeking to raise the economic and social standards of the natives, but had no intention of handing over governing power until the natives had become more advanced. They did not believe European higher education or the creation of an elite class to be in the best interests of the Africans.[7]

Ultimately, the Belgians could not ignore the independence of Ghana in 1957 or de Gaulle's offer of autonomy to neighboring Francophone Africa in 1958. In late 1959, after tribal fighting had erupted in the Congo, the Belgians convened a round-table conference with Congolese Africans in January 1960. To the surprise of the Belgians, the participants called for immediate independence. Under these pressures, the government in Brussels decided to hold elections in the territory in five months and to grant independence in six!

The timetable provided little opportunity to prepare the giant territory for freedom. The Congo had few university graduates and few trained senior civil servants or military officers. Nevertheless, elections were held in May. The Mouvement Congolais National won the most seats and its leader, Patrice Lumumba, a fiery nationalist, became prime minister. The declaration of independence on June 30, 1960 was followed within four days by a mutiny of the military, the Force Publique, demanding the dismissal of their Belgian officers. Unrest ensued and on July 11, the Belgians reintroduced their troops into Leopoldville (later Kinshasha); their declared purpose was to protect Belgian citizens.

On the same day that Belgian troops arrived in Leopoldville, the wily ruler of Katanga, Moshe Tshombe, declared the separate independence of the copper-rich province. While Tshombe prohibited Lumumba and other federal officials from entering the province, he welcomed back the Belgians. They ran the mines and paid royalties to Tshombe in Elizabethville (later Lumumbashi), not to Leopoldville.

After an appeal from Lumumba, the UN Security Council authorized the dispatch of military aid to the Congo government. The first troops arrived July 14. The UN presence immediately created difficulties with Lumumba, who wanted them to assist him in reasserting central authority over Katanga. When UN Secretary General Dag Hammarskjold resisted, Lumumba threatened to invade Katanga with his own forces. He asked for and received some help from the Soviet Union.

Tshombe, meanwhile, had raised the stakes by beginning to employ European mercenaries.

The deaths in 1961 of two prominent players in the Congo drama, Lumumba and UN Secretary General Dag Hammarskjold, complicated efforts to resolve the crisis. Sometime in January 1961, Lumumba, who had been captured and taken to Katanga, was killed—presumably murdered—under mysterious circumstances. Hammarskjold died in a plane crash en route to Ndola in Rhodesia on September 18, 1961.

Finally, on December 21, 1961, Tshombe agreed to renounce secession. Tshombe's agreement did not end the political turmoil, which continued until November 1965, when the Congolese army led by Mobutu took power.

This brief sketch gives only the barest outline of the political, diplomatic, and military maneuvering that went on during the first years of the existence of the Congo (later Zaire). It is against that background that the first of a series of African intrusions into the U.S. political process took place.

Tshombe, backed by the economic power of the Katangan mining interests, launched a major propaganda campaign on behalf of Katangan separatism in Europe and the United States. He was supported not only by Belgium but also by Britain, which did not wish to see a radical nationalist regime on the border of Rhodesia.

I was in the Embassy in London at the time, where I was responsible for consultations with the British on the Congo. I once asked a British diplomat friend, "Does the Foreign Office consult directly with the mining companies on the situation in Katanga?" His answer, "Nothing formal. You see, our ministers and the heads of the companies all went to the same schools. They speak to each other in unfinished sentences."

An article in the *TransAfrica Forum* for the fall of 1984 details Tshombe's public relations efforts in the United States:

> Katanga could also count on the propaganda efforts of its agent in the U.S., Michel Struelens, who reported some $240,000 in expenses as a foreign agent from 1960 to 1962, probably only a fraction of the funds he actually disbursed. Struelens had good contacts in the press and in the Congress among both Republican and Democratic legislators. Senator Thomas Dodd, Democrat of Connecticut and a member of the Foreign Relations Committee [the present senator's father], urged support of Tshombe as "the most solid bulwark against Communism". . . . The American Committee for Aid to Katanga Freedom Fighters organized letter writing campaigns, condemning UN and US actions against Katanga.[8]

Officially, the major U.S. concern was that the Congo turmoil not provide opportunities for the Soviets or Chinese in the heart of Africa. The "chaos-to-communism" fear took strong root in Washington. But counsels were divided on how this should be approached. Africa specialists recognized the unpopularity of the Katangan secession among most black Africans. The Organization of African Unity strongly supported maintaining the integrity of Africa's colonial borders, however illogical they may have been. Their reasoning was that if you begin breaking up major territories or condoning their disintegration, where does it end? Beyond that, in the period when decolonization was taking place, someone like Tshombe who consciously invited back the colonial power and hired white mercenaries was running against the tide. He also reportedly received assistance from the apartheid regime in South Africa. Most of the leaders of the new countries and their political elites were far more concerned with reducing dependence on former colonial powers and suspicious of those who did not share this view. On the basis of this analysis of broad African opinion, most Africa specialists believed that Western alliances with the Tshombes of Africa would help, not hurt, the Soviets among the other new nations of the continent.

The position of the United States in much of Africa was further compromised by widespread reports that the United States, through the CIA, had been involved in the murder of Lumumba. According to Stephen Weissman in *American Foreign Policy in the Congo 1960–1964*, the CIA was probably involved in the removal of Lumumba as prime minister but not in his death.[9]

But, in an argument that was to take place again and again in the next three decades, many senior politicians in Washington, regardless of party, were more attracted to the figure who accepted Western help without qualms, professed strong anti-communism, and appeared to be standing boldly against the forces of militant nationalism. They were alarmed by the African nationalist leader who mouthed Marxist principles, solicited help from the Soviets, and resisted cooperation with Western powers. Africans, for them, were divided into the "good" and the "doubtful."

Rhodesia/Zimbabwe

The diplomatic, military, and economic measures that followed the unilateral declaration of independence (UDI) by the white minority regime in Rhodesia in 1965 and led eventually to the establishment of Zimbabwe have been discussed earlier. As these steps were unfolding in Africa, a parallel debate was taking place in the United States, a debate every bit as virulent as that over the Congo and those on African issues that were to follow.[10]

When Ian Smith, the Rhodesian white leader, likened the Rhodesian declaration to the struggle of the American colonies he provided a sympathetic rhetorical base for conservatives in the United States sympathetic with the white minority government and angry at Britain for its lukewarm support for the U.S. in Vietnam. Once more, as in the debate over Katanga, the white regime was seen as the bulwark against communism in Africa.

A sample of the arguments used by supporters of Rhodesia is found in the introduction to a book, *The Real Case for Rhodesia*, by Charlton Chesterton, a South African writer:

Imagine:
An army composed of vast hordes of Africans, organized and led by the Chinese, equipped with every modern weapon by the Russians. Crossing the Zam-

bian border, this army penetrates deep into Rhodesia within a matter of hours. They sweep on, through Salisbury, through Bulawayo, across the Limpopo. With strength equivalent to that which countered even the American might in Vietnam, they cannot be stopped. . . .

Improbable? We Southern Africans know that it is likely rather than unlikely. But is this nightmare only ours? On the contrary—if the communists gain de facto control of Africa, it will be the beginning of the end for effective Western resistance.[11]

An echo of this white southern African sentiment is found in Washington in the words of Congressman Joseph Waggoner of Louisiana, who referred to Rhodesia as "the cornerstone of the nation's tenuous foothold in the entire Afro-Asian world." He continued, "If we are successful in our treacherous subversion of Rhodesia . . . we will have no friends on the continent."[12]

With such strong support from conservative members of Congress as well as business interests in Rhodesia, the Smith regime mounted a major campaign in the United States, centered in the office of the Rhodesian Information Service in Washington.

Invariably, when I spoke to audiences in U.S. cities on African policy, a man or woman would rise to ask questions, reading from yellow slips provided by the Rhodesian Information Service: "How can we let down our true friends in Africa?" "Do you want to see the communists take over the vital minerals of southern Africa?"

Britain had the responsibility for the solution to the Rhodesia question. The United States supported the continuing British efforts at sanctions and negotiation, but several issues required decisions in Washington.

Should the United States keep open its consulate in Salisbury?

Should the United States support UN sanctions against Rhodesia?

Should Kenneth Towsey, head of the Rhodesian Information Service in Washington, be accorded diplomatic status?

Should Ian Smith be received in Washington?

The Nixon White House provided little support for a hard line against Rhodesia. I once attempted to persuade Patrick Buchanan, then a special assistant to the president, that our interests lay in finding a way to majority rule in southern Africa. He replied, "Why should we support the Africans? We got only eight percent of the black votes."

Secretary of State William Rogers, on the other hand, took a broader view and ultimately persuaded President Nixon that the United States should close the consulate in Salisbury. Although Paul O'Neill, the consul, was withdrawn at the time of UDI, the office was not officially closed until March 17, 1970, after Smith declared a republic and severed all ties with the Queen of England. [13]

But not everyone agreed with the decision to close the consulate. Shortly after the closing, the president held a dinner on October 24, 1970 in honor of the twenty-fifth anniversary of the United Nations, at which the emperor of Ethiopia, Haile Selassie, was the guest of honor. Henry Kissinger, then national security adviser, wanted to keep the program short and discourage speeches, possibly on order from President Nixon. I was asked to dissuade the emperor from speaking. I failed. The emperor rose to speak after the dinner. After a few minutes, Dr. Kissinger wrote on the back of his place card, "Five minutes more and we reopen the consulate in Salisbury." But, to my relief, the emperor sat down shortly after that and the consulate remained closed.

We were less successful in maintaining sanctions.

Britain imposed a series of unilateral economic sanctions immediately after UDI. Nine days later, on November 20, 1965, the UN Security Council called on all states not to provide arms or oil. The Council followed up in December with bans on the export of copper, chrome, asbestos, and foodstuffs. Rhodesian funds were blocked in major capitals. One year later, when little progress had been made in reversing UDI, the Security Council declared the situation to "constitute a threat to international peace and security," thus making sanctions mandatory. Over the ensuing twelve years, until a settlement on independence was reached in 1980, sanctions were progressively tightened.

The United States supported the sanctions measures, except for two vetoes of proposals to cut off postal and telecommunications links and to tighten trade barriers among Rhodesia, South Africa, and Portuguese Mozambique. Both Britain and the United States also opposed Afro-Asian bloc efforts to promote the use of force—except to enforce the sea blockade preventing the supply of oil.[14]

The U.S. support for sanctions was unpopular with many conservative members of Congress, who did not like the United Nations in 1970 any more than they did in 1999, disagreed with the premises of the UN action and, as in the case of the Congo, contrasted Britain's punishment of anti-Communist Rhodesia with its trade with Vietnam, China, and Cuba. However, in 1971, they found a way to circumvent U.S. observance of the sanctions in legislation that ultimately became known as the Byrd Amendment.

Originally introduced by Representative James Collins, Democrat of Texas, the law prevented the United States from prohibiting the import of any strategic and critical material from a free world country for so long as the importation of a like material from a Communist country was not prohibited. The act was directed primarily at chrome, available in Rhodesia, but also in the Soviet Union.

Through a series of legislative maneuvers in which the proposal was initially rejected by the foreign affairs committees, the measure was attached by Senator Harry Byrd, Democrat of Virginia, to the Defense Procurement Bill and was passed and signed by President Nixon on November 17, 1971. In the Bureau of African Affairs, we sought to acquaint members of Congress with the implications for the United States in thus unilaterally ignoring a UN Security Council action, but we had little support from the Nixon administration. Not only were many in that administration unenthusiastic about African issues, but they were also involved in attempting to defeat a measure by Senator Mike Mansfield, Democrat of Montana, to withdraw troops from Vietnam. They needed conservative support in that effort.[15]

Joy greeted the passage of Section 503 of the Military Procurement Authorization Bill (the Byrd Amendment) in the offices of the Rhodesian Information

Service. "The 503 Club Marching Song," a parody to the tune of "O Tannenbaum," was sung; I figured in stanza 4:

(To be sung with wistful melancholy)
Oh, 503, oh, 503
We faced a mighty enemy;
Oh, 503, oh, 503
The State Department thwarted thee.
We ran afoul of David Newsom,
[Senator] Culver and [Congressman] Diggs—an awesome twosome;
The U.N. fought you mightily
And Harold Wilson [British Prime Minister] censured thee.[16]

With the establishment of the black majority government of Zimbabwe under Robert Mugabe on April 17, 1980, the sanctions issue and the Byrd Amendment became moot.

Two other issues occupied the political battleground during these years. Many in the Congressional Black Caucus sought to stop the activities of the Rhodesian Information Service on the grounds that its chief, Kenneth Towsey, was representing an "illegal government" and should be deported. Towsey, however, was in the United States as a permanent resident alien and could not be deported except for criminal acts. He conducted the affairs of the Rhodesian Information Office carefully to avoid any direct lobbying that might bring him into conflict with the law; he distributed information and made contacts with those interested, including members of Congress, but his activities were never determined to be illegal.

Some members of Congress, including particularly Senator S. I. Hayakawa, Republican of California, pressed for an official visit for Smith. He did finally come to the United States after Bishop Adel Muzorewa had been named prime minister of Rhodesia in a short-term solution to the problem. To the disappointment of Smith and his friends on Capitol Hill, he was received only in the State Department by the undersecretary for political affairs. I happened to hold the position at that time and presided over a somewhat sullen and inconclusive session.

The Nigerian Civil War

In July of 1969, I left my post as ambassador to Libya and returned home to California on leave, preparatory to taking up my new post as assistant secretary of state for African affairs. The day I arrived, the San Francisco Examiner carried a full-page advertisement addressed to Assistant Secretary of State David Newsom. In the center of the ad was the picture of a child with the bloated belly of kwashiorkor, a condition brought on by serious malnutrition. The message of the ad was, "If you want to save this child, get relief into Biafra." When I reached Washington some days later, my new desk was piled high with angry letters blaming the State Department for neglecting the starvation in Biafra. This was my introduction to another African issue that was to engulf the Washington political system.

Once more the United States faced—as it frequently would in the future—the conflict between political and humanitarian objectives, the power of a politically astute lobby, revelations of the limits of U.S. influence, and embedded African sensitivities about sovereignty and outside intervention. No brief account can fully reflect the passion exhibited on both sides of the issue at that time.[17]

The Eastern Province of Nigeria, populated largely by Ibo people, declared its secession from Nigeria and the establishment of the independent state of Biafra on May 30, 1967. The declaration by the leader of the new entity, Col. Odumegwu Ojukwu, followed riots against the Ibo people in the north of Nigeria and growing tension between the Eastern Province and the capital in Lagos. On July 6, forces of the Federal Military Government (FMG) crossed into Biafra and, in the ensuing campaign, surrounded the province, ultimately cutting it off from the outside.

Biafra ultimately collapsed in January 1970. During the thirty months of the war, an intense debate divided Washington—in the Congress, within the executive, and in the country beyond. U.S. and international efforts to bring a peaceful end to the conflict were not successful.

Within the State Department, the emphasis was on preserving relations with the FMG in Lagos. This reflected an assessment of African consensus, a recognition of African American attitudes, and apprehension that a disintegrating Nigeria could become another opportunity for the Soviets in Africa. The Soviets did supply some military equipment to the FMG during the war, although their aid was not a major factor in the outcome. The United States embargoed arms shipments to both sides.

Only four African countries—the Ivory Coast, Gabon, Tanzania, and Zambia—and Haiti recognized Biafra. Most African countries, aware of French support for Biafra, saw the secessionist effort as another attempt by outside powers to break up the continent's largest black nation. Britain, with its strong interests in Nigeria, also supported the unity of Nigeria and, as a traditional supplier, continued some arms shipments to the FMG.

Biafra had strong friends in the United States. A group of Catholic missionaries, the Holy Ghost fathers from Boston, had long worked in eastern Nigeria. With ties to Senator Edward Kennedy and other political figures, they mounted a campaign to apprise Americans of the starvation in Biafra being caused by the FMG blockade. Their efforts were complemented by a group of former Peace Corps volunteers who had served in the Eastern Province and by the effective efforts of Ibos who lived in the United States. Their emphasis was on the humanitarian disaster being created by the FMG's encirclement of Biafra. They benefited from a virtual absence of efforts by the Nigerian government in Lagos to present its point of view. The Nigerian attitude, as expressed to me by one official was, "We have the right on our side. We expect Americans to understand that."

The impact of the pressures was felt in the Congress and in the White House. In the Congress, the Black Caucus strongly favored support for one Nigeria, but other voices were more influenced by the reports of famine and disease. President Nixon, himself, was never enthusiastic about Nigeria and probably leaned toward

U.S. recognition of Biafra. In his presidential campaign, he had made a strong statement in support of Biafra:

> The terrible tragedy of the people of Biafra has now assumed catastrophic dimensions. . . . Until now efforts to relieve the Biafran people have been thwarted by the desire of the central government of Nigeria to pursue total and unconditional victory, and by the fear of the Ibo people that surrender means wholesale atrocities and genocide. But genocide is what is taking place right now—and starvation is the grim reaper.[18]

Throughout the war, a debate continued over the actual conditions within Biafra and over how to get relief into the beleaguered province. The U.S. Embassy in Lagos was under constant fire from the White House over its claim that reports of conditions within Biafra exaggerated the problem and over its resistance to any relief efforts that would violate the sovereignty of Nigeria. At one point, two representatives of the National Security Council traveled to Lagos to tell the American embassy how the White House viewed the issue.

The FMG opposed relief flights into Biafra, not only on the basis of sovereignty, but for fear that the relief planes would probably also carry arms. Nevertheless, a major night airlift was established with contract aircraft operating from Sao Tome. U.S. relief contributions to Biafra, both official and private, totaled $72.3 million, most of it carried by the airlift.

The end of the war brought arguments over conditions within the defeated enclave and a conflict between U.S. objectives and Nigerian sovereignty. At the request of the White House, two reports had been prepared to determine possible post-war relief requirements. One was by Dr. Karl Western of the Centers for Disease Control in Atlanta and the second by a team under a U.S. Army colonel, Eugene Dewey. Both projected major relief needs if starvation was to be avoided. Acceptance of the conclusions of both encountered the resistance of the Nigerians to outside post-war involvement.

In January 1970, I was sent to Lagos to join British Parliamentary Undersecretary Maurice Foley in an approach to General Yakubu Gowon, Nigeria's head of state. Our mission was to propose an international commission to survey the situation in the defeated province of Biafra. The impact of our mission was somewhat blunted by a premature British Broadcasting Company broadcast announcing the purpose of our visits. General Gowon received us separately and he was ready.

When I mentioned the purpose of my call, he turned around to the bookshelf behind him containing the Bruce Catton series on the American Civil War. "I have read about the Reconstruction after your civil war," he said. "I can assure you that we will treat the Eastern Province every bit as fairly as you treated the South—and, perhaps, more so."

And, by all accounts, including my own observations in a visit to the Eastern region in 1971, they did re-incorporate the East with remarkable consideration for the losers.

Angola

U.S. policies toward the Portuguese territories of Angola and Mozambique had long been a problem for Washington's approach to Africa. As conflicts with Lisbon grew and liberation movements expanded their activities, often with Soviet support, the United States was inhibited from overt support by obligations to Portugal, a NATO member and landlord of the important U.S. base in the Azores. With independence of the Portuguese territories in 1975, the problems for Washington did not decrease. Another African issue became the focus of congressional and national debate. And where the previous problems of the Congo and Rhodesia had had elements of the Cold War, Angola created an even more direct confrontation between the interests of Moscow and Washington and preoccupied policymakers, including Secretary of State Kissinger.

When the secretary came to Jakarta in December 1975, where I was ambassador, I could not get him greatly interested in Indonesia's problems. He wanted to talk about the Cubans in Angola.

By that time the three-way struggle among liberation movements that followed the independence of Angola from the Portuguese had begun. Even before Angola's independence, outside powers, including the United States, were supporting one or more of the movements. The United States, through the CIA, had long been providing modest assistance to Holden Roberto's Front for the National Liberation of Angola (FNLA). And so had China. China was also providing help to Jonas Savimbi's National Union for the Total Independence of Angola (UNITA). The Popular Movement for the Liberation of Angola (MPLA), led by Augustino Neto, had been receiving support from Cuba and from the Communist Party of Portugal. Soviet help had been intermittent.

An accord among the three movements broke down in February and March 1975 when Roberto's FNLA, with the largest military force, moved against Neto's MPLA in Luanda. Soviet arms shipments had already been on the way to the MPLA but were accelerated after the FNLA attack. Following the March attacks, Neto appealed to Havana for additional help. The Cubans responded initially with advisers, and, after a major South African incursion in October, Cuban help expanded, using both Cuban and Soviet aircraft. With that help, the MPLA was able to push back both the FNLA and UNITA and was in clear control of Luanda when independence came on November 11. By the end of January 1976, the Cuban presence was estimated to be in excess of 10,000.[19] Further, the entry of South African troops, seen as allies of Savimbi, clearly increased support in the rest of sub-Saharan Africa for the MPLA regime.[20]

Soviet actions and the Cuban presence were seen by the Ford administration as incompatible with détente and as a threat to American interests. In October 1975, Secretary Kissinger raised the matter directly with Soviet Ambassador Anatoly Dobrynin in Washington. Daniel Patrick Moynihan, then U.S. ambassador to the United Nations, alleged on December 14, 1975, that if the United States discontinued its opposition to Soviet activities in Angola, "the Communists will take over Angola, and thereby, considerably control the oil shipping lanes from the Persian Gulf to New York."[21] But the U.S. position was weakened, not only because Washington was known to be providing help to other Angolan groups, but because the question of involvement, whether covert or overt, had become a political issue in Washington. Once more the debate was joined on whether African developments, in which countries sought help from the Soviet Union and its allies, should be treated as global or regional matters.

Nathaniel Davis, then assistant secretary of state for African affairs, was asked to chair an interagency group to recommend a course of action. The group recommended against covert support for groups opposing the MPLA and, instead, recommended encouraging African diplomatic efforts to promote a solution. He gives this account in an article in *Foreign Affairs:*

> In essence the memo argued that covert intervention would not serve larger U.S. interests; that an attempted intervention could not be kept secret; and that a covert intervention would have to be so circumscribed as to fall between stools in any case—while the other side could escalate at will.[22]

Kissinger, who favored tougher action, quickly thereafter accepted Davis's resignation.

It was not only within the Bureau of African Affairs that doubts were raised about the wisdom of covert activity in Angola. At the beginning of 1976, the Senate and the House passed, with veto-proof margins, the Clark Amendment prohibiting further covert support in Angola. The views of the Congressional Black Caucus in a press release on December 17, 1975, are relevant to the story:

> The Congressional Black Caucus, concerned with the serious threat to international peace posed by the escalating civil war in Angola, deplores the intervention of non-Angolan powers in that conflict. The United States involvement is particularly disturbing. For, not only is it a covert operation, but it is contrary to the position of the Organization of African Unity (OAU) opposing all foreign intervention. It aligns the United States on the same side with the white minority regime in South Africa, and in so doing, compounds the harm to U.S. relations with independent, majority rule Africa, created by U.S. refusal to support majority rule in South Africa. Moreover, it is based on the false "domino theory" assumption that the U.S. must intervene to counter a so-called Soviet challenge.[23]

The Black Caucus and other African American groups favored U.S. ties and diplomatic recognition of the MPLA regime in Angola as the government recognized by the majority of African states. As long as the Cubans remained, this became politically impossible, even for the succeeding Carter administration.

In the Carter administration, in which I was undersecretary for political affairs in the State Department, the concern over the Cubans continued. They were threatening U.S. interests not only in Angola but in the Horn of Africa as well.[24] In 1979, I led a delegation to meet with Cubans to discuss the release of the prisoners captured in the ill-fated Bay of Pigs invasion of 1961. The Cubans wanted to discuss the U.S. embargo. Our firm instructions were that there could be no discussion of any other issue unless the Cubans agreed to leave Africa. The Cuban response was, "Our presence in Africa has been requested by African states and results from our own African heritage. It is no business of the United States."

In the Reagan administration, supporters of an active U.S. role in Angola took up the cause of Jonas Savimbi, the leader of UNITA. Despite an earlier record of Maoist support, connections with South Africa, and links to an increasingly megalomaniacal Mobutu in Zaire, Savimbi, backed by a skillful public relations program, emerged as a stalwart anti-Communist "freedom fighter." One of Washington's principal lobbying firms, Black, Manafort, Stone, and Kelly, was reportedly paid $600,000 per year by Savimbi and his supporters.[25] Their work included arranging a visit to Washington for Savimbi in January 1986, during which he met with the president and the secretaries of state and defense, spoke at the National Press Club, and was honored by conservative organizations. Jeane Kirkpatrick, Reagan's ambassador to the United Nations, called him "one of the few authentic heroes of our time."[26]

The Reagan administration was able to arrange the repeal of the Clark Amendment and resume help to Savimbi as part of a broader successful strategy that ultimately resulted in independence for Namibia and the withdrawal of the Cuban troops. As of 1999, however, while the Soviet-Cuban threat has passed into history, the fight for power and wealth between Savimbi and his opponents in Luanda continued in Angola with tragic results for all. What Ambassador Davis wrote in 1978 is still valid today:

> Angola was a tragedy. It was a tragedy for moderate blacks, for radical blacks wishing to fend off alien influences, for whites in southern Africa, for Mobutu, Kaunda, Roberto, Savimbi, soldiers of fortune, Zairian infantrymen, and countless others. Perhaps America's choices were impossible ones. I cannot assert any easy confidence in the likely success of the course of action favored by most of our task force on Angola in June 1975. But I think we would have done better at least to have tried that other course.[27]

South Africa

Although discrimination against blacks had existed in South Africa from the time Europeans first landed, it was institutionalized in the establishment of apartheid in 1948. The measures called for blacks to be segregated in homelands and townships outside major cities and to be severely restricted when in white areas. Race relations in South Africa were even more highlighted internationally with news of the killing of sixty-nine Africans outside a police post in Sharpeville on March 21, 1960.

In the United States, two camps formed, each supported by active lobbies. One favored close ties with the South African regime on the basis of its strategic importance, its minerals, and its anti-communism. This camp insisted that only by engagement—through business, diplomatic relations, and personal relations—could the United States ultimately influence race policies in South Africa. Sanctions, proponents argued, would hurt blacks more than whites. A code of conduct for U.S. business, drawn up by Rev. Leon Sullivan, a black clergyman from Philadelphia, called for a non-discrimination policy on the part of American businesses. Defense officials insisted that the United States should continue to have access to the Simonstown Naval Base, a key position on the route around Cape Horn. The more extreme position was represented by a map of Africa with red arrows from China and Russia sweeping down on the southern third of Africa.

The opposite camp pressed for completely curtailing U.S. contacts with South Africa and isolating the country through sanctions. They urged disinvestment by U.S. companies working in South Africa. The portfolios of major companies and public institutions were scrutinized to be sure they held no investments from companies also investing in South Africa. Opponents of any relationship with the Pretoria regime publicized their cause through dramatic demonstrations, often including leading public figures, outside the South African embassy in Washington.

As assistant secretary for African affairs in the first Nixon administration (1969–1973), I was involved in an internal debate over a statement of policy for southern Africa embodied in National Security Decision Memorandum No. 39 (NSSM39). The document represented the view of the Nixon administration that change could not be brought to southern Africa through violence and that white minority regimes would be in power for the foreseeable future. Information that leaked out gave the impression that the new administration was lifting previous barriers on U.S. relations with South Africa. In fact, when the dust settled, very few changes were made. Political realities brought home the limitations on U.S. relations with the apartheid regime. Many wanted increased U.S. naval visits to South Africa, for example, but backed away when faced with the possible publicity resulting from the separation of black and white U.S. servicemen once they went ashore. The memorandum provided for some increase in trade with Pretoria, including the sale of dual-purpose items that might have a military use. The possibility of the sale of executive jet aircraft received much attention; in the end, South Africa bought none from the United States.

In a highly charged debate in Washington, terms that are used to describe policy take on a life of their own. In a speech at Northwestern University in 1970, I described the Nixon administration policy as one of "communication" with South Africa. That term became the handle used to criticize the policy, just as "constructive engagement" served the same purpose for opponents of the Reagan policies years later.

I believed that, through continued communication, our relations with South Africa could be used to demonstrate that we favored a different racial path. I arranged the assignment of an African American diplomat to Pretoria for the first time. I visited the country with an African American deputy, Beverly Carter, a former newspaper publisher and candidate for Congress. We met prominent Africans as well as members of the government. Whether the visit helped relations, I cannot say. It did help us both understand the depth of difference in perspective.

During the visit we dined at the home of the Minister of Justice. I was seated next to the Minister's wife.

"Mr. Carter is very impressive," she said. "He is not like our black people."

"How many black people have you ever sat and talked with?" I asked.

"Why," she replied, "we sit and talk with our servants all the time."

"But have you ever had a conversation with a university-educated African?"

She thought a moment and then said, "No, I guess not."

The South African issue continued through the Ford and Carter administrations and then, in the conservative administration of Ronald Reagan, took an unexpected turn. A Republican House of Representatives, concerned about holding the black vote in the South, voted sanctions on South Africa. To forestall further congressional action, President Reagan signed an executive order implementing sanctions on September 9, 1985.

A few years later, under a new South African prime minister, F. W. de Klerk, the leader of the African National Congress, Nelson Mandela, was released in 1990 after twenty-seven years in prison and in 1994 became president of a majority-ruled South Africa. Once more, as in the previous cycles of independence, the leader of a feared "terrorist" organization was released to negotiate and lead the nation.

*   *   *

As one looks back at the African battles in Washington from the perspective of 1999, it is tempting to ask many questions. Was there ever a real Soviet and Cuban threat to U.S. interests in Africa? Was the U.S. manipulation of events in the Congo and Angola ultimately in the interests of the United States and of the peoples of the region? If the United States had followed the lead of the African consensus would the outcome have been any different?

Such questions cannot be fully answered. Decisions flow from the circumstances and political balances of a moment. Those who might have predicted the outcomes, whether favorable or unfavorable, would have been discredited by those who were determining policies. Would an assistant secretary of state for African affairs under any president in the 1970s or 1980s who predicted that Nelson Mandela would emerge as president of South Africa have kept his job?

If any lesson flows from the lobbying and political battles of these years it is that eventually the dynamics of individual countries and regions prevail. U.S. diplomacy has been successful where it has recognized and helped to channel such dynamics; where it has refused to recognize the true currents of African events, it has failed.

THIRTEEN

The General Assembly

To understand the negative attitudes in the United States toward the United Nations at the end of the century, one needs look no further than the half century of confrontation between the U.S. and Third World nations in the UN General Assembly (UNGA). Attacking the United States for its perceived support of colonialism, apartheid, and Israel; tying Zionism to racism; and challenging Western press freedom principles all struck sensitive nerves in Washington.

In that half century, the United States lost control of the international organization it had fostered in 1945.

Rhetoric and Votes

Although part of the disillusionment came about because Russian and Chinese vetoes in the UN Security Council (UNSC) frustrated U.S. designs, a principal reason can be found in the rhetoric and votes of Third World countries that came increasingly to dominate the UNGA.

Although developing countries in Asia, Africa, and Latin America were among the original members of the United Nations, the organization was dominated in its early years by industrial nations, led by the United States. With the deluge of independence in the 1960s, the balance changed irrevocably. While the United States retained its veto in the Security Council, it was no longer able to dominate the General Assembly. It was in this body for the rest of the century that the most direct confrontations between the U.S. and Third World nations occurred. Although the actions of the UNGA did not have legal force, the anti-American tone of much of the debate enhanced a basic dislike of the international organization, especially among U.S. conservatives.

For many of the new member nations, the secretariat and the specialized agencies of the international organization represented an opportunity for significant jobs for its citizens. In the view of the United States, such patronage created a bloated and unnecessary UN bureaucracy. The frequent demands from Washington for reform were resented in New York. So, also, were the efforts by the United States to reduce its share of the UN budget—as logical as that may have seemed from the United States point of view.

After 1961, with the selection of U Thant of Burma, secretaries general of the United Nations were either from Third World countries or were beholden to them for their political support, which often put these key UN officials on a collision course with the United States. In 1996, the United States openly opposed the re-election of an Egyptian, Boutros Boutros Ghali, to the post.

Washington sought various ways to influence Third World votes and rhetoric. Appeals were made to home governments, but it quickly became apparent that statements and votes were determined by the peer pressure of regional blocs—Arab, Latin American, Asian, African—in the Assembly. Often smaller countries sent their entire foreign ministries to the Assembly; no one remained behind to read the mail.

Confrontation came to a head in 1981 with the advent of the Reagan administration and a Republican Congress. For the new team in Washington, it was not only the frequent attacks on the United States in the UNGA but, even more, the fact that so many of the positions taken by Third World countries appeared to coincide with those of the Soviet Union. Jeane Kirkpatrick, the first Reagan UN ambassador, expressed the view of the administration when she testified before a Senate subcommittee in 1983:

> We must communicate that it is not possible to denounce us on Monday, vote against us on important issues of principle on Tuesday and Wednesday, and pick up assurances of support on Thursday and Friday. . . . Voting behavior should be one of the criteria we employ in deciding whether we will provide assistance.[1]

In 1986, the concept of linking aid to UN voting was enacted into law. The State Department was required thereafter to prepare an annual report on UN voting patterns. Third World nations resented the link as one additional "string" attached to decreasing levels of U.S. assistance. But despite the legislation and the reports, in practice the link was never absolute. U.S. aid procedures were never convenient for the fine-tuning that such a strategy might require, and other national interests intervened in decisions on economic and military aid.

Many delegates from developing countries seemed surprised at the sharp U.S. reaction to their rhetoric; they thought the United States should have "broad shoulders." They did not fully understand the resentment in Washington at attacks on the United States while Soviet misdemeanors went unnoticed. The explanation they often gave that "we expect more from you, the Americans," wore thin. They did not understand the degree to which their frequent anti-American attacks were undermining vital American support for the United Nations itself. And often the tone of the UN rhetoric was at variance with the generally friendly bilateral relations.

For the Third World nations, however, the issues on which their votes were being judged were "motherhood" issues: racism in South Africa and colonialism.

These were their primary concerns—not communism. The new nations in the Assembly varied greatly in size and outlook, but on these issues they were generally united—as they were on the question of the New International Economic Order. Other votes related to issues that were highly sensitive in the United States: Palestine and Israel and the New World Information Order.

Inherent in the U.S.–Third World differences were radically different approaches to the rules of the Assembly. When the new nations sought to expel South Africa and Israel from the Assembly, the United States opposed the action on grounds that the basis for expulsion in the Charter had not been met.

When Third World nations sought to bring up the contentious issues of South Africa and Palestine in meetings of the specialized agencies of the United Nations such as the World Health Organization or the International Postal Union, the United States opposed such efforts as not being germane to the work of the agency. Such U.S. opposition was essential if the tenuous support for these agencies in Congress was to be maintained.

For many of the proponents of more radical actions against those they saw as offending nations, these were "legalisms" created by the United States to defend outcast nations. The United States was seen not as a defender of the integrity of the UN Charter but as a defender of racism in South Africa and of Israel's aggression against Arab lands. (The U.S. insistence on maintaining South African and Israeli membership was also seen as inconsistent with the annual U.S. effort to exclude the People's Republic of China.)

Donald McHenry, the U.S. ambassador to the United Nations from 1979 to 1981, describes the problem in his essay "Confronting a Revolutionary Legacy":

> The new nations, dominant in number but not in financial or political power, had their own concepts of and priorities for the United Nations. "Legal niceties" was how the majority of new members, supported by many Communist countries, described rules such as the requirement for a two-thirds majority to commit the organization on one or another side of an "important question." Once again the United States found its sincerity doubted when it tried to honor human rights at the same time it respected traditional rules it helped to write. Thus, when South Africa's credentials were called into question at the United Nations in 1973, the United States argued that the nature of the South African government's racial policies had nothing to do with the legal status of the government issuing credentials. . . . In the Third World's view, the United States was still arguing legalisms when more important and overriding principles, such as racial equality, were the real issues at stake.[2]

Colonialism

In the early years of the United Nations, particularly when Eleanor Roosevelt was the U.S. representative, the United States had reasonably good relations with the representatives of the few newly independent countries.

The confrontation between the United States and Third World nations began in 1960 when the United States joined eight other Western countries in abstaining on a Declaration on the Granting of Independence to Colonial Countries and Peoples. The declaration had been proposed by Nikita Khrushchev of the Soviet Union. The Third World countries that drafted the declaration and discussed its importance in the General Assembly constantly referred to the Bandung conference and the spirit of Afro-Asian cooperation that called for the eradication of colonialism, which the Third World considered to be the greatest threat to international security.[3] For the nations that made up the Third World, the 1960 declaration represented the culmination of the principles they held most dear, and it became the cornerstone for Third World policies in the United Nations for the next thirty-five years.

In 1964, subcommittees were formed to consider American territories such as Guam, Samoa, the Cook Islands, and the U.S. Virgin Islands. As a result of initial foot-dragging by the United States on the implementation of the Declaration on the Granting of Independence to Colonial Countries and Peoples, the Third World sponsors of the resolutions now regarded the United States as a major colonial power and an obstruction in eradicating the colonialism hated throughout the Third World. (The Soviet Union's "territories" were never included in discussions on this issue.)

By 1970, frustration had firmly set in on both sides of the debate over the Declaration. The U.S. representative expressed before the General Assembly his "regret that despite the long association of my country as a member of the Special Committee [on implementing the declaration] not a single one of its suggested amendments to the program of action had been adopted."[4] Representatives from Third World countries, on the other hand, continued to attack the United States and its "imperialist" practices, passing in 1970 a resolution that condemned the drafting of indigenous populations to fight in "colonial" wars after it was pointed out that Virgin Islanders had died in Vietnam.[5] Representatives from Burma, Chile, India, Indonesia, and Somalia all spoke out in the General Assembly against the deteriorating conditions in colonial territories, a situation they again attributed to the circumstances in southern Africa.[6]

Continuing a pattern established over the previous ten years, the United States (joined only by Australia, New Zealand, and South Africa), consistently voted against and, by the end of the decade, abstained from declarations on colonialism. U.S. policymakers believed that these declarations did not sufficiently recognize the right of people in colonial territories to determine their own status (as in Puerto Rico). They also did not believe that all contacts with South Africa were to be condemned, or that military bases interfered with a country's right to self-determination.[7] Although one could argue that the United States had valid claims, continued American reluctance to support the implementation of the 1960 Declaration remained a sore point with Third World countries.

In 1980, the General Assembly adopted a new plan of action for the full implementation of the 1960 Declaration, a resolution that passed on December 11 by a 120-6-20 vote. The United States voted against this plan because of "excesses of language in almost every paragraph" that it could not support.[8] Of particular concern for the United States was language that called for armed struggles by colonial peoples against their oppressors, and "the unqualified condemnation of foreign investment and military activities in non self-governing territories."[9] The United States found itself criticized not only for supporting South Africa and Israel, but also for its trade practices, which Third World nations increasingly viewed as neo-colonialist by the end of the 1970s.[10]

The United States voted against the proposed program of activities to celebrate the twenty-fifth anniversary of the 1960 Declaration in 1984 and the following year, joined only by Israel and the UK, voted against the resolution on the twenty-fifth anniversary because "it clung to an outdated presumption that imperialism and colonial domination remained the predominant reality."[11]

The contrasting viewpoints held by the United States and the Third World did not change much over the following ten years. In 1990 the United States (with only the UK) again voted against resolutions commemorating the thirtieth anniversary of the 1960 Declaration. On the suggestion of Third World nations, the General Assembly declared the 1990s the International Decade for Eradication of Colonialism, a motion that passed without a vote. Throughout the decade, however, the United States continued to vote against resolutions calling for implementation of the 1960 Declaration for the same reasons it had voted against this resolution for 30 years. An American UN representative stated in 1994 that the United States "remained concerned about the evidence of old thinking still contained in the text," wording that called again for dismantling military bases and specifically criticized the United States for failing to hold a referendum on Puerto Rico.[12] The United States believed by the 1990s that colonialism was a thing of the past and that former colonial possessions no longer had reason to view imperialism with such alarm.

South Africa

The Declaration stressed that racial discrimination, particularly that practiced by South Africa, remained one of the most vile manifestations of colonialism and needed to be eliminated immediately.[13] Thus, from the outset of the General Assembly's war on colonialism, the situation in South Africa lay at its heart. The United States based its abstention on Soviet support for the draft document, a patronage that the United States considered hypocritical because the Soviet Union represented "the arch practitioner of a new and lethal colonialism."[14]

The next year, in 1961, the Third World nations introduced a stronger resolution calling apartheid in South Africa a threat to international peace and security and proposing economic sanctions and the expulsion of South Africa from the United Nations. The divide between the Western industrialized powers and the Third World over apartheid became even clearer in 1962. In that year, the UN representative from the Soviet Union called South Africa "a sanctuary for colonialism and racialism" and deplored alleged NATO arms shipments to Pretoria.[15] Resolution 1761, adopted on November 6, 1962, called for sanctions and expulsion from the United Nations again, and referred to the actions of some member states that "indirectly provide encouragement to the Government of South Africa."[16] Although no specific countries were mentioned in the resolution, the paragraph targeted the United States and its NATO allies in hopes that they would respond to this indirect pressure.

The following year, 1964, the United States was specifically named. A resolution called for "the United States, the United Kingdom, and France, permanent members of the Security Council" to take effective measures to meet the present situation in South Africa.[17] The belief had taken shape by 1963–1964 that the United States and its NATO allies represented the largest obstacle to ending apartheid, and this belief would serve as the linchpin for future attacks on the United States in the years to come. The United States continued to maintain that, as deplorable as the circumstances might be in South Africa, they did not constitute "a threat to international peace and security," language that authorized military intervention under the UN Charter's Chapter VII.

In the years that followed, little changed in the basic positions of both sides, although the language used in both resolutions and debates continued to grow more caustic. The General Assembly and a new Special Committee on Apartheid began to call apartheid a "crime against humanity," and explicit attacks were directed at the United States and other trading partners of South Africa. The chairman of the Special Committee issued the following report in 1966:

> The danger of a bloody racial conflict in the Southern part of Africa has become all the greater because of the attitude of non-cooperation shown by the major trading partners of South Africa in seeking a peaceful solution. Their refusal to join the Special Committee on Apartheid, their reluctance to contribute to the humanitarian programs established by the United Nations—for assisting the families of political prisoners and for aiding South Africans abroad in their education and training—clearly show the unwillingness of the major trading powers of South Africa, in particular the United Kingdom, France, and the United States, to cooperate fully in implementing the decisions taken by the competent organs of the UN.[18]

Representatives from Afghanistan, Algeria, Colombia, the Congo, Czechoslovakia, Ethiopia, Guatemala, Hungary, India, Iran, Jamaica, Madagascar, Morocco, Pakistan, the Philippines, Poland, Rwanda, Trinidad and Tobago, Syria, and Zambia (among others) all spoke out in the next two years against the apathy of South Africa's trading partners in fighting apartheid. By the late 1960s, the situation in South Africa formed the link between the other major issues the Third World nations considered vital. The failure to stop apartheid in South Africa came to be seen by the Third World as a serious threat to ending colonialism and establishing the principles of the Declaration to Eradicate Colonialism. At the same time, the Third World viewed the continued trade between the West and South Africa, resulting in Pretoria's expanded wealth, as a major stumbling block in establishing a new trading system that would end poverty in former colonial countries. The arms dealing between NATO countries and Pretoria and subsequent nuclear capabilities of South Africa formed the basis of numerous resolutions proposed by Third World countries condemning the slow pace of disarmament. Finally, Third World countries began after 1967 to draw parallels between the South African situation and the Palestinian question, and resolutions began to combine condemnations of Western aid to apartheid and "Zionist imperialism" in the same breath, striking a particularly sensitive chord in Washington.

Ensuing years saw apartheid compared with nazism, called "an evil," and consistently labeled a threat to international peace. Resolutions passed by the General Assembly, the Economic and Security Council, the Commission on Human Rights, and the International Conference on Human Rights all agreed on the nature of apartheid and the need to implement strict sanctions against Pretoria. As the number of resolutions calling for cultural, sporting, and other economic boycotts passed by the General Assembly increased, so the dissatisfaction among Third World countries grew as the South African government continued its policies. Trade between South Africa and the West continued to increase in the late 1960s and early 1970s as well, prompting severe condemnations from many countries. The United States claimed that maintaining normal diplomatic and economic relationships with South Africa would better allow the United States "to urge South Africa's Government to reform its policy,"[19] a claim repeated several times. Third World countries called the American intransigence "a mockery of the UN"[20] and noted that the West continued to give "more weight to economic considerations than to moral principles."[21] For most of the countries that constituted the UN General Assembly, American failure to support sanctions against South Africa "had not only emboldened South Africa to assume a defiant attitude towards the UN but was also undermining the prestige and authority of the organization."[22]

In the wake of South Africa's 1975 use of troops in Angola and the June 1976 massacre in Soweto, General Assembly resolutions and debate grew increasingly shrill, condemning the "triple veto" in the Security Council that prevented an arms embargo while noting that Pretoria had used weapons received from the West in pursuing its repressions. The United States, France, and Great Britain now were deemed "accomplices in the inhuman practices of racial discrimination, apartheid, and colonialism perpetrated" in South Africa.[23]

The death of anti-apartheid leader Stephen Biko on September 12, 1977, resulted in the United States finally agreeing to a mandatory arms embargo after years of reports that South African repressions used Western guns. UN Secretary General Kurt Waldheim stated that the resolution marked the first time in the organization's 32-year history that action had been taken under Chapter VII of the UN Charter against a member state. The General Assembly continued to press for more sanctions in its resolutions, again voted against by the United States.

In 1978, the United States continued to vote against resolutions on the relations between South Africa and Israel, a resolution calling for an oil embargo, a resolution requesting no nuclear collaboration with Pretoria, a resolution requesting no economic collaboration with South Africa, a resolution on "the situation in South Africa" calling for comprehensive sanctions, and a resolution calling for no military collaboration with Pretoria in the wake of revelations that the arms embargo had not been met. The United States abstained from resolutions praising the work of the Special Committee on Apartheid and on apartheid in sports. In 1978, the United States voted for only two resolutions on South Africa, one to honor the memory of leaders killed fighting apartheid and a second that called for the dissemination of more information on apartheid throughout the world.[24] Beyond words, the United States continued to advocate very little action against South Africa.

Reports that South Africa had exploded a nuclear device in 1979 led to a new round of condemnations, as Barbados, Guyana, India, Cameroon, and others spoke of "the hypocrisy of those who condemn South Africa's practices while conniving with it."[25] Despite these calls and similar ones for "those who had urged an international boycott of the 1980 Olympic Games to take the lead in imposing a boycott on Pretoria" the following year,[26] the United States continued to vote against or abstain from every General Assembly resolution (all sponsored by Third World countries) calling for action against South Africa. In 1981, the representative from India noted before the General Assembly that the question of apartheid "was still the central issue facing the General Assembly, even after decades of discussions in various forums aimed at eliminating that pernicious evil," pointing the finger in the process at those nations that refused to implement decisions against South Africa.[27]

After thirty years of discussing the issue of race conflict in southern Africa, the division between the Third World and the United States over the issue had only grown wider, illustrated by an American UN representative in 1982, who stated that the U.S. policy of "'constructive engagement' was more likely to bring about positive changes in South Africa than would confrontation, punishment, and isolation, which was the philosophical basis" of all UN resolutions.[28] After decades of inability to end apartheid because of continued support from Western nations, Third World countries found the remarks unacceptable, for in the words of the Egyptian representative, "constructive engagement had already not borne fruit."[29]

The United States continued to defend its policies throughout the 1980s in addition to voting against resolutions containing what it called "contentious language," even when the General Assembly dropped such language in 1987 (which the United States noted). Although anti-apartheid measures had passed the U.S. House and Senate in 1986, nothing had changed in the UN General Assembly or in the eyes of the Third World, whose nations continued to consider the United States as the primary obstacle to eradicating colonialism. The election of F. W. de Klerk as President of South Africa in 1989 brought with it some liberalizing measures, and the General Assembly pressed for even more, emboldened by Special Committee reports that economic sanctions had contributed to P. W. Botha's resignation. Despite these reports, the United States continued to vote against resolutions calling for increased international pressure, a trend that continued as apartheid began to crumble. In 1992, on the eve of apartheid's fall, the United States found itself the only country voting against an oil embargo and joined Great Britain in opposing a resolution calling for no military collaboration with Pretoria.[30] Nelson Mandela's election as president of South Africa in May 1994 brought an end to General Assembly discussion of apartheid for the first time since 1946.

Palestine

Throughout most of the 1960s, UN debates on the Middle East remained largely a Security Council affair, although one that developed along Cold War lines. Responding to various Syrian and Israeli complaints over illegal military actions, the Soviet Union sided with the Arab states and the United States with its Cold War ally, Israel, creating a stalemate in the Security Council by the mid-1960s. In 1964, the heads of state of member states of the Arab League sent a declaration adopted at their Alexandria Conference to the Security Council that first mentioned the Palestinian people as central to peace in the region. Setting the contours of later debate, the resolution expressed hope that the UN would "uphold and restore the rights of Palestinian people to their homeland."[31] The resolution criticized Israel and its repeated accusations of Syrian violations of the UN Charter, stating that Israel "hardly qualified to accuse other states" of such violations.[32] In response to the Arab declaration, on October 19 Israel issued a letter that claimed the Arab Conference's purpose was the liquidation of Israel.[33] The battle lines had been drawn. Thereafter, Israel resisted any role for UN organs in peace-making with the Palestinians.

In 1966, several nations again brought the Palestinian question before the UN. Jordan, Mali, Nigeria, and Uganda all expressed the belief that year that lasting peace in the region depended upon the Security Council addressing the whole substance of the Palestinian problem. Their calls formed the majority opinion the following year, when hostilities broke out in the Arab-Israeli War. When the fighting began in 1967, vigorous debate about how to contain it began almost immediately in both the Security Council and the General Assembly.

In the wake of the 1967 war, debate over the Middle East again returned solely to the Security Council. The foreign minister of the United Arab Republic (the brief union between Egypt and Syria) denounced Israel's "racist colonialism" before the Security Council, while the Syrian representative called the conflict "the culmination of Western colonial domination which the United States had inherited through the retrogressive policies of its government," concluding that "nothing but catastrophe would result unless and until the rights of the Palestinian people were understood and recognized."[34] The 1967 war and Israel's occupation of territories that ensued produced the rallying cry for Third World opposition to Israel and its ally, the United States: no peace could take hold in the region without recognition of Palestinian rights. The following year brought calls for the Palestine Liberation Organization (PLO) to participate in General Assembly discussions, and the United States voted against the only General Assembly resolution on the issue because it stated that "the problem of the Palestinian Arab refugees has arisen from the denial of their inalienable rights under the Charter of the UN and Universal Declaration of Human Rights."[35]

The early 1970s brought a cascade of condemnations against Israel and the United States from the nations of the Third World. Resolutions noting Israel's refusal to cooperate, its violation of human rights in the occupied territories, its failure to comply with the Geneva conventions on prisoners of war, and its continued defiance of the UN all passed every year despite United States objections. In addition, virtually every resolution contained the language that "the respect for the rights of the Palestinians is an indispensable element in the establishment of a just and lasting peace in the Middle East."[36] The representatives of Arab states, joined by other Third World nations, annually raised calls deploring American military aid to Israel, assistance that allowed Israel to ignore UN resolutions. The calls, eerily similar to debates on South Africa, charged that "nothing had enabled Israel to evade its obligations more than its reliance on United States support."[37] If the United States had served as apartheid's "reluctant uncle," it now had become the wicked stepbrother of Israel's policies toward the Palestinians in the eyes of the Third World.

The General Assembly continuously condemned Israeli occupation of territories in the Middle East, while the UN Human Rights Committee reported every year on Israeli violations in the region. (The United States always voted against the committee's findings because they did not examine Arab or Palestinian violations). African and Asian states accused Israel of hindering international efforts at creating peace because Israeli policies presented faits accomplis in the occupied territories,[38] and by 1973 the Third World linked Israeli practices in the occupied territories to colonialism and racism practiced in South Africa.

In 1974, at the request of 56 UN members, mostly from the Third World, the PLO was invited to participate in deliberations on the Palestinian question. The United States was in a minority on two votes calling for such representation. PLO Chairman Yasser Arafat spoke before the General Assembly on November 13 using moderate language and uttered the famous phrase that he carried an olive branch in one hand and a freedom fighter's gun in the other, imploring the West to "not let the olive branch fall from my hand."[39]

The Camp David Accords, signed amid great fanfare in the United States in 1978, did not meet with universal acclaim within the United Nations. Arab members called Sadat's visit to Israel and subsequent peace "a tragedy for every free Arab,"[40] while General Assembly resolutions passed after the accords condemned them as invalid because they were outside the framework of the UN and did not recognize the Palestinian question as the heart of the Middle Eastern conflicts. Despite the attempt to broker a peace in the Middle East, American insistence that the Palestinian question did not lie at the heart of the matter continued to widen the gulf between the United States and the Third World. Until very late in the debate, the United States insisted that the issue was between Israel and its neighbors and not between Israel and the Palestinians. The divide grew even wider in 1980 after Israel passed its "Basic Law" declaring Jerusalem its capital and expanded its settlements in the occupied territories.

The General Assembly resolved that the November 1981 strategic agreements between the United States and Israel "encouraged Israel to pursue expansionist policies,"[41] while a resolution sponsored by Bangladesh, Cuba, Guyana, India, Laos, Malaysia, Mongolia, Nigeria, Pakistan, Sri Lanka, Vietnam, and Yugoslavia argued that Israel would not be able to continue with its policies without the material and moral support of the United States. The resolution referred to Israel as "the United States' gendarme in the Middle East."[42] Other non-aligned countries called continued American vetoes in the Security Council "far more dangerous than missiles" because in their view they encouraged Israeli expansion.[43]

The rest of the decade followed a similar pattern. The number of resolutions condemning Israeli actions and violations of Palestinian rights increased, while the United States consistently voted against them all, on many occasions, as one U.S. representative put it, "because the text mentioned the PLO, which the United States did not recognize and which, by refusing to recognize Israel, had impeded the Middle East peace process."[44]

The Palestinian intifadah, or uprising, of 1988 again demonstrated the wide disparity in views between the Third World and the United States. General Assembly resolutions praised the Palestinians for fighting back, while the United States abhorred the fighting and even tried to close down the PLO's observer mission in New York. When that failed, the United States denied Yasser Arafat a visa to enter the country to speak before the General Assembly. Appalled by the American actions, the General Assembly convened instead in Geneva to hear Arafat speak and adopted a resolution that accepted his declaration of a Palestinian state while designating "Palestine" to be used in official declarations in place of "PLO." Only the United States and Israel objected to these resolutions.[45]

Zionism and Racism

An even more contentious and emotional issue was to surface in the General Assembly in 1975. In a meeting of the Subcommittee on Near Eastern and South Asian Affairs of the Senate Committee on Foreign Relations on March 30, 1990, Senator Daniel Patrick Moynihan stated that the purpose of the meeting was to consider:

> United Nations Resolution 3379 of 1975 which declared Zionism to be a form of racism and which was perhaps the low point in the history of the behavior of the General Assembly and of the campaign led at that time by the Soviet Union to discredit both the nation of Israel, its principal allies and friends around the world and, in the process of doing so to politicize, at a level heretofore unknown, the activities of the General Assembly. Those are essentially political activities in any event, but the Soviets chose to use them as instruments of totalitarian propaganda, distortion, and lying that we came to associate with the totalitarian state.
>
> It emerged in time that the Zionism resolution had its origins in a two-part article in Pravda written by the deputy foreign editor which appeared in 1971. . . .

It appeared at the International Women's Conference in Mexico City sponsored by the United Nations in the summer of 1975 and then, of course, appeared
in Geneva at UNESCO and finally in the third committee of the General Assembly in 1975.[46]

The resolution was finally repealed by the General Assembly on December 16,
1991, under strong U.S. pressure. But the antagonism toward the General Assembly
in much of the American body politic remained.

The New World Information Order

In 1976, Third World countries in the General Assembly raised another issue striking at the heart of a fundamental American principle: freedom of the press. Taking a cue from the New International Economic Order, they launched the New
World Information and Communications Order (NWIO), directed at what they
perceived as inequities in the flows of information, news, and communication
technologies. The initiative expressed the broad resentment of many Third World
countries at what they believed was overly negative reporting on their internal conditions and policies. The United States, on the other hand, saw the demands for a
new information order as a direct threat to the American principle of a free press
and to access for U.S. media organizations to developing countries. Major media
organizations were mobilized to fight the initiative.

The General Assembly referred the matter to the UN Education, Scientific,
and Cultural Organization (UNESCO). The subsequent withdrawal of the United
States from that organization was due in part to the support for the NWIO within
UNESCO. Although that may have been the ostensible reason, Washington was
also dissatisfied with the leadership of UNESCO, and some in Congress were looking for an occasion to show their general displeasure with the United Nations.

Until the mid-1960s, the focus of debate on the flow of information within
the United Nations, particularly in UNESCO, consisted of talk about the "free flow
of information" and the use of mass media to build "modern" societies in the
Third World.[47] By the middle of that decade, however, increasing criticism had developed around what Third World countries perceived to be the overwhelming
domination of Western mass media and news agencies.

Complaints of the proponents of the NWIO centered on what they regarded
as an imbalance in the flow of information between capitalist developed countries
and the rest of the world, the content of the flow in each direction, and control
over the flow of information. Third World complaints targeted the United States
most frequently, often accusing Anglo-American news agencies (such as Associated
Press, United Press International, Reuters, and Columbia Broadcasting System) of
cultural and media imperialism. Critics charged that the dominant role played by
Western media has distorted and excluded authentic cultural values and expression
in Third World countries and has presented them to the world through Western
eyes.[48] They much preferred that Western news agencies prominently display the
positive news disseminated by Third World government agencies.

Third World nations began to articulate their dissatisfaction more and more frequently throughout the early 1970s, charging that information about Third World countries that enters the world news system emphasized their fragility, instability, and corruption and suggested that economic imbalances stemmed not from European colonialism and neo-colonial forces but from their own inability to sustain development. Views of Third World problems presented by the dominant Western media ultimately filtered back into the developing world, which depends on the same media for information. Third World countries argued that distorted, negative treatment of their problems in the media neglected the facts and real issues facing their nations and impeded their attempts to develop.[49] What was needed, the developing world claimed, was a global change in telecommunications, news flows, intellectual property rights, and international advertising.

D. R. Mankekar, former chairman of the Coordinating Committee of the Non-Aligned Countries' Press Agencies Pool, expressed Third World views of the western domination of the news quite clearly:

> They [the West] fail to realize that their obduracy is being construed by the Third World as a disguised attempt to tighten on them the grip of colonialist hegemony through the Western media in the name of freedom of information.[50]

Western control over the flow of information, then, constituted a form of colonialism in the eyes of the Third World, and thus represented a direct threat to the national sovereignty of the developing nations.

These views were presented to UNESCO, which in 1977 established the International Commission for the Study of Communications Problems, chaired by a liberal Irish politician, Sean MacBride. Amadou-Mahtar M'Bow, director-general of UNESCO, stated the goals of the commission:

> It is essential that all men and women, in all social and cultural environments, should be given the opportunity of joining in the process of collective thinking thus initiated, for new ideas must be developed and more positive measures must be taken to shake off the prevailing inertia. With the coming of a new world communication order, each people must be able to learn from the others, while at the same time conveying to them its own understanding of its own condition and its own view of world affairs. Mankind will then have made a decisive step forward on the path to freedom, democracy, and fellowship.[51]

MacBride echoed these thoughts as he commented upon the state of affairs in the flow of information throughout the world:

> In the 1970s international debates on communications issues had stridently reached points of confrontation in many areas. Third World protests against the dominant flow of news from the industrialized countries were often construed as attacks on the free flow of information. Defenders of journalistic freedom were labeled intruders on national sovereignty. Varying concepts of news values and the role, rights, and responsibilities of journalists were widely contended, as was the potential contribution of the mass media to the solution of major world problems.[52]

The commission, established "to study the totality of communication problems in modern societies," began its work in December 1977 and published its final
report in 1980. The group, which included the American journalist Elie Abel and
the Colombian writer Gabriel Garcia Marquez, concluded that communications
issues "are structurally linked to wider socio-economic and cultural patterns,"
while communication problems "assume a highly political character which is the
basic reason why they are at the center of the stage today in national and international arenas."[53] Despite some disagreements over the next step, the commission
published a massive report that included a plan for future action that called for the
regulation of transnational corporations and the "right" of nations to use their
means of information.[54] The recommendations later formed the basis of UNESCO
Resolution 4/19, which listed the eleven objectives of the new information order:

1. Elimination of the imbalances and inequalities which characterize the
   present situation;
2. Elimination of the negative effects of certain monopolies, public or private,
   and excessive concentrations;
3. Removal of internal and external obstacles to a free flow and wider and
   better balanced dissemination of information and ideas;
4. Plurality of sources and channels of information;
5. Freedom of the press and information;
6. Freedom of journalists and all professionals in the communication media,
   a freedom inseparable from responsibility;
7. The capacity of developing countries to achieve improvement of their own
   situations, notably by providing their own equipment, by training their
   personnel, by improving their infrastructure and by making their information and communication media suitable to their needs and aspirations;
8. The sincere will of developed countries to help them attain these objectives;
9. Respect for each people's cultural identity and for the right of each nation
   to inform the world public about its interests, its aspirations and its social
   and cultural values;
10. Respect for the right of all peoples to participate in international exchanges
    of information on the basis of equality, justice, and mutual benefit;
11. Respect for the right of the public, of ethnic and social groups and of in-
    dividuals to have access to information sources and to participate actively
    in the communication process.[55]

Although the resolution contained language preserving freedom of the press,
U.S. media organizations argued strongly that the tone represented a capitulation
to those who would restrict such freedom. The U.S. organizations offered to assist
in the training of journalists and in the establishment of Third World press organizations. Although some such assistance was provided, the NWIO represented a
continuing suspicion, if not resentment, of Western media organizations in the
Third World. Although the issue remains, in a globe that is becoming more and
more linked with electronics that know no borders, the issue is becoming moot

while the new means of communication are becoming less amenable to control and more and more threatening to indigenous cultures and local government censorship. The recollection of this UN effort to curb a fundamental U.S. principle, however, remains one of the elements in the negative attitudes toward the international organization within the United States.

FOURTEEN

The Twenty-First–Century Agenda

This book began with the premise that solutions to some of the most significant foreign policy problems facing the United States in the twenty-first century will depend substantially on effective relations with nations that emerged from colonialism in the twentieth century.

Subsequent chapters have examined the breakup of the European empires and the perceptions and attitudes generated in the imperial age and the bearing of these sensitivities on relations with the United States. At the conclusion of this examination, it is appropriate to ask whether the experiences under colonialism remain relevant to the development of U.S.–Third World relations in the next century.

A Changing World

Certainly the latter years of the twentieth century have brought many changes in the global landscape.

The Cold War confrontation between the Western powers and the Soviet bloc of nations that dominated international relations for four decades has ended. Problems created by alliances and military presences in the Third World during the East-West confrontation have abated.

Issues such as colonialism and apartheid that divided the United States from much of the developing world have disappeared from the agenda of the UN General Assembly.

New generations, more influenced by globalization, have emerged. The Internet has created an international communicating elite in which major developing countries such as India have played a significant role.

Economic realities and free market challenges have changed attitudes toward foreign investment. The newer nations, however, have developed at different paces; some, such as South Korea, joined the industrial ranks. Others, such as Nigeria and

Indonesia, have suffered from lack of internal cohesion, corruption, and poor governance and have lagged behind.

Common opposition to Western and racial dominance created a fragile solidarity among the new nations. The solidarity was to some degree a rhetorical myth made possible by common experiences and common suspicions of the West. That solidarity has eroded. As one observer, Ambassador Teresita Schaffer, has written:

> The Third World has become increasingly fragmented as both economic growth and different political interests have affected different countries in different ways. This process was already under way in the early 1980s, when I remember the lack of Third World solidarity at the Geneva GATT ministerial. It became more pronounced after the end of the Cold War. By now differences in attitude and especially in policy between, say, Brazil, India, Singapore, Burma, Yemen, South Africa, Zimbabwe, and Cote d'Ivoire are quite pronounced. One can no longer assume that the G-77 will vote in unison in any forum where real consequences are likely to follow from the vote.[1]

The changes should provide new opportunities for the United States. But the world has not totally changed.

An Unchanged World

Sensitivities over race, sovereignty, intervention, and income disparities remain. The Asian countries reacted negatively to efforts by the United States and the International Monetary Fund to dictate terms of recovery to them during the 1999 Asian financial crisis. Many Indonesians reacted strongly against the idea of white Australian troops entering East Timor as part of a UN peace-keeping force in August of that year. Many Third World nations, despite the Serbian atrocities in Kosovo, saw the NATO attacks in 1999 as an unwelcome violation of national sovereignty. The old feelings still lie beneath the surfaces of Third World countries.

The gap between the richer and poorer countries remains and is growing, especially in Africa. The same issues of debt relief, conditions of trade, access to technology, and resource transfers that were the agenda of the NIEO are alive at the end of the century. As the abortive World Trade Organization meeting in Seattle in December 1999 and the efforts to shut down the World Bank and IMF meetings in Washington in April 2000 demonstrated, a major gap in the perceptions of free trade benefits divides the industrial and developing worlds.

The U.S. Interests

Should the United States still care about these sensitivities and pay attention to these issues?

The United States has significant interests in the developing nations. Almost 50 percent of U.S. exports go to member nations of the Group of 77. The nation is heavily dependent on imports for oil, vital minerals, and agricultural products that come from Third World countries.

And the fulfillment of a large number of the stated U.S. foreign policy objectives will depend on satisfactory relations with Third World countries. Take a look at the details of the U.S. International Affairs Strategic Plan published in September 1977[2.] The plan lists sixteen strategic goals—an agenda for the twenty-first century:

- Ensure that local and regional instabilities do not threaten the security and well-being of the United States or its allies.
- Eliminate the threat to the United States and its allies from weapons of mass destruction or destabilizing conventional arms.
- Open foreign markets to free the flow of goods, services, and capital.
- Expand U.S. exports to $1.2 trillion by 2000.
- Increase global economic growth.
- Promote broad-based economic growth in developing and transitional economies.
- Enhance the ability of American citizens to travel and live abroad securely.
- Control how immigrants and non-immigrants enter and remain in the United States.
- Minimize the impact of international crime on the United States and its citizens.
- Reduce significantly from 1997 levels the entry of illegal drugs into the United States.
- Reduce international terrorist attacks, especially against the United States and its citizens.
- Increase foreign government adherence to democratic practices and respect for human rights.
- Prevent or minimize the human costs of conflict and natural disasters.
- Secure a sustainable global environment in order to protect the United States and its citizens from the effects of international environmental degradation.
- Stabilize world population growth.
- Protect human health and reduce the spread of infectious diseases.

The fulfillment of every one of these goals will require a degree of cooperation between the new nations of the twentieth century and the United States. And that means developing U.S. policies and attitudes that can establish such cooperation.

The residual problems of Kashmir, Cyprus, and the Middle East still threaten global stability. Eliminating weapons of mass destruction requires effective communication with the nations of the Middle East, India, Pakistan, the two Koreas, China, and Taiwan.

Population growth, regional unrest, the spread of disease, and environmental degradation threaten the health of industrial societies, including the United States, and have roots in the developing world. Terrorism, crime, and drugs from nations beyond U.S. borders directly affect American citizens. Many developing countries have yet to establish sound institutions, let alone democracy; continuing oppression, poverty, and civil unrest spark demands for U.S. intervention.

In pursuit of these issues, Washington will need to establish a sufficient degree of diplomatic acceptance and access. In many cases, political leaders in Third World countries will need to make difficult decisions to satisfy U.S. interests. Those will be hard, if not impossible, if the local political climate precludes cooperation because of real or imagined actions by the United States.

The records of the last half century hold many examples of the chance remark by a U.S. official, legislator, or journalist that has been seen as insulting to the pride or sovereignty of an Asian or African nation and has made cooperation difficult. The publication of comments by a Peace Corps volunteer in Nigeria in the 1960s seriously disrupted normal diplomatic communication with that key African country. Such incidents cannot be prevented, but their existence illustrates problems of communication that are too often ignored.

U.S. researchers may not be able to get vital statistics on epidemics in an African country because of American comments on its health system.

Intelligence vital to the detection of crime or terrorism will not be available if a country is deeply suspicious of the United States.

The encouragement of democracy or human rights in a country requires the quiet establishment of a common interest in the pursuit of these goals.

Even humanitarian relief will be blocked if the recipient country senses an ulterior motive on the part of the donor.

In today's world, national objectives will seldom be achieved by military means. This puts greater responsibility on diplomatic approaches that include a willingness to negotiate and a capacity to understand and recognize the political and cultural dynamics of another country and society. Americans, who tend to see the rest of the world in their own image, have not demonstrated a marked capacity to empathize with and understand other countries and societies.

In its relations with the rest of the world, the United States wants to be liked and to have what Americans believe to be generous largesse appreciated. Neither is a realistic expectation. Americans are more thin-skinned than they will admit. Political rhetoric critical of the United States abroad is often a facile way for political figures to gain popularity. The anti-imperialist appeal is not dead. Decolonization represented a major world revolution; the rhetoric of the revolution does not fade overnight. What is important is not what is said, but what a government is prepared to do, perhaps quietly, to assist a U.S. interest.

Envy and Admiration

In the modern world, international relations are at the mercy of images. Globalization and communications have perpetuated images, many of them created in the United States—whether it be McDonald's or Mickey Mouse. To those affected by the global reach of American commerce or the threat to cultures of U.S. entertainment, these images have become symbols of resentment and dislike. Globalization has brought benefits to many, but to others who are culturally and economically affected by the spread of American influence, the new internationalization of life is seen as a new form of imperialism with a U.S. label.

The gap created by history and cultures is still wide between the United States and much of the Third World. The sensitivities of the latter lie very near the surface. Some ask, "Will not globalization begin to erode this gap?" For a tiny population of elites around the world, this might be true. But globalization and the rapid development of the Internet have other results. They increase the threat to older cultures and the resentment of the spread and popularity of Western (read American) culture. They will not erase the rivalries, the histories, the ambitions that continue to fuel the world's unrest.

Given its wealth and power, the United States will continue to be viewed by many in the world with a mixture of envy, admiration, and distaste. Its ideas and aggressive technology challenge conventional societies. In a world of multiple humanitarian crises, disintegrating nations, and civil and ethnic wars, the United States is looked to for leadership and is integral to global action but is considered imperialistic if it acts unilaterally. Washington's admonitions to others to cease conflict or shape up their economies are often seen as arrogant. Although the World Bank and the International Monetary Fund are international organizations, they are widely seen as U.S. instruments, and Americans suffer the blame for unpopular actions and policies.

The United States remains a dream for thousands who want to come to savor the freedom, the opportunities, and the glamour of America. Such a desire should not be taken as an indication of acceptance of U.S. society and policies. Some of the sharpest critics of U.S. foreign policies come from ethnic and immigrant communities.

Much of the world is ignorant about the United States, basing their concepts on America's entertainment exports and often on cliches about America that were commonly propagated by Europeans in the colonial period. U.S. advances in meeting admitted problems of racism, ethnic relations, and poverty are obscured by attention to isolated incidents. Future relations between the United States and the Third World will be affected not only by U.S. ignorance about the developing world, but also by Third World ignorance of the United States.

The end of the Cold War has freed the United States from the need to identify with and pay undue attention to authoritarian regimes. More consistent policies with respect to democracy and human rights should be possible. But reaching understandings with ambitious, charismatic, clever Third World leaders who wield effective authoritarian control may never be possible. The United States could not relate effectively to either Sukarno of Indonesia or Nkrumah of Ghana. Saddam Hussein is beyond diplomacy. Nevertheless, each of these leaders in their countries and regions—including Saddam—can garner support and touch nerves of anti-Western sentiment. Diplomatic approaches to countries, such as Iran, where, in

1999 elements unfriendly to the United States were still in a strong position, run the risk of politically embarrassing rebuffs.

Major regional disputes still put the United States on the spot, but as progress is made in the Middle East, Cyprus and—possibly—even Kashmir, this obstacle to the U.S. relationship to key Third World nations should fade. In certain sections of the Islamic world, however, the U.S. identification with Israel's presence in Jerusalem will continue to breed anti-American feeling. Only a genuine peace between the Israelis and the Palestinians, seen as such in the Muslim world, will eventually reduce that feeling.

But the difficulties should not inhibit efforts to reach out to the Third World. The United States has achieved significant—if, at times, partial—fulfillment of objectives in Third World areas. The Israeli-Palestinian peace process, negotiations on the independence of Namibia, and cooperation in the identification and control of diseases in Africa stand out as examples.

It is difficult, however, to be optimistic that the achievement of U.S. objectives in the Third World in the twenty-first century will be any easier than they were in the twentieth century. As previous chapters have shown, history and local political and economic conditions have created nations that do not relate easily to the dynamic, assertive, rich American giant.

No approach to the Third World is likely to be free of vulnerability to rejection, misunderstanding, unreasonable demands or exploitation. For the United States, several attitudinal difficulties stand in the way.

Through most of the last half of the twentieth century, the cry of the Third World was "anti-imperial," continuing even into independence. Given the power and wealth of the United States, it was attacked as the new imperialist. Although some of the criticism represented genuine anger at some U.S. policies, much was rhetorical habit. In some countries, it was safer for politicians to attack Washington than to criticize their own country. Inescapably, because of its economic and military power, the United States remains the target of criticism for the failure of the world to resolve its inequities.

But the Third World has paid a price for these gratuitous attacks in a general disenchantment with the Third World in the United States. This was especially true during the Cold War period when similar barbs did not appear to be leveled at the Soviet Union. But the effects linger at the end of the century.

Disillusionment

The United States—and especially the conservative Congress—has become disillusioned with the Third World and the instruments of international relations created after World War II. By 1999, the portion of the federal budget for international relations had dropped 50 percent in real dollars since 1980.

The United Nations is no longer looked upon as an aid to U.S. diplomacy as the United States tends more and more to "go-it-alone." At the end of 1999, U.S. payments to the United Nations were heavily in arrears.

The disillusionment extends particularly to foreign aid, whether bilateral or through international lending agencies. Such aid is less and less popular because many in America doubt its effectiveness and the benefits to U.S. interests. With the end of the Cold War, one of the principal rationales for assistance was lost. In 1997, the United States ranked twenty-first, behind Spain and Italy, in the proportion of its per capita gross national product devoted to foreign assistance. As a *Washington Post* writer stated, "While America has enjoyed one of its most prosperous decades ever in the 1990s, it also has set a record for stinginess. For as long as people have kept track, never has the United States given a smaller share of its money to the world's poorest."[3]

It is true that much aid was ineffective, the victim of political priorities and poor planning and implementation. Professor Carol Lancaster, former senior official of the Agency for International Development (AID), gave this assessment of U.S. aid to Africa:

> Extraordinary high levels of aid relative to the size of its economies have gone to the region [Africa] over an extended period. At the same time, economic development has been disappointing by almost any standard. Foreign aid, which is supposed to promote development, has had some real successes in Africa, proving that it can be effective. But it has frequently proven unsatisfactory in impact and its positive results unsustainable over the long run.[4]

Jim Hoagland of *The Washington Post* commented on a recent presentation to a World Bank gathering by its president, James D. Wolfenson:

> Wolfenson, a successful investment banker in his native Australia and then in New York, displays missionary zeal in focusing on the problems the world's poor have in plugging into globalization . . .
>
> He worries that development assistance from the world's affluent countries has declined from $60 billion 10 years ago to $35 billion today, even as Third World countries have adopted free market systems and learned to use aid more effectively.
>
> "Two billion people live on less than $2 a day." Almost as many "do not have access to clean water. The significant gains the world made in women's education are being reversed. We live in a world that gradually is getting worse and worse. It is not hopeless, but we must do something about it now."[5]

Fear

Fear plays a role in the U.S. approach to the Third World.

On the heels of Saddam Hussein's invasion of Kuwait, the revelations of his weapons of mass destruction, the World Trade Center bombings, and acts of terrorism against U.S. citizens and installations, Americans have become genuinely afraid of threats from the Third World. This fear has compounded the difficulties of responding to challenges from these nations. Military responses are frustrated by risk aversion at home, lack of full cooperation from nations in affected regions abroad, and the shadowy nature of the targets. Fear makes fortresses of our diplomatic establishments abroad, inhibiting both essential access to local publics and the gathering of essential information.

Much of the fear is directed at Islam, with insufficient discernment of the differences within that important world religion. At the end of the century, Islamic fundamentalism risked becoming the new "adversary" of the United States.

There is also a fear of negotiation. The U.S. system is founded on the principle of compromise, yet it is ironic that many Americans consider diplomatic negotiations a sign of weakness. Washington has achieved important objectives through negotiation in the Middle East, Asia, and the United Nations but, regrettably, each major negotiation has faced U.S. domestic opposition, complicating the complete fulfillment of each agreement. This attitude is particularly striking given the general failure of the United States to achieve all its objectives by military means, whether in Iraq, Somalia, or Cuba.

The Panama Canal treaties were ratified only after acrimonious Senate debate. The Reagan administration refused to sign the Law of the Sea Treaty. U.S. politics interfered with a follow-up to the Madrid conference on the Middle East. Congress refused to appropriate the funds for the full implementation of the agreement with North Korea. At the end of 1999, it rejected ratification of the Comprehensive Test Ban Treaty. And more than sixty other treaties, negotiated in good faith by the United States, remain unratified by the U.S. Senate.

Unilateralism

In cases where U.S. objectives relating to terrorism or weapons of mass destruction have been resisted, the United States has tended to impose unilateral economic sanctions. Where sanctions have been successful, they have had a single, easily understood, and unchanging objective. The most recent example has been the willingness in 1999 of Muammar Qadhafi of Libya to turn over those who allegedly bombed the Pan American aircraft over Lockerbie, Scotland, in 1988. The sanctions imposed on Saddam Hussein of Iraq have been less successful. While various rationales were stated for the imposition of sanctions, it was clear that Washington's true intent was the overthrow of Saddam. The same is true of the embargo against Castro's Cuba. Proud and power-hungry Third World leaders are unlikely to yield to sanctions that call for their own demise. Thus sanctions become an unsatisfying alternative to force; the United States faces the dual problems of friendly governments that undermine the sanctions and sympathy for the victims in regions such as the Middle East.

Intervention

The achievement of key objectives of U.S. foreign policy may require intervention in the internal affairs of other countries—striking directly at one of the most sensitive principles in the Third World. To eliminate weapons of mass destruction, ensure non-proliferation of nuclear technology, and combat terrorism requires the collection of intelligence, cooperation with local authorities, and, often, candid diplomatic encounters. External remedies for economic collapses carry harsh demands for cutting government payrolls, ending subsidies, and curtailing corruption. Environmental discussions may deal not only with embarrassing ecological conditions but also with ending favors to leaders and their cronies. Migration touches on both the economy and family planning. More and more, especially with the rampant AIDS epidemic, health issues are on the diplomatic agenda. The U.S. reports, statements, and diplomatic pressures on questions of dissidents, torture, detentions, religious freedom, and democracy can strike at the basis of a regime's survival.

With the end of the Cold War, the nature of U.S. intervention has changed. Whatever its nature, however, each intervention risks awakening thoughts of past imperialism. During the confrontation with the Soviets, both overt and covert interventions were designed to block the advance of an adversary. Although military interventions have occurred in Somalia, Kosovo, and Bosnia and are continuing in Iraq, such interventions have had primarily humanitarian objectives. U.S. interventions in sovereign states are more likely in the future to involve human rights, democracy, or religious freedom.

In Conclusion

Given these obstacles, how can the United States interact effectively with a world composed in part of nations that are fragmented, poor, disillusioned, often corrupt, and frequently torn by violent strife? There is no magic answer, but in countries where stability exists and U.S. interests are clear, it should be possible to overcome the inhibitions of their Third World heritage and further the positive changes now taking place.

Americans and the U.S. political system are not prepared at the beginning of the twenty-first century to make any special effort to improve communication with Third World nations. Under these circumstances it would be naive to propose drastic reversals of current U.S. attitudes. Nevertheless, in light of the many ways that threats from the Third World may ultimately affect the United States, it is not unreasonable to hope that future circumstances will bring a reorientation of directions. One can only hope it will not be too late.

Understanding the political realities of the Third World does not mean accepting them. If, however, the United States is to gain the essential cooperation of significant Third World states in its pursuit of key foreign policy objectives, Washington must find ways to overcome the suspicions and ignorance of the United States that have prevailed over the past fifty years in many Third World countries.

Despite basic differences, the United States continues to command respect in much of the Third World. Recognition of Third World problems and responses that display a respect for the dignity and independence of the peoples of Asia, the Middle East, Africa, and Latin America can make possible more effective cooperation without sacrificing fundamental U.S. interests.

Obviously, cooperation with any country will depend in large measure on U.S. bilateral relations, but global Third World grievances remain as obstacles. The payment of full U.S. arrearages to the United Nations, support for the Israeli-Palestinian peace process, and agreement to the global environmental treaty will help.

Although times have changed, President John F. Kennedy, with his empathy for the newly independent nations, illustrated one path. He listened.

Of all the U.S. presidents, John Kennedy displayed the greatest genuine interest in the Third World. Abroad, he was probably the most popular of U.S. leaders. Arthur Schlesinger's description of Kennedy's interest illustrates both the approach and the obstacles. The analysis is as true in 2000 as it was in 1960:

> Kennedy became, in effect, Secretary of State for the Third World. With his consuming intellectual curiosity, he generally knew more about the Middle East, for example, than most of the officials on the seventh floor of the State Department; and the Assistant Secretaries in charge of the developing areas dealt as much with him as with the Secretary of State. Moreover, he conducted his Third World campaign to an unprecedented degree through talks and correspondence with heads of state. He well understood that personalities exert a disproportionate influence in new states without stable political systems, and he resolved to turn the situation to his own purposes.
>
> The leaders of the new nations, it must be said, did not always make this task easier. They were often ungenerous and resentful, driven by historic frustrations and rancor and brimming over with sensitivity and vanity. Moreover, anti-American bravado was always a good way to excite a crowd and strike a pose for national virility. The President, understanding this as part of the process, resolved not to be diverted by pinpricks. He was sometimes greatly tried, and on occasion the dignity of the United States required some form of response. But most of the time he was faithful to the spirit of Andrew Jackson who in 1829 had called on his fellow countrymen, in the event of foreign provocation, "to exhibit the forbearance becoming a powerful nation rather than the sensibility belonging to a gallant people."
>
> And so the new President set out to adjust American thinking to a world where the cold war was no longer the single reality and to help the new countries find their own roads to national dignity and international harmony. But in his own government, he immediately ran head-on against a set of inherited policies on colonialism, on neutralism, and on foreign assistance, deeply imbedded in the minds of government officials and the structure of the executive branch.[6]

Kennedy's popularity did not necessarily translate into U.S. successes, but it did establish a measure of respect for the United States and its leadership. He created the impression that in the new world that was emerging, the United States was interested, was willing to learn, and did not have all the answers. He understood the importance of individuals in the Third World.

He was willing to listen patiently—an approach rare among Americans. Listening—although it may be arduous at times—often provides insights into a speaker's thinking and politics that are important to an understanding of the problem at hand.

But listening is an art. It requires distinguishing between what people believe the foreigner wants to hear and what the speaker really thinks or believes. It requires a degree of humility on the part of the listener. Dialogues in the Third World are not appropriate settings for reminders of the "superpower" status of the United States—the assertion comes across as arrogance.

Listening and personal attention go hand in hand. Kennedy had more visitors from Third World countries during his brief time in office than any other president. In lands where individual leadership is important, this attention to the pride and status of leaders is a great help to diplomacy.

Effective communication with the Third World also requires some limits on rhetoric that seems to promise more than can be delivered. Terms such as "freedom" or "support" can create expectations and result in disappointments.

Whether they have fled a Saddam Hussein or a Fidel Castro, exiles who dream unrealistically of a triumphant return to their homeland are often assisted in the United States. Such encouragement only exposes U.S. weakness and reinforces an imperial image in the region concerned.

The new century will undoubtedly see changes in such countries as Iraq and Cuba, but the likelihood is that they will come from within without the help of the United States.

When former Senator Edmund S. Muskie became secretary of state, he remarked to his staff, "I can see that my job is just politics—but on an international scale." Those Americans who have related effectively to Third World nations have understood that other nations have politics, too. But many in both the Congress and the executive branch are sadly unwilling to accept that others may be constrained by local political considerations, just as they are. Efforts by diplomats to explain to U.S. officials why another country's official cannot perform as the United States wishes because of local political circumstances—often circumstances that carry serious risk—have been met by the comment, "That's their problem. Why are you defending them?" Politics can be a high-risk enterprise in many Third World countries where too close an association with a major power can bring dismissal, disgrace, exile, or death.

One legacy of past attitudes toward the new nations is a sense that the United States knows best and has little need either to consult or involve those of another country in U.S. decisions. Consultation and involvement, even if at times difficult and unsuccessful, go far to remove an image of imperial overlordship. The United States could also benefit from more consultation with Europeans on Third World matters. They, after all, know these countries in some cases better than the Americans.

The United States cannot be successful with Third World nations unless it takes the United Nations seriously. For all the problems inherent in the UN system, it is, for much of the world, the sole legitimator for international action. This is true in Europe as well as Asia, Africa, and Latin America.

Finally, the United States, with its wealth, cannot be effective diplomatically in the rest of the world unless it finds better ways to use portions of that wealth to raise the standards of living in other countries. Given threats of disease, migration, and environmental degradation, such use of wealth is in the U.S. interest. Trade and investment that take into account the needs and sensitivities of other nations should play a major part. Continued encouragement should be given to private U.S. foundations that have played so important a role in many of the Third World countries. Since the early 1980s, the share of U.S. foundation giving to domestic and overseas recipients for international activities—from education to human rights to the arts to religion—has increased substantially. In 1997, 10.8 percent of total grant dollars was spent on international programs, more than double the share reported in 1982.[7]

But whatever other resources may be used, the United States cannot ignore official assistance. J. Brian Atwood, administrator of AID under President Clinton, said it eloquently in an essay in *The Christian Science Monitor:*

> It's time to end the hypocrisy. Globalization is leaving out about two-thirds of the world. Either we should invest real money in the global model we are promoting, or we should erect the barriers to keep out these poor countries when their internal problems boil over. The US, with its military budget of $275 billion and its foreign assistance budget of $12 billion may already have made its choice. But have we done so consciously? Or are we victims of inertia?
>
> We are fast approaching a world in which 10 percent of the people control 90 percent of the wealth. We hear rhetoric about a more equitable world where America's vision of a democratic, market-based globe can be realized, but it isn't matched by our resource allocations.[8]

America can turn its back on the Third World, saying these nations are not worthy of our attention and our largesse, that they are hypocritical, ungrateful, and dangerous to our interests. We Americans can recognize that we are on one planet together and that their troubles are America's troubles.

In the new century, the United States, can envelop itself in its imperial mantle and stand aside and declare, demand, prescribe, and manipulate, or it can, with some humility, throw off the cloak and recognize that effective power comes through understanding and relating to others—as difficult as this may sometimes be.

In the twenty-first century, the Third World will increasingly thrust itself into America's deliberations—through migrations, environmental degradation, disease, terrorism, and weapons. It is not too early to recognize that although the United States may not be the imperial power some claim it to be, it shares a major responsibility to respond to this thrust.

Backgrounds of Liberation Leaders

These charts illustrating the varied backgrounds and activities of selected independence leaders represent only a portion of the many men and women who played key roles in this drama. The backgrounds of others, such as Julius Nyerere, Hastings Banda, and Agostinho Neto, are included in the text.

Christopher Sutton, a University of Virginia graduate student, prepared the charts.

Leader	Circumstances of birth	Circumstances of education	When and how did they become involved in the independence movement or colonial administration?	What made them take the course they ultimately followed?	When did they organize independence movements?	How did they manifest opposition to colonial rule?	Were they imprisoned? Exiled? How long?	When and under what circumstances were concessions made? With what result?
Amilcar Cabral	Born September 12, 1924 in Bafata, Portuguese Guinea. Son of Cape Verdean parents; father was a teacher; mother managed a hotel.	Sent to the Liceu Gil Eane in Sao Vicente, Cape Verde for secondary education. Graduated from University of Lisbon Institute of Agronomy with honors in 1950.	Entered colonial agricultural service in 1950, at which time he traveled extensively in Guinea.	His years in Lisbon (1945–1952) changed the intellectual Cabral into an African nationalist. Exposed to and influenced by Communist/ Marxist thought. Cabral rejected his privileged position in Portuguese system and began to think of himself as an African nationalist/socialist.	First effort to organize nationalist movement in Guinea was the "Recreation Association" in 1954, which led to the short lived Movimento Para Independencia Nacional da Guine Portuguesa. On Sept. 19, 1956, Cabral and others formed Partido Africano de Independencia de Guine e Cabo Verde (PAIGC), the nationalist revolutionary party. In Dec. 1956, Cabral met with Neto to form the Movimento Popular de Libertacao de Angola (MPLA). In 1961, he organized the Conferencia de Organizacoes Nacionalists das Colonias Portuguesas in Tunis, which sought to unify all African Portuguese colonies.	Strikes staged in 1959, which were severely repressed by colonial regime. After repression, Cabral changed tactics to guerilla warfare. Wrote a number of works on African liberation, culture, history, and class formation.	No.	In 1973, the PAIGC was able to declare itself the government of an independent Guinea-Bissau. The April 1974 overthrow of the Portuguese regime marked the end of colonialism in Africa. However, before the regime fell, it assassinated Cabral in a plot to regain control, killing him on January 20, 1973. Official date of independence is September 10, 1974.

Mohandas Gandhi	Born October 2, 1869, in Porbandar, India. Son of moderately wealthy chief minister of the town. Vaisya caste (merchant class) family.	Primary school in Porbandar. Joined Samaldes College in Bhavnagar. Law School at Inner Temple, a law college in London.	In South Africa in 1894, he worked to defend Indian suffrage. Formed Natal Indian Congress.	Amritsar massacre in the Punjab in 1919 led Gandhi to take stand on nationalism and independence.	In autumn 1920, he refashioned the Indian National Congress into a grassroots nationalist organization.	Non-violent resistance (satyagraha), which consisted of boycotts, marches, fasts.	Arrested March 22, 1922 and sentenced to 6 yrs, though released after an appendicitis operation. Imprisoned December 1931 but released after fasting. Arrested again in 1946.	After embarking on an-other fast, Britain's new constitution was changed to treat untouchables fairly. Demanded imme-diate withdrawal of British in summer of 1942, be-cause of British-promoted discord. Labour Party triumph in 1945 and the Mountbatten plan of June 3, 1947, set the day of independence and the mode of partition.
Ho Chi Minh	Born May 19, 1890, in Hoang Tru, Vietnam. Son of poor, minor government official dismissed for activity against the French.	Between ages 14 and 18 he studied at grammar school in Hue.	He became a strong nationalist and socialist while living in France from 1917–1923, where he joined the Communist Party, and wrote extensively on Vietnamese nationalism.	His travels in Europe and the Soviet Union, as well as his address on Vietnamese nationalism at the Versailles Peace Conference after World War I led him to action.	Joined French Communist Party in 1920. In December 1924, he went to Canton, China, to recruit the first cadres of the Thanh Niem (Vietnamese Revolutionary Youth Association). Formed Viet Minh in January 1941.	Guerilla warfare. He also wrote numerous articles on nationalism in France and while in prison wrote a book, Notebook from Prison, that called for revolution.	In 1942, sentenced to 18 months' prison by Chiang Kai-shek. In 1939, sentenced to 2 years' prison in Hong Kong.	Japanese invasion coupled with Japanese defeat in WWII led communists to declare independence on September 2, 1945. In March 1946 the French recognized Vietnam Democratic Republic as free state within Indo-chinese Federation; how-ever, they refused to grant independence. The waning power of the French and defeat at Dien Bien Phu on May 7, 1954, forced the French to negotiate via the Geneva Accords, which stated that Vietnam was to be united and indepen-dent after the elections of 1956. Guerilla warfare resumed in 1959, and Ho died before negotiations took place.

Leader	Circumstances of birth	Circumstances of education	When and how did they become involved in the independence movement or colonial administration?	What made them take the course they ultimately followed?	When did they organize independence movements?	How did they manifest opposition to colonial rule?	Were they imprisoned? Exiled? How long?	When and under what circumstances were concessions made? With what result?
Felix Houphouet-Boigny	Born October 18, 1905? at Yamoussoukro, Côte d'Ivoire, French West Africa. Son of a wealthy chief.	Educated at Bingonville; attended medical school at Dakar, Senegal.	In 1944, he organized the African planters' movement to seek equality with European planters. Elected to French National Assembly in 1945; re-elected in 1946.	In October 1946 elected president of Reassemblent Africain (RDA), a movement seeking emancipation of Africans. Realizing that political mobilization and coalition-building was important, he founded the Party of Côte d'Ivoire (PDCI) in 1946.	Advocated autonomy within the French Community rather than independence. Wanted more autonomy for territories, but believed that political and economic ties with France would be beneficial.	He did not advocate opposition to colonials. Wished to stay in de Gaulle's new French African Community.	No	Charles de Gaulle offered French territories referendum on whether to join federal community of West African states or become independent. Houphouet-Boigny campaigned and won right to stay within community, with limited French governing authority. However, Houphouet-Boigny and PDCI campaigned and won independence in 1960 after France gave all states complete autonomy.
Muhammad Ali Jinnah	Born December 25, 1876, in Karachi, India. Son of prosperous merchant.	Taught at home and at Sind-Madrassat. He then went to London and joined Lincoln's Inn, a legislative society.	Participated in 1906 Calcutta session of the Indian National Congress (INC). Four years later he was elected to Imperial Legislative Council.	Election of 1937 saw absolute majority of INC in 6 provinces; Jinnah decides not to include the Muslim League in formation of provincial governments, and an all-Congress government resulted.	On March 22 and 23, 1940, in Lahore, the Muslim League adopted resolution to form separate Muslim state.	Strove to keep peace between Muslim and Hindus through Legislative Assembly, roundtable conference, and through his 14 Points, which espoused his views on a successful federal form of government.	No.	Riots between Muslims and Hindus forced Indians to accept partition, as they knew they would face civil war or a weak federation if they did not concede. Independence on August 14, 1947.

Jomo Kenyatta	Born in 1890? in Khgaweri, Kenya. Son of peasant father of tribal Kikuyu descent.	Attended Thogoto Presbyterian Mission School. Started at about age 10 and finished at about age 15. Spent 2 years at Moscow State University. Earned advanced degree in anthropology from London School of Economics.	Joined Kikuyu Central Association (KCA) in early 1922.	Ascendance as general secretary of KCA in 1927, and subsequent visit to London to discuss Kikuyu land rights. Publishing of *Muigwithania*, a native-language journal.	Joined KCA political protest movement in 1922. Elected president of Kenya African Union and organized mass nationalist party.	Wrote about Kikuyu interests for English newspapers. *Muigwithania* garnered political support from Kikuyu peoples. Printed pamphlets.	Arrested Oct. 21, 1952, for having directed the Mau Mau rebellion. Sentenced to 7 years' imprisonment, although he spent 9 years in prison.	In 1932, Kenyatta testified to Carter Land Commission and got compensation for Kikuyu lands. As a result of increased demands, Britain steered Kenya toward majority rule (1960). At London Conference in 1962, he negotiated constitutional terms which led to independence. Kenyan African National Union (KANU) won election of 1963, forming provisional government, with full independence on December 12, 1963, with Kenyatta as Prime Minister.
Patrice Lumumba	Born in Onalua, Belgian Congo, on July 2, 1925. A member of the small Batetela tribe.	Protestant mission school. Largely self-educated.	Became president of Congolese trade union of government employees. Became active in Belgian Liberal Party. Wrote essays and poems for journals.	Imprisoned on grounds of embezzlement. After release from prison, founded the Congolese National Movement (MNC), the first nationwide Congolese political party. Attended the first Pan-African Conference in Accra.	In October 1958, he organized the MNC, an organization that visualized independence for the Congo.	In June 1959, MNC and other groups petitioned Belgians for individual liberties. Thereafter, Lumumba began to hold speeches advocating independence. Launched journal *Independence* in 1960 to express grievances. MNC boycotted elections of 1960.	Imprisoned and sentenced for 12 months in 1956. Charged and imprisoned for inciting a riot in 1959, but released to attend Brussels roundtable conference in 1960.	Believing that their political associates would take over the government, Belgium conceded to the boycott of elections and riots by allowing free elections and independence. The election was held in May 1960, in which the MNC won a landslide victory, humiliating the Belgians. Formal independence was gained on June 23, 1960.

Leader	Circumstances of birth	Circumstances of education	When and how did they become involved in the independence movement or colonial administration?	What made them take the course they ultimately followed?	When did they organize independence movements?	How did they manifest opposition to colonial rule?	Were they imprisoned? Exiled? How long?	When and under which circumstances were concessions made? With what result?
Samora Machel	Born in Xilenbene, Gaza Province, Mozambique, on Sept. 29, 1933. Son of pastor.	Primary school at Catholic mission school. Took course for a career in nursing in Xai-Xai and Lourenço Marques, now Maputo.	Fled Portuguese secret police to Tanzania in 1963, when he joined Frente de Liberticao de Mocambique (FRELIMO).	Medical work in medical institutions in South Africa, along with injustices suffered by his parents and deaths of his brothers convinced him to reject his *assimilado* status. Decision to join FRELIMO catapulted Machel as leader in revolutionary movement. Deeply impressed by meeting with Eduardo Mondlane in 1961.	Established FRELIMO's first training base and commanded first assault on Portuguese positions in September 1964. Became FRELIMO's Secretary of Defense in 1964. Elected President of FRELIMO in 1970.	Guerilla warfare starting in 1964. Machel established FRELIMO's Nachingwea Center for Political and Military Training. Wrote articles advocating liberation.	No.	Frustrations of Portuguese junior officers in a conventionally trained European infantry fighting a counter-insurgency campaign in Africa, contributed to the officers' coup in Lisbon, April 1974. Overthrow of Portuguese regime and signing of cease-fire and transitional government provisions on September 7, 1974 led to Mozambique independence on June 25, 1975, with Machel as president of the new republic.
Nelson Mandela	Born July 19, 1918, in Transkei province of South Africa. Son of a chief of Xhosa-speaking Tembu Tribe.	Attended school at palace of Tembu regent after father's death. At age 19 went to Clarkesbury Secondary School. Attended University College of Fort Hare and University of Witwatersrand for law degree.	Joined African National Congress (ANC) in 1944 and in 1949 became one of its leaders.	After massacre of unarmed Africans by police in 1960 and subsequent banning of ANC, he began to advocate a militant stance for liberation.	Ascendance to leadership of ANC in 1949.	Passive resistance, boycotts, strikes; later, though, he advocated acts of sabotage and terrorism.	In 1962, he was sentenced to 5 years in prison for advocating sabotage. On June 11, 1964, sentenced to life in prison. Released by de Klerk in 1990.	The ascendance of F. W. de Klerk to presidency led to more talks of reconciliation. De Klerk accepted almost all of Harare Declaration of 1989, which called for release of political prisoners, lifting of bans on all organizations, and removal of troops from townships. ANC thus called off its terror tactics. New constitution was drawn. The first multi-party, multi-racial elections held April 1994. Mandela inaugurated as president on May 10, 1994.

Eduardo Mondlane						
Born 1920 in Manjacaze, Mozambique. Son of a regent of a clan of the Tsonga people, who had fought in resistance against the Portuguese.	Rudimentary school in Manjacaze, beginning at age 12. Mission primary school in Lourenco Marques. Agricultural training at the American Methodist Episcopal Mission in Khambane. Douglas Laing Smith Secondary School in South Africa in 1944, later matriculating to University of Witwatersrand in South Africa. Brief study at University of Lisbon before traveling to United States for B.A. at Oberlin College. M.A. and Ph.D in anthropology from Northwestern University.	While studying in South Africa, Mondlane became involved in nationalistic political activities. While in Lisbon, Mondlane came to know other anticolonial nationalists, such as Agostinho Neto and Amilcar Cabral.	Under the auspices of the United Nations Trusteeship Council, Mondlane traveled to Mozambique in 1961. The support of the people convinced Mondlane of the need for African liberation.	Formed connections with resistance groups upon 1961 trip to Mozambique. On June 25, 1962, the Frente de Libertacao de Mocambique, or the Front for the Liberation of Mozambique (FRELIMO), was founded, with Mondlane as president.	Guerilla warfare. Extensive traveling to the West in order to campaign on behalf of the Mozambican cause. Wrote numerous articles promoting liberation; published one book, *The Struggle for Mozambique*, in 1969.	In 1948, Mondlane was expelled from South Africa as result of his political activities. Upon his return, the Portuguese sent Mondlane to Portugal because of his nationalistic stance. After 1 year of harassment by secret police, he left Portugal for the United States.	Between 1964 and 1968, 1/3 of Mozambique liberated by guerillas. Mondlane killed in 1969 by mail bomb in Dar es Salaam, Tanzania, at height of resistance movement. Mondlane succeeded by Samora Machel. Officers' coup in Portugal in April, 1974, paved way for liberation of Mozambique. Official day of independence on June 25, 1975.

Leader	Circumstances of birth	Circumstances of education	When and how did they become involved in the independence movement or colonial administration?	What made them take the course they ultimately followed?	When did they organize independence movements?	How did they manifest opposition to colonial rule?	Were they imprisoned? Exiled? How long?	When and under what circumstances were concessions made? With what result?
Robert Gabriel Mugabe	Born February 21, 1924, in Kutama, Southern Rhodesia. Son of wealthy village carpenter.	Trained as teacher in Roman Catholic mission school. Studied at University College of Fort Hare, South Africa. Law degree through correspondence from prison.	Aided Reverend Ndabaningi Sithole for Zimbabwe African National Union (ZANU) as breakaway from Zimbabwe African People's Union.	Imprisonment for subversive speech against British government. Led coup from prison in 1974 deposing Sithole as ZANU's leader.	Formed ZANU in 1963.	Public meetings under the auspices of ZANU denying European culture; boycotts; guerilla civil war.	Imprisoned for 11 years.	After guerilla war and ascension of Margaret Thatcher to power, the British announced plans to decolonize in 1979. Elections were set for 1980, at which time Zimbabwe (Rhodesia) gained independence.
Gamal-Abdel Nasser	Born January 15, 1918, in Alexandria, Egypt. Son of a minor postal worker.	Started education at age 8. Secondary school mostly in Alexandria. Attended law school for several months, but graduated from Royal Military Academy as 2nd Lieutenant.	Participated in anti-British demonstrations during his teenage years; joined Young Egypt, a nationalist organization, in 1934	The war in Palestine after World War II angered Arabs and led Nasser to realize the weakness of the Arab states. At that time the Free Officers began to organize and establish connections with the military and civil society.	While serving in the army, Nasser, along with Zakaria Mohieddine, Abdel Hikim Amer, and Anwar as-Sadat formed Free Officers, a nationalist organization that hoped to oust the British forces and the Egyptian royal family.	As a young boy, Nasser demonstrated. Nationalist pamphlets appeared in 1949; later, the Free Officers smuggled arms to guerillas fighting the British.	No.	After "Black Saturday," during which Britons were killed in mob fashion, King Farouk dismissed the Wafd government. Subsequently, the Free Officers planned a coup for July 23, 1952, overthrowing the puppet king. In January 1956, Nasser announced the promulgation of a new constitution claiming Egypt a socialist Arab state.

Jawaharlal Nehru	Born November 14, 1889, in Allahabad, India. Son of wealthy lawyer and one of Gandhi's lieutenants. Sister later became first woman president of UN General Assembly.	Until 16, he was educated at home by tutors. In 1905, he went to Harrow, in England. Then he went to Trinity College and spent 3 years earning honors degree in natural science. He qualified as a barrister after 2 years at the Inner Temple, a law society.	Nehru and his father became active in nationalist causes after meeting Gandhi and being introduced to the Indian National Congress (INC).	Fervent post-World War I nationalist activity and government repression. Amritsar massacre in April 1919.	Apprenticed with INC from 1919–1929; in 1923 and 1927 he served separate 2-year terms as general secretary of the INC. He presided over the Lahore session of the INC in 1929, which proclaimed complete independence as its goal.	Passive resistance, boycotts, marches.	Served 9 periods of detention; longest was almost 3 years ending in June 1945. In all, his time in jail amounted to about 9 years.	The Japanese attacked India via Burma, and Churchill made attempts to patch the constitutional problem. However, the INC would accept nothing less than full independence. The Party passed the Quit India resolution on Aug. 8, 1942, which subsequently led to the banning of the INC and widespread protests and terrorist activity. Labour Party triumph in 1945 and the Mountbatten Plan of June 3, 1947, set the day of independence and the mode of partition.
Kwame Nkrumah	Born in Nkroful, Ghana, on September 21, 1909. Son of moderately wealthy goldsmith.	Educated at Catholic mission schools and graduated from Achimota College in 1931. Received degrees in economics and sociology at Lincoln University in the United States; postgraduate degree from University of Pennsylvania.	Helped organize Pan-African Congress in 1945.	In 1947, he accepted invitation to join the United Gold Coast Convention (UGCC), where he saw that the populace was pressing for change.	1947 joined the United Gold Coast Convention (UGCC).	Organized the UGCC and set up party branches in every town to prepare for self-rule. Participated in demonstrations, boycotts, and strikes. Convened the Constitutional Assembly to draft constitution.	Arrested for leading demonstrations, but let go after 8 weeks to minimize further unrest. Arrested Jan 1950 and received 1-year sentence.	Britain set up the Commission of Inquiry that recommended a more democratic constitution for Ghana. Boycotts succeeded in forcing the British to agree to lower prices in February 1948. Election of Convention People's Party (CPP) in 1951 demonstrated inability of British to govern any longer. Decolonizing began with ascendance of Nkrumah as prime minister. Full independence on March 6, 1957.

Leader	Circumstances of birth	Circumstances of education	When and how did they become involved in the independence movement or colonial administration?	What made them take the course they ultimately followed?	When did they organize independence movements?	How did they manifest opposition to colonial rule?	Were they imprisoned? Exiled? How long?	When and under what circumstances were concessions made? With what result?
Sam Nujoma	Born May 12, 1929, in Owambo, South-West Africa (Namibia). Son of peasant parents.	Primary School, 1937–1948, in Ovamboland. Secondary education at St. Barnabas School, 1949–1954, in Windhoek.	Joined labor movement after becoming a railway worker.	Inequities in contract labor system and unfairness toward blacks.	1957, founded the Ovamboland People's Congress, the forerunner to the South-West African People's Organization (SWAPO).	Boycotted removals of "natives" from Windhoek. SWAPO staged guerilla war against South Africa and compelled the United Nations to condemn South Africa's continued presence in Namibia.	Imprisoned for a week in 1959, released and fled before trial. Returned in 1989 after 30 years.	1971, the International Court of Justice upheld UN authority of Namibia, and demanded South Africa to withdraw. UN Resolution 435 was passed in 1977, largely a work of Nujoma and Western powers, which laid out provisions for UN-supervised elections. South Africa retreated on April 1, 1989. Elections were held in Nov. 1989. March 21, 1990, is formal day of independence.
Leopold Sedar Senghor	Born October 9, 1906, in Joal, Senegal, French West Africa. Son of wealthy trader of the Serer tribe.	Roman Catholic school. At age 20 transferred to secondary school in Dakar. In 1928, he was granted partial scholarship to Paris and studied at the Lycee Louis-le-Grand and the Sorbonne.	Fought in World War II. Member of French Constituent Assembly. Founded Senegalese Democratic Bloc in 1948 and pushed for reforms that would make French Union a true federation of equal states.	In 1956, the French Parliament passed *loi cadre*, a resolution giving a large amount of self-rule to the territories, which Senghor opposed. Senghor founded and supported parties dedicated to federal African unity.	Late 1948, Senghor founded the Bloc Democratique Senegalais (BDS).	Published paper, *La Condition Humaine* (The Human Condition), in which he sought to educate the masses and mobilize them into political action. Leading advocate of negritude.	No.	French troubles in 1957 culminated in the dissolution of the Fourth Republic in 1958, and de Gaulle's offer of referendum sparked fervor. Senegal and Soudan entered into the Mali Federation, although Dahomey and Upper Volta failed to do so. Senegal and Soudan became an autonomous federation in 1961, with Senegal breaking away from the federation in January 1961 and declaring itself an independent state.

Sukarno	Born June 6, 1901, in Surabaja, Java, Dutch East Indies. Son of poor Javanese schoolteacher.	At age 15, sent to secondary school in Surabaja, then to Bandung Technical Institute, where he acquired civil engineering degree.	In 1925 formed the Algemeene Sudiee Club (General Study Club), which was an overtly political organization with independence as its goal.	Partai Komonis Indonesia, Indonesian Communist Party (PKI) rebellion was crushed in 1926–1927. The Sarekat Islam, or Islamic Union, waned in activity, and nationalism came to the fore.	Study Club founded the Partai Nasional Indonesia, or Indonesian Nationalist Party (PNI), in 1927.	Public meetings denouncing colonial rule, coalition building of rival ethnicities and religions, development of Malay/Indonesian language to promote communication.	Imprisoned by Dutch for 2 years, for challenging colonialism, from 1929–1931. Spent 8 years in exile (1933–1942). Released when Japanese invaded.	After Japan surrendered, Sukarno declared independence on August 17, 1945. Dutch tried to regain Indonesia, but were condemned by the United States and the United Nations for their actions, and were eventually fought off. Formally transferred power on Dec. 27, 1949.
Ahmed Sékou Touré	Born Jan. 9, 1952, in Faraneh, French Guinea. Son of poor, uneducated parents. Claimed to be grandson of nineteenth-century activist, resistant to French rule.	Attended French technical school for 1 year at Conakry, but expelled for leading a "food riot."	Became administrative assistant in postal service; subsequently took interest in labor movement and organized the first successful strike (76 days) in French West Africa.	Became active in politics in the Reassemblent Democratique Africain (RDA). Barred from taking position in French National Assembly in 1951 and in 1954 but finally allowed to take seat in 1955.	Touré led Parti Democratique de Guinee (PDG), beginning in 1947, and trade union movement, demanding a voice in labor and better working conditions. After de Gaulle's offer of referendum for self-determination in 1958, he campaigned for independence.	Led wave of strikes between 1945 and 1952, which put pressure on colonials for better pay. Wrote extensively in L'Ouvier (The Worker), denouncing miserable living conditions.	Imprisoned for 3 days in June, 1960, to silence his work with labor.	Labor movement led to increased aid in 1951 and 1953. French defeat at Dien Bien Phu and the Algerian Independence of 1954 heightened fervor for independence and raised doubts about France's infallibility. July 18, 1958, PDG and RDA issued declaration for right to determine independence, just as the Fourth Republic of France crumbled. France conceded, thinking that Guinea would soon rejoin the Federation. On October 2, 1958, Guinea voted, gained independence.

NOTES

INTRODUCTION

1. How to refer to the group of formerly colonial, generally poor countries has been a constant dilemma for journalists, academics, and politicians. "Undeveloped" and "less developed" were considered pejorative. "Developing" has come to be accepted as has, with reservations, "Third World." In his article "Is There a Third World?" (*Current History* 98, no. 631 [November 1999]: 355), Martin W. Lewis describes the dilemma:

> The term "third world" can easily be construed as insulting, not to mention confusing and contradictory. Why on earth would we want to relegate this, or any other part of the world, to a third position? "The global zone of poverty," as a colleague of mine recently pointed out, "is not a third world at all, but is rather at least two-thirds of the entire world." After wrestling at length with these and other conceptual challenges, I have tried to drop the word from my geographical lexicon altogether. But this is no easy task. The "three worlds" notion is deeply imbedded in professional as well as popular geography, and most alternatives, including the even simpler "North-South" formula entail headaches of their own.

2. Described in Santha Rama Rau, *Home to India* (New York and London: Harper and Brothers, 1944), 28.

3. Michael Howard, "The Bewildered American Raj: Reflections on a Democracy's Foreign Policy," *Harper's Magazine* (March 1985): 55–60.

4. David D. Newsom, "Exporting America," *California Monthly* (September 1949): 12–13.

5. James Reston, "History's Revenge," *New York Times*, June 23, 1983.

6. Letter from author from American Embassy, Jakarta, to the Honorable Carol C. Laise, Assistant Secretary for Public Affairs, November 5, 1974.

7. Robert J. Samuelson, "End of the Third World," *The Washington Post*, July 18, 1990, A23.

1. THE MARCH OF EMPIRE

1. Daniel Boorstin, *The Discoverers* (New York: Random House, 1983), 163. Boorstin describes the caravel thus: "These remarkable little vessels were large enough to hold an explorer's supplies for a small crew of about twenty, who usually slept on deck but in bad weather went below. The caravel displaced about fifty tons, was about seventy feet in length and about twenty-five feet in the beam, and carried two or three lateen sails" (164).

2. Rouhollah K. Ramazani, *The Persian Gulf: Iran's Role* (Charlottesville: University of Virginia Press, 1972), 11.

3. "The History of European Overseas Expansion: European Expansion since 1763," *Encyclopedia Britannica, CD98.*

4. Quoted in Brian Lapping, *End of Empire* (London: Granada Publishing, 1985), 448.

5. Ibid., 450.

6. Ibid.

7. John Henrik Clarke, "Time of Troubles (1402–1828)," 335. Chapter 9 of A. Adu Boahen, et al., *The Horizon History of Africa* (New York: American Heritage Publishing, 1971), 353–375.

8. A. Adu Boahen, "The Coming of the Europeans," in *The Horizon History of Africa*, by A. Adu Boahen et al. (New York: American Heritage Publishing Co., 1971), 318.

9. Lapping, *The End of Empire,* 232.

10. Ibid., 153–154.

11. Ibid., 191.

12. The United States had consular courts for U.S. citizens in Morocco and Oman until the 1930s, when Congress abolished the right to negotiate such privileges except in the case of U.S. service personnel abroad. Even that exception, embodied in status-of-forces agreements, would haunt Washington in future years.

13. William L. Langer, ed., *An Encyclopedia of World History* (Boston Houghton Mifflin Co., 1962), 1117.

14. As quoted in Samuel Eliot Morison, *The Oxford History of the American People* (New York: Oxford University Press, 1965), 414.

15. Ibid., 826.

2. THE NATURE OF IMPERIALISM

1. Lapping, *End of Empire,* 21.

2. See Appendix, "Backgrounds of Liberation Leaders."

3. "Philippines: History: The Spanish Period," *Encyclopedia Britannica, CD98.*

4. Multatuli [Eduard Douwes Dekker], *Max Havelaar; or, The Coffee Auctions of the Dutch Trading Company* (Sijthoff Leyden/Heinemann London, 1967), 211.

5. Donald Easum (former assistant secretary for Africa and ambassador to Upper Volta and Nigeria) to author, December 4, 1999.

6. Stephen, Neill, *A History of Christian Missions* (Harmondsworth, Middlesex, England: Penguin Books), 323.

7. Ibid., 324.

8. Ibid, 432.

9. "Christianity: The Christian Community; Protestant Missions 1500–1950," *Encyclopedia Britannica, CD98.*

10. Quoted in Neill, *A History of Christian Mission,* 426.

11. Chinua Achebe, *Things Fall Apart* (Nairobi: East African Educational Publishers, African Writer Series, 1962), 130ff.

12. Stanlake Samkange, "Wars of Resistance," in *The Horizon History of Africa,* by A. Adu Boahen et al. (New York: American Heritage Publishing Co., 1971), 403.

13. Multatuli, *Max Havalaar,* 215.

14. As told to me by Robert Stimson of the *Times of India* in 1940.

15. Byron Farwell, *Armies of the Raj* (New York: W.W. Norton and Co., 1989).

16. Conversation with Andrew Stewart, May 5, 1999.

17. Lapping, *End of Empire,* 27–28.

3. INDEPENDENCE

1. Mien Soedarpo, *Reminiscences of the Past* (Jakarta: The Sejati Foundation, 1994), 47.

2. For a full discussion of the constraints on today's nation-state see Adam Watson, *The Limits of Independence* (London and New York: Routledge, 1997).

3. Information based on Chris Cook and David Killingray, *African Political Facts since 1945* (London: Macmillan, 1991), and *Facts On File.*

4. John Keegan, *War and Our World* (London: Hutchinson, 1998), 66.

5. Quoted in Lapping, *End of Empire,* 484.

6. Meg Greenfield, "Gambling on Democracy," *The Washington Post,* November 10, 1982, A31.

7. Robert J. McMahon, *Colonialism and Cold War: The United States and the Struggle for Indonesian Independence, 1945–1949* (Ithaca, N.Y.: Cornell University Press, 1981), 39.

8. Quoted in ibid., 75.

9. Paul Gardner, *Shared Hopes, Separate Fears: Fifty Years of U.S.-Indonesian Relations* (Boulder and Oxford: Westview Press, 1997), 3.

10. McMahon, *Colonialism and Cold War,* 56.

11. Walter Lippmann, *Public Opinion* (New York: Free Press Paperbacks, 1997), 214–215.

12. William Dunseath Eaton, Harry C. Read, and Edmund McKenna, *Woodrow Wilson: His Life and Work* (Washington, D.C.: J. Thomas, 1924), 418.

13. Quoted in McMahon, *Colonialism and Cold War,* 69.

14. Quoted in ibid., 59.

15. Quoted in ibid., 54.

16. Quoted in Lapping, *End of Empire,* 6.

17. Quoted in McMahon, *Colonialism and Cold War,* 55.

18. James MacGregor Burns, *Roosevelt: The Lion and the Fox* (San Diego: Harcourt Brace Jovanovich), 459.

19. *Foreign Relations of the United States 1945,* VI, 293. (Hereafter *FRUS.*)

20. Dean Acheson, *Present At the Creation* (New York: W.W. Norton, 1969), 671.

21. Ibid., 673.

22. McMahon, *Colonialism and Cold War,* 62.

23. From Franklin D. Roosevelt, *FDR: His Personal Letters,* vol. 2, ed. Elliott Roosevelt (New York: Duell, Sloan, and Pearce, 1947), 1304. Quoted in Gardner, *Shared Hopes, Separate Fears,* 5.

24. See Chapter 10.

25. *New York Times,* July 3, 1957, 5.

4. FREEDOM IN ASIA

1. McMahon, *Colonialism and Cold War,* 22–23.

2. For more on the U.S. role, see Chapter 11.

3. "Philippines: History: The Period of US Influence," *Encyclopedia Britannica CD98,* 2.

4. The French Union was a political entity from 1946 to 1958 that was comprised of Metropolitan France (France proper and Corsica) and its overseas territories.

5. Statement by Gerald Da Cruz quoted in Lapping, *End of Empire,* 163.

6. Yogesh Chadha, *Rediscovering Gandhi* (London: Arrow Books, 1997), 53.

7. Quoted in Lapping, *End of Empire,* 29.

8. Ibid.

9. Bipan Chandra, et al. *India's Struggle for Independence* (New Delhi: Penguin Books India, 1989), 80–81.

10. Lapping, *End of Empire,* 35.

11. For a more complete account see Chadha, *Rediscovering Gandhi,* 237ff.

12. Lord Irwin became Lord Halifax, Foreign Secretary under Neville Chamberlain and subsequently ambassador to the United States.

13. Speech at Mansion House, London, November 10, 1942.

14. Quoted in Chadha, *Rediscovering Gandhi,* 300.

5. FICTIONAL INDEPENDENCE

1. R. K. Ramazani, *Revolutionary Iran: Challenge and Response in the Middle East* (Baltimore and London: Johns Hopkins University Press, 1988), 201.

2. Letter from R. K. Ramazani to author, November 26, 1999. The subject of the status-of-forces agreement is also discussed at greater length in R. K. Ramazani, *Iran's Foreign Policy, 1941–1973* (Charlottesville: University of Virginia Press, 1975), 361–363.

3. See George Antonius, *The Arab Awakening* (Beirut: Khayats, 1938).

4. Quoted in George Lenczowski, *The Middle East in World Affairs,* 4th ed. (Ithaca, N.Y., and London: Cornell University Press, 1980), 77.

5. Quoted in ibid., 85.

6. Ibid., 485.

7. Lapping, *End of Empire,* 107.

8. Lenczowski, *Middle East in World Affairs,* 520.

9. Ibid., 529.

10. Roger Kirk to author, November 11, 1999. Senator Walter F. George, Democrat of Georgia, was a member of the Senate Foreign Relations Committee.

11. Lapping, *End of Empire*, 320.

12. Ibid.

13. From Hansard, quoted in ibid., 321.

14. Ibid., 336.

15. Ibid., 349.

6. THE GULF AND THE PENINSULA

1. An agreement that gave Britain responsibility for Kuwait's foreign and defense affairs, so-called because it was signed in a date garden.

2. Rouhollah K. Ramazani, *The Persian Gulf: Iran's Role* (Charlottesville: University of Virginia Press, 1972), 56–68.

3. For more on Yemen as it was in 1945, see Chapter XVII, "The Land of the Imam" in Richard H. Sanger, *The Arabian Peninsula* (Freeport, N.Y.: Books for Libraries Press, 1970), 235–252.

4. Quoted in Lapping, *End of Empire*, 283.

5. Ibid., 294.

6. Ibid., 295.

7. Ibid., 302–303.

8. Elizabeth Monroe, *Britain's Moment in the Middle East* (London: Chatto and Windus, 1981), 214.

9. Lapping, *End of Empire*, 310.

7. AFRICA I

1. Lapping, *End of Empire*, 369–370.

2. Quoted in ibid., 371.

3. Ibid., 383.

4. Ibid., 435.

5. Immanuel Wallerstein, "Africa for the Africans," in *The Horizon History of Africa*, by A. Adu Boahen et al. (New York: American Heritage Publishing Co., 1971), 497–498.

6. Quoted in Francis Terry McNamara, *France in Black Africa* (Washington, D.C.: National Defense University Press, 1989), 49.

7. Quoted in ibid., 51.

8. Ibid., 59.

9. Ibid., 98.

10. William Drozdiak, "French Ties To Africa Undergo Key Change," *The Washington Post*, January 22, 1994, A10.

11. Ibid.

12. Ibid.

13. McNamara, *France in Black Africa*, 165.

14. For more details on Foccart, see ibid., 186–198 and Foccart's memoirs, *Foccart Parle* (Paris: Fayard/Jeune Afrique, 1995). Jim Farley was a prominent Democratic Party operative in the Franklin Roosevelt administration, well known for his capacity to remember names.

15. McNamara, *France in Black Africa*, 128–129.

16. Ibid., 108.

17. The details of Leopold's rule are graphically described in Adam Hochschild, *King Leopold's Ghost* (Boston and New York: Houghton Mifflin Co., 1999).

8. AFRICA II

1. Quoted in Lapping, *End of Empire*, 13–14.

2. Peter Calvocoressi, *World Politics since 1945*, 7th ed. (London and New York: Longman, 1996), 740.

3. In 1969, when the last full census was taken in Rhodesia/Zimbabwe, the population consisted of 4,818,000 Africans, 228,044 Europeans, and 23,525 Asians. R. Kent Rasmussen, *Historical Dictionary of Rhodesia/Zimbabwe* (Metuchen, N.J.: Scarecrow Press, 1979).

4. Lapping, *End of Empire*, 490.

5. Ibid., 506.

6. Ibid., 507.

7. Quoted in ibid., 397.

8. Ibid., 404.

9. Ibid., 407.

10. Quoted in ibid., 417. For indications that Macharia may have been bribed by the government, see ibid., 415.

11. Ibid., 425–426.

12. Quoted in ibid., 442.

9. THE LEGACY OF THE TWENTIETH CENTURY

1. "India: Progress and Plans," *The Washington Post,* October 6, 1998, A13.

2. Edward Said, *Orientalism* (New York: Vintage Books, 1994).

3. *Ujama* was a form of village collectivization introduced in Tanzania by Julius Nyerere in the 1960s.

4. Researcher Stephen Norris has contributed text to this section.

5. G. H. Jansen, *Nonalignment and the Afro-Asian States* (New York: Frederick A. Praeger, 1966), 29.

6. Ibid.

7. Panch Sheel is Hindi for "five principles." The principles include mutual respect for other nations, territorial integrity and sovereignty, non-aggression, non-interference in internal affairs, and peaceful coexistence. *Encyclopedia Britannica CD98.*

8. Daniel Yergin, *The Prize* (New York: Simon and Schuster, 1991), 706.

9. Ian Skeet, *OPEC: Twenty-five Years of Prices and Politics* (Cambridge: Cambridge University Press, 1988), 153.

10. ECONOMICS

1. The U.S. plan for the reconstruction of war-damaged Western Europe.

2. For a summary of the Dutch-nationalist conflict, see Chapter 4. For more complete accounts of the negotiations leading to independence, see Gardner, *Shared Hopes, Separate Fears;* and McMahon, *Colonialism and Cold War.*

3. Quoted in Gardner, *Shared Hopes, Separate Fears,* 34.

4. Quoted in McMahon, *Colonialism and the Cold War,* 256.

5. Quoted in Gardner, *Shared Hopes, Separate Fears,* 88.

6. Henry Kissinger, *Years of Upheaval* (Boston and Toronto: Little Brown and Co., 1982), 885.

7. *State Department Bulletin,* May 27, 1974, 572.

8. Adapted from the text of UN General Assembly Resolution 3201, cited above, 573.

9. *State Department Bulletin,* May 27, 1974, 569.

10. *State Department Bulletin,* October 13, 1975, 557.

11. Ibid., 558.

12. *State Department Bulletin,* May 27, 1974, 571.

13. *State Department Bulletin,* February 3, 1975, 147.

14. Kissinger, *Years of Upheaval,* 1092.

15. USIS Wireless File, No. 93, May 14, 1975.

16. Ibid.

17. This anecdote is also in my book *Diplomacy and the American Democracy* (Bloomington and Indianapolis: Indiana University Press, 1988), 86–87.

18. *Department of State Bulletin,* September 22, 1975, 426.

19. Ibid., 430.

20. "Turnaround at U.N." *New York Times,* September 18, 1975, 40.

21. Ibid.

22. USIA Backgrounder, Wireless File, May 6, 1976, No. 17/76-EB, 4.

23. Ibid. 8.

24. Michael T. Kaufman, "Extent of Kissinger Offer Surprises Parley Aides," *New York Times,* May 8, 1976, 3.

25. Ibid.

26. Calvocoressi, *World Politics since 1945,* 184.

27. For a more complete discussion of the problems of foreign aid see my *Diplomacy and the American Democracy,* 161–178.

28. In his inaugural address in January 1949, President Truman proposed, as the fourth recommendation of his speech, a program of technical assistance for poorer countries. This became known as the Point Four program.

11. THE COLD WAR

1. Quoted in Waldemar Gallman, *Iraq under General Nuri* (Baltimore: Johns Hopkins Press, 1964), 22.

2. Elmer Plischke, ed., *Contemporary U.S. Foreign Policy* (Westport, Conn.: Greenwood Press, 1991), 440.

3. Ibid., 187.

4. Ibid., 188.

5. Author's recollection of an account of the visit by Ambassador John Jernegan, who accompanied Richards.

6. Plischke, *Contemporary U.S. Foreign Policy,* 438–439.

7. Ibid., 440.

8. South Korea, Thailand, Philippines, New Zealand, and Australia.

9. *FRUS 1945,* VI, 293.

10. Ibid., 300.

11. *FRUS 1948,* VI, 28.

12. *FRUS 1949,* VII, 13–14.

13. Ibid.

14. Ibid., 55–56.

15. Ibid., 57–58.

16. *FRUS 1949,* VII, 106.

17. *FRUS 1950,* VI, 694.

18. Ibid., 697.

19. See Robert Schulzinger, *A Time for War: The United States and Vietnam, 1941–1975* (London and New York: Oxford University Press, 1997).

20. *FRUS 1950,* V, 1461–1463.

21. Author's recollection.

22. Gallman, *Iraq under General Nuri,* 194–195.

23. Dennis Kux, *India and the United States: Estranged Democracies* (Washington, D.C.: National Defense University Press, 1992), 267.

12. AFRICA, RACE, AND POLITICS

1. William B. Helmreich, comp., *Afro-Americans and Africa: Black Nationalism at the Crossroads* (Westport, Conn.: Greenwood Press, 1977), x.

2. Arthur Schlesinger, Jr., *A Thousand Days* (Boston: Houghton Mifflin Co., 1965), 560.

3. William Roger Louis and Ronald Robinson, "Empire preserv'd," *Time Literary Supplement,* May 5, 1995, 14–16.

4. Dean Rusk, as told to Richard Rusk, *As I Saw It* (New York and London: W.W. Norton & Co. 1990.), 273–274.

5. Schlesinger, *A Thousand Days,* 561.

6. Chester A. Crocker, *High Noon In Southern Africa* (New York and London: W.W. Norton and Co., 1992), 254–255.

7. George McGhee, *Envoy to the Middle World* (New York: Harper and Row, 1983), 159.

8. William Minter, "The Limits of Liberal Africa Policy: Lessons from the Congo Crisis," *TransAfrica Forum* 2, no. 3 (Fall 1984): 38.

9. For a full account of the last days of Lumumba, see Stephen R. Weissman, *American Foreign Policy in the Congo, 1960–1964* (Ithaca and London: Cornell University Press, 1974), 85–99, 107.

10. Rhodesian UDI came in the midst of the civil rights debate in the administration of Lyndon B. Johnson.

11. Charlton Chesterton, *The Real Case for Rhodesia* (Honeydew, Transvaal: Janssonius and Heyns, 1973), 9.

12. Quoted in Thomas J. Noer, *Black Liberation: The US and White Rule in Africa 1948–68* (Columbia: University of Missouri Press, 1985), 209.

13. For a more complete account of steps leading up to the closing of the consulate in Salisbury, see Anthony Lake, *The Tar Baby Option* (New York: Columbia University Press, 1976), 134–144.

14. For a full discussion of Rhodesian sanctions see Harry R. Strack, *Sanctions: The Case of Rhodesia* (Syracuse, N.Y.: Syracuse University Press, 1978), esp. 16–21.

15. For a full case study of the Byrd Amendment, see ibid., 146–164.

16. Quoted in Lake, *The Tar Baby Option*, 227.

17. For a more complete account of the Biafran relief issue see Joseph E. Thompson, *American Policy and African Famine: The Nigeria-Biafra War, 1966–1970* (Westport, Conn.: Greenwood Press, 1990).

18. Statement by Republic candidate Nixon on September 9, 1968, quoted in Suzanne Cronje, *The World and Nigeria* (London: Sidgwick and Jackson, 1972), 226.

19. For a more detailed account of the complex military maneuvers at the time of Angolan independence see Raymond L. Garthoff, *Detente and Confrontation* (Washington, D.C.: The Brookings Institution, 1985), 502–537.

20. Donald Easum, at the time U.S. ambassador to Nigeria, wrote in a letter to the author on December 4, 1999, "Joe Garba, Nigerian Foreign Minister at the time, summoned me immediately upon learning of the South African action. He said he was under instruction to inform me that unless I could obtain from Kissinger a disavowal of the South African action or at least a statement to the effect that the U.S. had nothing to do with it, Nigerian policy would swing immediately from trying to mediate between the various African factions to full support and exclusive recognition of the MPLA and a pledge of military training and other assistance. I received nothing from Kissinger."

21. *Facts On File*, February 14, 1975, 270.

22. Nathaniel Davis, "The Angola Decision of 1975," *Foreign Affairs* 57, no. 1 (Fall 1978): 113.

23. *Hearings before the Subcommittee on International Resources, Food and Energy of the Committee on International Relations, House of Representatives, Ninety-Fourth Congress, November 5, 1975, February 26, and March 10, 1976* (Washington, D.C.: U.S. Government Printing Office, 1976), Appendix 10.

24. The Ethiopian revolutionary regime that overthrew Haile Selassie in 1974 called on Cuba to assist in thwarting a Somali effort to retake the Ogaden province, scene of many years of conflict. With Soviet airlift help, the Cubans responded with a substantial military force. The Carter administration, and especially National Security Adviser Zbigniew Brzezinski, saw this as a major threat against U.S. interests.

25. For a fuller description of the lobbying effort on behalf of Savimbi, see the author's *The Public Dimension of Foreign Policy* (Bloomington and Indianapolis: Indiana University Press, 1996), 195.

26. Elaine Windrich, *The Cold War Guerilla: Jonas Savimbi, the U.S. Media, and the Angolan War* (New York: Greenwood Press, 1992), 50.

27. Ibid., 124.

13. THE GENERAL ASSEMBLY

1. Quoted in Charles W. Kegley, Jr., and Steven W. Hook, "U.S. Foreign Aid and U.N. Voting: Did Reagan's Linkage Strategy Buy Deference or Defiance?," *International Studies Quarterly* 35 (1991): 296.

2. Donald F. McHenry, "Confronting a Revolutionary Legacy," in *Estrangement: America and the World,* ed. Sanford J. Ungar (New York and Oxford: Oxford University Press, 1985), 95.

3. *Yearbook of the United Nations 1960* (New York: Office of Public Information, 1960), 44.

4. *Yearbook of the United Nations 1970* (New York: Office of Public Information, 1970), 693.

5. Ibid., 694.

6. Ibid., 695.

7. See, for example, comments made regarding the 1977 version of the resolution in *Yearbook of the United Nations 1977* (New York: Office of Public Information, 1977), 828–897.

8. *Yearbook of the United Nations 1980* (New York: Office of Public Information, 1980), 1052.

9. Ibid.

10. Ibid., 706–708.

11. *Yearbook of the United Nations 1985* (New York: Office of Public Information, 1985), 1063.

12. *Yearbook of the United Nations 1994* (New York: Office of Public Information, 1994), 186.

13. Ibid., 47.

14. Ibid., 48.

15. *Yearbook of the United Nations 1962* (New York: Office of Public Information, 1962), 96.

16. Ibid., 100.

17. *Yearbook of the United Nations 1964* (New York: Office of Public Information, 1964), 106–120.

18. *Yearbook of the United Nations 1966* (New York: Office of Public Information, 1966), 82.

19. *Yearbook of the United Nations 1968* (New York: Office of Public Information, 1968), 108.

20. *Yearbook of the United Nations 1969* (New York: Office of Public Information, 1969), 99.

21. Ibid.

22. Ibid.

23. *Yearbook of the United Nations 1976* (New York: Office of Public Information, 1976), 582.

24. These resolutions can be found in *Yearbook of the United Nations 1978* (New York: Office of Public Information, 1978), 183–219.

25. *Yearbook of the United Nations 1979* (New York: Office of Public Information, 1979), 167–205.

26. *Yearbook of the United Nations 1980* (New York: Office of Public Information, 1980), 194–243.

27. *Yearbook of the United Nations 1981* (New York: Office of Public Information, 1981), 159.

28. *Yearbook of the United Nations 1982* (New York: Office of Public Information, 1982), 258.

29. Ibid.

30. *Yearbook of the United Nations 1992* (New York: Office of Public Information, 1992), 151–168.

31. *Yearbook of the United Nations 1964, 176.*

32. Ibid.

33. Ibid.

34. *Yearbook of the United Nations 1968, 273–274.*

35. *Yearbook of the United Nations 1969, 242.*

36. See, for example, *Yearbook of the United Nations 1970* (New York: Office of Public Information, 1970), 261.

37. Made by the Egyptian foreign minister before the General Assembly in 1971. See *Yearbook of the United Nations 1971* (New York: Office of Public Information, 1971), 170.

38. See *Yearbook of the United Nations 1972* (New York: Office of Public Information, 1972), 156–208.

39. *Yearbook of the United Nations 1974* (New York: Office of Public Information, 1974), 221.

40. See *Yearbook of the United Nations 1977* (New York: Office of Public Information, 1977), 290.

41. *Yearbook of the United Nations 1982, 388.*

42. Ibid., 390.

43. Ibid., 401.

44. *Yearbook of the United Nations 1983* (New York: Office of Public Information, 1983), 285.

45. *Yearbook of the United Nations 1988* (New York: Office of Public Information, 1988), 201–267.

46. *Hearing before the Subcommittee on Near Eastern and South Asian Affairs of the Committee on Foreign Relations United States Senate, One Hundred First Congress, Second Session, March 30, 1990* (Washington, D.C.: U.S. Government Printing Office, 1990), 1.

47. Geoffrey Reeves, *Communications and the "Third World"* (London: Routledge, 1993), 101.

48. Ibid., 101–102.

49. Ibid.

50. D. R. Mankekar, *Whose Freedom? Whose Order? A Plea for a New International Information Order by the Third World.* (Delhi: Clarion Books, 1981), viii.

51. Quoted in Sean MacBride, et al., *Many Voices, One World: Communication and Society, Today and Tomorrow* (Paris: UNESCO, 1980), xv.

52. Ibid., xvii.

53. Ibid., xix.

54. For the full report, see ibid.

55. Reproduced in Mark Alleyne, *International Power and International Communication* (London: Macmillan, 1995), 119–120. The original document is UNESCO Res. 4/19 "On the International Commission for the Study of Communication Problems" (Belgrade, 21 October 1980), sec. VI, 14.

14. THE TWENTY-FIRST–CENTURY AGENDA

1. Ambassador Teresita Schaffer in a letter to the author, November 26, 1999.

2. *United States Strategic Plan for International Affairs,* Department of State Publication 10505, released September 1997.

3. Karen DeYoung, "Giving Less: The Decline in Foreign Aid," *The Washington Post,* November 25, 1999, A1.

4. Carol Lancaster, *Aid to Africa: So Much To Do—So Little Done* (Chicago and London: University of Chicago Press, 1999), 220.

5. Jim Hoagland, "Richer and Poorer," *The Washington Post,* April 25, 1999, B7.

6. Schlesinger, *A Thousand Days,* 509.

7. *Foundation Giving: Yearbook of Facts and Figures on Private, Corporate, and Community Foundations* (Washington, D.C.: The Foundation Center, 1999), 76.

8. J. Brian Atwood, "Trade, Not Aid," *Christian Science Monitor,* July 6, 1999, 11.

BIBLIOGRAPHY

BOOKS

Achebe, Chinua. *Things Fall Apart.* Nairobi: East African Educational Publishers, 1994.

Acheson, Dean. *Present at the Creation.* New York: W.W. Norton and Company, 1969.

Aldcroft, Derek H., and Ross E. Catterall, eds. *Rich Nations, Poor Nations: The Long-Run Perspective.* Brookfield, Vt.: E. Elgar, 1996.

Anderson, David M., and David Killingray, eds. *Policing and Decolonization: Politics, Nationalism, and the Police, 1917–1965.* New York: Manchester University Press, 1992.

Anderson, Lisa. *The State and Social Transformation in Tunisia and Libya, 1830–1980.* Princeton, N.J.: Princeton University Press, 1986.

Antonius, George. *The Arab Awakening.* Beirut: Khayats, 1938.

Appadorai. *The Bandung Conference.* New Delhi: Indian Council of World Affairs, 1955.

Armstrong, Hamilton Fish, ed. *Fifty Years of Foreign Affairs.* New York: Praeger, 1972.

Aseka, Eric. *Jomo Kenyatta.* Nairobi: East African Educational Publishers, 1992.

Azvedo, Mario. *Historical Dictionary of Mozambique.* Metuchen, N.J.: Scarecrow Press, 1991.

Barber, Benjamin R. *Jihad vs. McWorld: How Globalism and Tribalism are Reshaping the World.* New York: Ballantine Books, 1996.

Bendana, Alejandro. *Power Lines: U.S. Domination in the New World Order.* New York: Olive Branch Press, 1996.

Berger, Elena L. *Labour, Race, and Colonial Rule: The Copperbelt from 1924 to Independence.* Oxford: Clarendon Press, 1974.

Bill, Scott L. *Empire and Cold War: The Roots of US-Third World Antagonism, 1945–1947.* New York: St. Martin's Press, 1990.

Birmingham, David. *Kwame Nkrumah: The Father of African Nationalism.* Athens, Ohio: Ohio University Press, 1998.

Bohannan, Paul, and Philip Curtin. *Africa and Africans.* Garden City, N.Y.: The Natural History Press, 1971.

Boorstin, Daniel J. *The Discoverers: A History of Man's Search to Know His World and Himself.* New York: Random House, 1983.

Borstelmann, Thomas. *Apartheid's Reluctant Uncle: The United States and Southern Africa in the Early Cold War.* New York: Oxford University Press, 1993.

Broad, Dave, and Lori Foster, eds. *The New World Order and the Third World.* Cheektowaga, N.Y.: Black Rose Books, 1992.

Broadhead, Susan H. *Historical Dictionary of Angola.* Metuchen, N.J.: Scarecrow Press, 1992.

Brockman, Norbert C. *An African Biographical Dictionary.* Santa Barbara, Calif.: ABC-CLIO, 1994.

Brown, L. Carl, ed. *Center Stage.* New York: Holmes and Meier, 1990.

Brzezinski, Zbigniew. *Power and Principle.* New York: Farrar, Straus, Giroux, 1983.

Burns, James MacGregor. *Roosevelt: The Lion and the Fox.* New York: Harcourt Brace Jovanovich, 1956.

Cain, P. J., and A. G. Hopkins. *British Imperialism: Crisis and Deconstruction, 1914–1990.* New York: Longman, 1993.

Calvocoressi, Peter. *World Politics since 1945.* 7th ed. New York and London: Longman, 1996.

Chadha, Yogesh. *Rediscovering Gandhi.* London: Arrow Books, 1997.

Chandra, Bipan. *India's Struggle for Independence 1857–1947.* New York: Penguin, 1989.

Chesterton, Charlton. *The Real Case for Rhodesia.* Honeydew, Transvaal: Janssonius and Heyns, 1973.

Christison, Kathleen. *Perceptions of Palestine: Their Influence on U.S. Middle Eastern Policy.* Berkeley: University of California Press, 1999.

Coates, Austin. *Rizal: Philippine Nationalist and Martyr.* Hong Kong: Oxford University Press, 1968.

Collins, Larry, and Dominique Lapierre. *Freedom at Midnight.* New York: Simon and Schuster, 1975.

Colvin, Ian. *The Rise and Fall of Moise Tshombe.* London: Leslie Frewin, 1968.

Crocker, Chester A. *High Noon in Southern Africa.* New York: W.W. Norton and Company, 1992.

Crosby, Cynthia A. *A Historical Dictionary of Malawi.* 2nd ed. Metuchen, N.J.: Scarecrow Press, 1993.

David, Stephen R. *Choosing Sides: Alignment and Realignment in the Third World.* Baltimore: Johns Hopkins University Press, 1991.

Deibel, Terry L., and John Lewis Gaddis, eds. *Containment.* 2 vols. Washington, D.C.: National Defense University, 1986.

Denham, Mark E. and Mark Owen Lombardi, eds. *Perspectives on Third-World Sovereignty: The Postmodern Paradox.* New York: St. Martin's Press, 1996.

Desai, Uday, ed. *Ecological Policy and Politics in Developing Countries.* Albany, N.Y.: SUNY Press, 1998.

Dirlik, Arif. *The Postcolonial Aura: Third World Criticism in the Age of Global Capitalism.* Boulder, Colo.: Westview Press, 1997.

Donaldson, Robert. *Soviet Policy toward India and Ideology and Strategy.* Cambridge, Mass.: Harvard University Press, 1974.

Doty, Roxanne Lynn. *Imperial Encounters: The Politics of Representation in North-South Relations.* Minneapolis: University of Minnesota Press, 1996.

Dougherty, James E., and Robert. L. Pfaltagraff, Jr. *American Foreign Policy: FDR to Reagan.* New York: Harper and Row, 1986.

Duiker, William. *Historical Dictionary of Vietnam.* 2nd ed. Lanham, Md.: Scarecrow Press, 1998.

———. *Nationalism and Revolution in Divided Vietnam.* New York: McGraw-Hill, 1995.

Duncan, P. J. S. *The Soviet Union and India.* London: Routledge, 1989.

Escobar, Arturo. *Encountering Development: The Making and Unmaking of the Third World.* Princeton, N.J.: Princeton University Press, 1995.

———. *Facing the Challenge: Responses to the Report of the South Commission.* Atlantic Highlands, N.J.: Zed Books, 1993.

Farwell, Byron. *Armies of the Raj.* New York: W.W. Norton and Company, 1989.

Frankel, Benjamin., ed. *The Cold War, 1945–1991.* Detroit: Gale Research, 1992.

Friedman, Thomas L. *The Lexus and the Olive Tree.* New York: Farrar, Straus, Giroux, 1999.

Fursenko, Aleksandr, and Timothy Naftali. *One Hell of a Gamble: Khrushehev, Castro, and Kennedy, 1958–1964.* New York: W.W. Norton and Company, 1997.

Gaillard Philippe. *Foccart Parle.* Paris: Fayard/Jeune Afrique, 1995.

Galbraith, John Kenneth. *A Life in Our Times.* New York: Ballantine Books, 1981.

Gallman, Waldemar J. *Iraq under General Nuri.* Baltimore: Johns Hopkins Press, 1964.

Gardner, Paul F. *Shared Hopes, Separate Fears: Fifty Years of U.S.-Indonesian Relations.* Boulder, Colo.: Westview Press, 1997.

Gerber, Haim. *The Social Origins of the Modern Middle East.* Boulder, Colo.: Lynne Rienner Publishers, 1987.

Glickman, Harvey, ed. *Political Leaders of Contemporary Africa South of the Sahara.* Westport, Conn.: Greenwood Press, 1992.

Goldthorpe, J. E. *The Sociology of Post-Colonial Societies: Economic Disparity, Cultural Diversity, and Development.* New York: Cambridge University Press, 1996.

Gonzalez, Alfonso, and Jim Norwine, eds. *The New Third World.* Boulder, Colo.: Westview Press, 1998.

Grammy, Abbas P., and C. K. Bragg. *United States-Third World Relations in the New World Order.* New York: Nova Science Publishers, 1996.

Green, Marshall. *Indonesia: Crisis and Transformation, 1965–1968.* Washington, D.C.: Compass Publishing, 1990.

Grotpeter, John J., Brian V. Siegel, and James R. Pletcher. *Historical Dictionary of Zambia.* 2nd ed. Lanham, Md.: Scarecrow Press, 1998.

Hadjor, Kofi Buenor. *Nkrumah and Ghana: The Dilemma of Post-Colonial Power.* New York: Kegan Paul International, 1988.

Halberstam, David. *Ho.* New York: Random House, 1971.

Handelman, Howard. *The Challenge of Third World Development.* Upper Saddle River, N.J.: Prentice Hall, 1996.

Heathcote, T. A. *The Military in British India.* New York: Manchester University Press, 1995.

Heggoy, Alf Andrew. *Historical Dictionary of Algeria.* Metuchen, N.J.: Scarecrow Press, 1991.

Helmreich, William, ed. *Afro-Americans and Africa: Black Nationalism at the Crossroads.* Westport, Conn.: Greenwood, 1977.

Hochschild, Adam. *King Leopold's Ghost: A Story of Greed, Terror, and Heroism in Colonial Africa.* New York: First Mariner Books, 1998.

Hoogvelt, Ankie M. M. *Globalization and the Postcolonial World: The New Political Economy of Development.* Baltimore: Johns Hopkins University Press, 1997.

Human Development Report 1997. New York: Oxford University Press, 1997.

Ignatyev, Oleg. *Secret Weapon in Africa.* Moscow: Progress Publishers, 1977.

Indo-US Strategic Symposium. *The United States and India in the Post-Soviet World: Proceedings of the Third Indo-US Strategic Symposium* [Warrenton, Virginia, 1992]. Washington, D.C.: The University, 1993.

International Council Conference, 1987. *U.S. Policies and Foreign Perceptions: Report of the United States Information Agency International Council Conference.* Washington, D.C.: United States Information Agency, 1988.

Jackson, Robert H. *Quasi-States: Sovereignty, International Relations, and the Third World.* New York: Cambridge University Press, 1990.

Jansen, G. H. *Nonalignment and the Afro-Asian States.* New York: Frederick A. Praeger, 1966.

Jessup, Philip C. *The Birth of Nations.* New York: Columbia University Press, 1974.

Josephy, Alvin M., Jr., ed. *The Horizon History of Africa.* New York: American Heritage Publishing Company, 1971.

Judd, Denis. *Empire: The British Imperial Experience from 1765 to the Present.* New York: Basic Books, 1997.

Kahin, Audrey R., and George McT. Kahin. *Subversion as Foreign Policy.* Seattle: University of Washington Press, 1995.

Kaplan, Robert. *The Ends of the Earth.* New York: Random House, 1996.

Karabell, Zachary. *Architects of Invention: The United States, the Third World, and the Cold War, 1946–1962.* Baton Rouge: Louisiana State University Press, 1999.

Kiely, Ray, and Phil Marfleet, eds. *Globalization and the Third World.* New York: Routledge, 1998.

Kissinger, Henry. *Years of Upheaval.* Boston: Little, Brown, & Company, 1982.

Kolko, Gabriel. *Confronting the Third World: United States Foreign Policy, 1945–1980.* New York: Pantheon, 1988.

Kux, Dennis. *India and the United States.* Washington, D.C.: National Defense University Press, 1993.

Lancaster, Carol. *Aid to Africa: So Much to Do, So Little Done.* Chicago: University of Chicago Press, 1999.

Langer, William L., ed. *An Encyclopedia of World History.* Boston: Houghton Mifflin Company, 1952.

Lapping, Brian. *End of Empire.* London: Granada Publishing, 1985.

Lenczowski, George. *The Middle East in World Affairs.* 4th ed. Ithaca, N.Y.: Cornell University Press, 1980.

Lippmann, Walter. *Public Opinion.* New York: Free Press, 1997.

Malik, Hafeez. *Soviet-Pakistan Relations and Post-Soviet Dynamics, 1947–1992.* London: Macmillan, 1994.

Mansingh, Surjit. *Historical Dictionary of India.* Lanham, Md.: Scarecrow Press, 1996.

Mason, Mike. *Development and Disorder.* Hanover, N.H.: University Press of New England, 1997.

Mastny, Vojtech. *The Cold War and Soviet Insecurity: The Stalin Years.* London: Oxford University Press, 1996.

McGhee, George. *Envoy to the Middle World: Adventures in Diplomacy.* New York: Harper and Row, 1969.

McIntyre, David W. *British Decolonization, 1946–1997: When, Why, and How Did the British Empire Fall?* Basingstoke: Macmillan, 1998.

McMahon, Robert J. *Colonialism and Cold War: The United States and the Struggle for Indonesian Independence, 1945–1949.* Ithaca, N.Y.: Cornell University Press, 1981.

———. *The Limits of Empire: The United States and Southeast Asia since World War II.* New York: Columbia University Press, 1999.

McNamara, Francis Terry. *France in Black Africa.* Washington, D.C.: National Defense University Press, 1989.

McPherson, K. *Jinnah.* Hemel Hempstead, England: Prentice-Hall International, 1980.

Memmi, Albert. *The Colonizer and the Colonized.* Boston: Beacon, 1967.

Menezes, S. L. *Fidelity and Honour: The Indian Army from the Seventeenth to the Twenty-First Century.* New Delhi: Viking, 1993.

Miller, Marian A. A. *The Third World in Global Environmental Politics.* Boulder, Colo.: Lynne Rienner, 1995.

Mittelman, James H. *Out from Underdevelopment Revisited: Changing Global Structures and the Remaking of the Third World.* London: Macmillan Press, 1997.

Mondlane, Eduardo. *The Struggle for Mozambique.* Baltimore: Penguin, 1970.

Monroe, Elizabeth. *Britain's Moment in the Middle East.* London: Chatto and Windus, 1981.

Morison, Samuel Eliot. *The Oxford History of the American People.* New York: Oxford University Press, 1965.

Morrissey, Oliver, Brian Smith, and Edward Horesh. *British Aid and International Trade.* Philadelphia: Open University Press, 1992.

Mosley, Paul. *Foreign Aid: Its Defense and Reform.* Lexington: University of Kentucky Press, 1987.

Multatuli. *Max Havelaar.* New York: London House and Maxwell, 1967.

Murphy, Robert. *Diplomat among Warriors.* Garden City, N.Y.: Doubleday and Company, 1964.

Nandy, Ashis. *The Intimate Enemy.* Oxford: Oxford University Press, 1983.

Narton, Craig. *Black Earth, Red Star: A History of Soviet Security Policy, 1917–1991.* Ithaca, N.Y.: Cornell University Press, 1992.

Neill, Stephen. *A History of Christian Missions.* Baltimore: Penguin, 1977.

Obiozor, George A. *The United States and the Nigerian Civil War.* Lagos: Nigerian Institute for International Affairs, 1993.

Ofcansky, Thomas P., and Rodger Yeager. *Historical Dictionary of Tanzania.* 2nd ed. Lanham, Md.: Scarecrow Press, 1997.

Ogot, Bethwell A. *Historical Dictionary of Kenya.* Metuchen, N.J.: Scarecrow Press, 1981.

Omissi, David. *The Sepoy and the Raj.* London: Macmillan Press, 1994.

Osso, Nyaknno, ed. *Who's Who in Nigeria.* Lagos: Newswatch, 1990.

Oveweso, Sivan. *The Post-Gowon Nigerian Accounts of the Civil War, 1975–1990: A Preliminary Review.* Lagos: Africa Peace Research Institute, 1992.

Parama, Roy. *Indian Traffic: Identities in Question in Colonial and Postcolonial India.* Berkeley: University of California Press, 1998.

Paxton, John, ed. *The Statesman's Yearbook.* 111th ed. New York: St. Martin's Press, 1974.

Peters, Jonathan. *A Dance of Masks: Senghor, Achebe, Soyinka.* Washington, D.C.: Three Continents Press, 1978.

Phillips, Claude S. *The African Political Dictionary.* Santa Barbara, Calif.: ABC-CLIO, 1984.

Plischke, Elmer, ed. *Contemporary U.S. Foreign Policy.* Westport, Conn.: Greenwood Press, 1991.

Polak, H. S., and H. N. Barilsford, Lord Pethick-Lawrence. *Mahatma Gandhi.* London: Odhams Press, 1949.

Pye, Lucian W. *Politics, Personality, and Nation Building: Burma's Search for Identity.* New Haven, Conn.: Yale University Press, 1962.

Quandt, William B. *Revolution and Political Leadership: Algeria 1954–1968.* Cambridge, Mass.: M.I.T. Press, 1969.

Rama Rau, Santha. *Home to India.* New York and London: Harper and Brothers, 1944.

Ramazani, R. K. *The Foreign Policy of Iran, 1500–1941: A Developing Nation in World Affairs.* Charlottesville: University Press of Virginia, 1966.

———. *Iran's Foreign Policy: A Study of Foreign Policy in Modernizing Nations.* Charlottesville: University Press of Virginia, 1975.

———. *The Persian Gulf: Iran's Role.* Charlottesville: University Press of Virginia, 1972.

———. *Revolutionary Iran.* Baltimore: Johns Hopkins University Press, 1988.

———. *The United States and Iran: The Patterns of Influence.* New York: Praeger Publishers, 1982.

Rasmussen, R. Kent. *Historical Dictionary of Rhodesia.* Metuchen, N.J.: Scarecrow Press, 1979.

Ricklefs, M. C. *A History of Modern Indonesia.* Bloomington: Indiana University Press, 1981.

Romulo, Carlos. *The Meaning of Bandung.* Durham: University of North Carolina Press, 1956.

Rothermund, Dietmar. *Mahatma Gandhi.* New Delhi: Manohar, 1991.

Ruane, Kevin. *War and Revolution in Vietnam, 1930–1975.* London: UCL Press, 1998.

Rubinstein, Alvin. *Moscow's Third World Strategy.* Princeton, N.J.: Princeton University Press, 1989.

Ryan, N.J. *The Making of Modern Malaysia.* London: Oxford University Press, 1967.

Ryrie, William. *First World, Third World.* New York: St. Martin's, 1995.

Sanger, Richard. *The Arabian Peninsula.* Freeport, N.Y.: Books for Libraries Press, 1970.

Schulzinger, Robert. *A Time for War: The United States and Vietnam, 1941–1975.* Oxford: Oxford University Press, 1997.

Schlesinger, Arthur M., Jr. *A Thousand Days: John F. Kennedy in the White House.* Boston: Houghton Mifflin Company, 1965.

Service, Robert. *A History of 20th Century Russia.* Cambridge, Mass.: Harvard University Press, 1997.

Shultz, George P. *Turmoil and Triumph.* New York: Maxwell Macmillan International, 1993.

Sick, Gary. *All Fall Down: America's Tragic Encounter with Iran.* New York: Random House, 1985.

Skeet, Ian. *OPEC: Twenty-Five Years of Prices and Politics.* New York: Cambridge University Press, 1988.

Skinner, Elliott P. *African Americans and U.S. Policy toward Africa, 1850–1924.* Washington, D.C.: Howard University Press, 1992.

Sloan, Henry, Kieran Dugan, and Judith Graham, eds. *Current Biography Yearbook 1986.* New York: H. W. Wilson Company, 1986.

Smith, David. *Mugabe.* Salisbury, Zimbabwe: Pioneer Head, 1981.

Smith, Roger C. *Vanguard of Empire: Ships of Exploration in the Age of Columbus.* New York: Oxford University Press, 1993.

Snow, Donald M. *Distant Thunder: Patterns of Conflict in the Developing World.* 3rd ed. New York: Longman, 1997.

Soedarpo, Mien. *Reminiscences of the Past.* Jakarta: Sejati Foundation, 1994.

South Commission. *The Challenge to the South.* New York: Oxford University Press, 1990.

Steinberg, S. H., ed. *The Statesman's Yearbook*. 105th ed. New York: St. Martin's Press, 1969.

Stempel, John D. *Inside the Iranian Revolution*. Bloomington: Indiana University Press, 1981.

Stephens, Robert. *Nasser: A Political Biography*. New York: Simon and Schuster, 1971.

Stone, Martin. *The Agony of Algeria*. New York: Columbia University Press, 1997.

Strack, Harry R. *Sanctions: The Case of Rhodesia*. Syracuse, N.Y.: Syracuse University Press, 1978.

The United States and India in the Post-Soviet World: Proceedings of the Third Indo-U.S. Strategic Symposium. Washington, D.C.: National Defense University Press, 1993.

Thompson, Joseph E. *American Policy and African Famine*. New York: Greenwood Press, 1990.

Thornton, Thomas Perry, ed. *Anti Americanism: Origins and Context*. Newbury Park, Calif.: Sage Publications, 1988.

Todd, Judith. *The Right to Say No*. London: Sidgwick and Jackson, 1972.

Ungar, Sanford J., ed. *Estrangement: America and the World*. New York: Oxford University Press, 1985.

United Nations. *Yearbook of the United Nations* 1960, 1961, 1962, 1963, 1964, 1965, 1966, 1967, 1968, 1969, 1970, 1971, 1972, 1973, 1974, 1976, 1977, 1978, 1979, 1980, 1981, 1982, 1983, 1984, 1985, 1987, 1988, 1992, 1993, 1994. New York: Office of Public Information.

United States–Viet-Nam Relations, 1945–1967. Washington, D.C.: U.S. Government Printing Office, 1971.

United States Consulate, Jakarta. *Despatches from United States Consuls in Batavia, Java, Netherlands East Indies, 1818–1906*. Washington, D.C.: National Archives, 1969.

United States Information Agency. *U.S. Policies and Foreign Perceptions: Report of the United States Information Agency. International Council Conference*. Washington, D.C., October 7–9, 1987. Washington, D.C.: The United States Information Agency, 1988.

Vincent, R. J., ed. *Foreign Policy and Human Rights*. Cambridge: Cambridge University Press, 1986.

Wallerstein, Immanuel. "Africa for the Africans." In *The Horizon History of Africa*, ed. Alvin M. Josephy, Jr. New York: American Heritage Publishing Company, 1971, pp. 497–498.

Weatherby, Joseph. *The Other World: Issues and Politics of the Developing World*. 3rd ed. New York: Longman, 1997.

Wepman, Dennis. *Jomo Kenyatta*. New York: Chelsea House Publishers, 1985.

White, John. *The Politics of Foreign Aid*. London: The Bodley Head, 1974.

Williams, William Appleman, et al., eds. *America in Vietnam: A Documentary History*. Garden City, N.Y.: Anchor Press, 1985.

Williams, G. Mennen. *Africa for the Africans*. Grand Rapids, Mich.: William B. Eerdmans Publishing Company, 1969.

Woodward, Peter. *Nasser*. New York: Longman, 1992.

Yergin, Daniel. *The Prize: The Epic Quest for Oil, Money, and Power*. New York: Simon and Schuster, 1991.

Zubok, Vladislav, and Constantine Pleshakov. *Inside the Kremlin's Cold War: From Stalin to Khrushchev*. Cambridge, Mass.: Harvard University Press, 1996.

JOURNAL ARTICLES

Abede, Ermia. "The Horn, The Cold War, and Documents from the Former East-Bloc: An Ethiopian View." *Cold War International History Project Bulletin* 8–9 (Winter 1996): 45.

Barber, Benjamin R. "Jihad vs. McWorld." *The Atlantic Monthly* (March 1992): 53–63.

Davis, Nathaniel. "The Angola Decision of 1975." *Foreign Affairs* 57, no. 1 (Fall 1976): 113.

Drozdiak, William. "French Ties to Africa Undergo Key Change." *The Washington Post*, January 22, 1994, A10.

Gies, Piero. "Havana's Policy in Africa, 1959–1975: New Evidence From Cuban Archives." *Cold War International History Project Bulletin* 8–9 (Winter 1996): 5–18.

Henze, Paul. "Moscow, Mengistu, and the Horn: Difficult Choices for the Kremlin." *Cold War International History Project Bulletin* 8–9 (Winter 1996): 45.

"Kaplan, Robert D. "The Coming Anarchy." *Atlantic Monthly* (February 1994): 44–76.

———. "Proportionalism." *Atlantic Monthly* (August 1996).

Kaufman, Michael T. "Extent of Kissinger Offer Surprises Parley Aides." *New York Times,* May 8, 1976, 3.

Kindleberger, Charles P. "The International Monetary System." In *America in the World Economy,* by Charles P. Kindleberger. New York: Foreign Policy Association, 1977, 91–103.

Kobrin, Stephen J. "The MAI and the Clash of Globalizations." *Foreign Policy* (Fall 1998): 97–109.

Lewis, Bernard. "The West and the Middle East." *Foreign Affairs* (January-February 1997): 114–130.

Lewis, Martin. "Is There a Third World?" *Current History* (November 1999): 355–358.

Litvin, Daniel. "Dirt Poor: A Survey of Development and the Environment." *The Economist* (March 21, 1998): 1–16.

Louis, William Roger, and Ronald Robinson. "Empire Preserv'd." *Times Literary Supplement* (May 5, 1995): 14–16.

Murphy, Craig N. "What the Third World Wants: An Interpretation of the Development and Meaning of the New International Economic Order Ideology." *International Studies Quarterly* 27: 55–76.

Perkovich, George. "Think Again: Nonproliferation." *Foreign Policy* (Fall 1998): 12–23.

Repetto, Robert, and Jonathan Lash. "Planetary Roulette: Gambling with the Climate." *Foreign Policy* (Fall 1997): 85–98.

State Department Bulletin. May 27, 1974; February 3, 1975; September 22, 1975; October 13, 1975. Washington, D.C.: U.S. Government Printing Office.

Stiglitz, Joseph F. "Trade and the Developing World: A New Agenda." *Current History* (November 1999): 387–393.

Strang, David. "Global Patterns of Decolonization, 1500–1987." *International Quarterly* 35 (1991): 429–454.

———. "From Dependency to Sovereignty: An Event History Analysis of Decolonization, 1870–1987." *American Sociological Review* 55 (1990): 846–860.

Westad, Odd Arne. "Moscow and the Angolan Crisis, 1974–1976: A New Pattern of Intervention." *Cold War International History Project Bulletin* 8–9 (Winter 1996): 40.

INDEX

Page references in italics refer to maps.

Abbas the Great, 14
Abdul Rahman, Tunku, 23
Abu Musa, independence of, 88
Acheson, Dean, 51–52, 136, 152, 154, 161
Aden, 24
Africa: African American support, 159–160, 162, 169, 172; Angola, 110, 111–113, 116, 171–172; Belgian Africa, 107–108; Benin, 20; Berlin African Conference, 21–22; Biafra, 168–170, 221*n*7; Brazzaville conference, 102–103; Buganda and Bunyoro, 120; French Africa, 101–107; Gabon, 21; Gambia, 101; Ghana, 97–100; Horn of Africa, 95–96; impact of Islam, 19; Kenya, 117–119; Lagos, 20; Malawi independence, 19; Matabele tribe, 18, 19; Mauritania, 21; missionary efforts in, 35; Namibia, 110; Nigeria, 20, 100–101; Northern Territories, 20; Nyasaland, 113–117; Pemba, 120; Portuguese territories, 111–113; Rhodesia, 113–117; "scramble for," 17–22; settler countries, 109–120; Shona nation, 18; Sierra Leone, 101; slave trade, 19–21; South Africa, 64, 110, 175, 180–184; South West African Peoples' Organization (SWAPO), 110; Sudan, 96–97; Tanzania, 119–120; Uganda, 120; U.S. aid to, 159–175; Zambesia, 18–19; Zambia independence, 19; Zanzibar, 120; Zimbabwe independence, 19
Afrikaaner settlements, 17–18
Agency for International Development (AID), 197, 202
Aguinaldo, Emilio, 38, 59
Ahmad Bey Arabi, 22
Ahmed, Imam, 151
Alatas, Ali, 141
Albuquerque, Alfonso de, 15
Algeria: French seizure of, 22, 52; independence of, 82–83; National Liberation Front (FLN), 82–83; Secret Army Organization (OAS), 83
Amboyna, 15, 38
American colonies, 17
American Foreign Policy in the Congo 1960–1964 (Weissman), 165
Amin, Idi, 38, 44, 161
Amritsar massacre, 38, 66
Anglo-Iranian Oil Company, 25, 71–72
Angola, 13; anti-colonial resistance, 110, 111–112; Chinese support of UNITA, 171; Communist threat, 171–172; Cuban troops, 110, 112–

113, 116; Frente Nacional de Libertação de Angola (FNLA), 111–112; Movimento Popular de Libertação de Angola (MPLA), 111–113; National Liberation of Angola (FNLA), 171; Popular Movement for the Liberation of Angola (MPLA), 171; slave trading, 20; União Nacional para a Independência Total de Angola (UNITA), 111–113; U.S. support of movements, 171–173
Annan, 16
Arab states, 72–73
Arden-Clarke, Charles, 100
Armitage, Robert, 114
As I Saw It (Rusk), 161
Ashanti, 20
Asian financial crisis, 192
Assab, port of, 21–22
Atlantic Charter, 48, 50–51
Attlee, Clement, 98
Averoff, Evangelos, 85

Baghdad Pact, 75–76, 78–79, 80, 148–151
Bahrein, 24, 87–88
Bahrein Petroleum Company (Bapco), 88
Baldwin, Stanley, 66
Balfour declaration, 76
Balladur, Edouard, 105
Banda, Hastings, 113–117
Bandung conference, 129–130
Banerjea, Surendranath, 65
Bangladesh, 44
Bantam, 15
Baring, Evelyn, 118, 119
Batavia, 46
Belgium: acquisition of Burundi and Rwanda, 21; Belgian Africa, 107–108; Congo colony, 21, 163–165; education in colonies, 32–33; Leopold II, 107–108
Biko, Stephen, 182
Bismarck, Otto von, 21
Black Hole of Calcutta, 29
Boers, 18, 110
Bokassa, Jean-Bedelle, 161
Botha, P. W., 183
Botswana, 18
Bourguiba, Habib, 52
Boutros-Ghali, Boutros, 177
Boxer Rebellion, 26
Britain's Moment in the Middle East (Monroe), 93
British East India Company, 15–16
British Petroleum, 89
British South African Company (BSAC), 18–19

Brown, Irving, 52
Brown, Ted, 160
Bruce, David K. E., 153–154
Bunker, Ellsworth, 57
Burns, Alan, 98
Burundi, 21, 107–108
Byrd, Harry, 167
Byrd Amendment, 167–168, 221*n*5

Cabral, Amilcar, 204
Caffrey, Jefferson, 152, 153
Calvocoressi, Peter, 112, 144
Cambodia, 16
Cameroon, Republic of, 21, *94*
Canada, 17
Cape Bojador, 13, 14
Cape of Good Hope, 14
Cape Verde Islands, 14
caravel ships, 13, 215*n*
Carmichael, Stokely, 160
Carter, Beverly, 174
Catholicism, 34
Cebu, 14, 15
Central African Republic, 21
Central Intelligence Agency (CIA), activities in
    Third World, 25, 126, 165, 171, 221*n*9
Central Treaty Organization, 151
Ceylon, 14
Chad, 21
Chandernagor, 16
Chiang Kai-shek, 61
China: Boxer Rebellion, 26; British colonies
    in, 25–26; extra-territoriality, 26, 216*n*2;
    incorporation of nation-states, 44; Mao
    Tse Dung, 47; Opium Wars, 25–26; Peking
    Conventions, 26; Treaty of Bogue, 26;
    Treaty of Tientsin, 26
Chosen. *See* Korea
Christianity, 34–36
Churchill, Winston, 100; drafting the Atlantic
    Charter, 50–51; opposition to India inde-
    pendence, 67, 69
Clarke, John Henrik, 19
Cochin, 14
Cochin China, 16
Coen, Jan Picterazoon, 38
Cohen, Andrew, 98–99, 120
Cold War: end of, 5, 7, 8, 191, 192, 195, 199; im-
    pact on Congo independence, 108; impact
    on U.S. policy toward Third World, 53, 147–
    158; U.S. covert activities, 157–158
Colonialism and Cold War (McMahon), 48
colonization, pattern of, 20
Columbus, Christopher, 14
Compagnie Française de Petrol, 89
Congo, 107–108, 163–165
Congo Brazzaville, 21
Creasy, Gerald, 98

Creech-Jones, Arthur, 98–99
Cripps, Stafford, 51
Crocker, Chester, 162
Crusaders, slave trading, 19–21
Cuba: after U.S. war with Spain, 59; aid to An-
    gola, 112–113, 162, 171–173; independence
    of, 27
Cyprus, 13; British leasing of, 22; independence
    of, 83–86; National Organization of Cypriot
    Fighters (EOKA), 85

Dahomey, 20, 21
Danquah, Joseph, 98, 100
Davies, John Paton, 50
Davis, Nathaniel, 172
de Gaulle, Charles: Algerian independence, 83;
    control of Indochina, 61–62, 152; on French
    Africa, 102
de Klerk, F. W., 110, 175, 183
Dewey, George, 27, 59
Diego Garcia, 104
Diggs, Charles, 160
Discoverers, The (Boorstin), 13, 215*n*
Djibouti, 95–96
Dominican Republic, 27–28
Doolittle, Hooker, 52
Douglas, Lewis, 153
Drake, Francis, 14, 15
Duce, James Terry, 89
Dulles, John Foster, 121; Eisenhower Doctrine,
    148–151; withdrawal of support to Egypt, 80
Dundas, Ambrose, 33
Dutch East Indies: Chinese favored position, 37;
    economic impact of decolonization, 45–46;
    forced agricultural production, 38; Japa-
    nese conquest of, 26–27; maintaining con-
    trol, 30–31; Roosevelt's considerations, 52;
    U.S. access to oil resources, 50
Dutch East Indies Company, 15, 17–18, 34
Dyer, Reginald, 38, 66

Eannes, Gil, 13, 14
East African Protectorate, 21
East India Company, 34
East Timor, 13, 44, 192
economics, expectations of the U.S., 134–146
Eden, Anthony, 84
Egypt: Baghdad Pact, 78–79, 80, 148–151; British
    Middle East Command, 73; British occupa-
    tion of, 21, 22–23; Egyptian Communist
    Party, 78; Free Officers, 78, 79; indepen-
    dence of, 78; Khedive Ismail, 22; Muslim
    Brotherhood, 78; refusal of Soviet aid, 79–
    80; revolt by Ahmad Bey Arabi, 22; Suez
    Canal Company, 22, 81
Eisenhower, Dwight D.: Eisenhower Doctrine,
    148–151; Middle East Defense Organization
    (MEDO), 148–151

End of Empire (Lapping), 29, 76, 85–86, 93, 98–99, 114, 118–119

Enders, Tom, 141

England: acquisition of Bechuanaland, 18; acquisition of Malaya, 16–17; acquisition of northern Cameroon and Tanganyika, 21; acquisition of Singapore, 16; alliance with Sherif Hussein, 73; Amritsar massacre, 38, 66; Anglo-Egyptian treaty, 78, 79; Anglo-Persian Oil Company, 25; annexing Lagos, 20; Baghdad Pact, 78–79, 148–151; British Somaliland, 96; British South African Company (BSAC), 18–19; Charles II, 16; Christian missions, 34; claims of Ottoman empire, 72–74; colonies in China, 25–26; colony in Zambesia, 18–19; colony of Northern Rhodesia, 19; control of Aden, 90–93; control of Sudan, 23; controlling India, 16, 30–33, 36, 67–69; "date-garden agreement" for Kuwait, 87; East African Protectorate, 21; education in colonies, 32–33; geographic division of India, 67, 68–69; Ghana independence, 97–100; independence of Cyprus, 83–86; independence of West Indian colonies, 101; internationalized Palestine, 76–78; Iran's oil resources, 71–72; Iraq territory, 23; New World settlements, 15; Nyasaland colony, 19; oil resources in the Gulf, 71–72, 88–89; Opium Wars in China, 25–26; overthrow of Mussadeq, 25; Palestine territory, 23, 77–78; presence in Suez Canal, 24, 78; protectorate of Egypt, 22–23; protectorate of Kenya, 21; protectorate of Uganda, 21; protectorate of Zanzibar, 21; Regulating Act, 16; Rhodesia colonies, 18–19; Saudi-British treaty, 88; settlement on Ternate, 15; Seven Years War, 16; Straits Settlements, 16–17; Sykes-Picot Agreement, 23–24, 73; Treaty of Bogue, 26; Treaty of London, 73; treaty with Transjordan, 75–76

Entente Cordiale, 22

Envoy to the Middle World (McGhee), 163

Eritrea, 22, 95–96

Eteki, William, 143

Ethiopia, 21–22, *94*, 95–96

extra-territoriality, defined, 26, 216*m*2

Facing Mount Kenya (Kenyatta), 117

Falle, Sam, 93

Foccart, Jacques, 106

Foley, Maurice, 170

Foot, Hugh, 85

Foote, Walter A., 46

Ford, Gerald, 58

Formosa (Taiwan), 26, *54*

Franc Zone in French Africa, 105

France: acquisition of Senegal, 20; Algeria independence, 22, 82–83; Annan protectorate, 16; bid for Morocco, 22, 26; Cambodia protectorate, 16; capture of Madras, 16; Cochin China settlement, 16; colonial issues with U.S., 51–52; colonies in China, 26; control and education in colonies, 31–32, 36; Franco-Lebanese agreement, 75; Franco-Syrian treaty, 75; independence of Djibouti, 96; independence of Indochina, 61–62; independence of Tunisia and Morocco, 82; Indochinese War, 61–62; language control, 36, 106–107; Laos protectorate, 16; Lebanon territory, 23; North and South Vietnam, 62; Peking Conventions, 26; protectorate of Tunisia, 22; protectorate over Madagascar, 20; racial tolerance, 33; Seven Years War, 16; suppression in Malagasy, 38; Sykes-Picot Agreement, 23–24, 73; Syrian territory, 23; Tonkin protectorate, 16; Treaty of London, 73; Treaty of Paris, 16; Treaty of Tientsin, 26

France in Black Africa (McNamara), 104

French Africa, 21, 101–107

French Cameroon, 21

Funze, Ralph, 32

Gama, Vasco da, 14

Gambia, 101

Gandhi, Indira, 126

Gandhi, Mohandas, 63–69, 205

Gbedema, Komla, 99–100

Germany: colonies and protectorates in Africa, 21; ports in Japan, 26–27; Treaty of Versailles, 21

Ghana, 13; independence of, 97–100; Portuguese trading post, 14; slave trading in, 20, 21

Gladstone, William, 65

Glubb, John, 76, 81

Goa, 14, 16

Gold Coast (Ghana), slave trading, 20

Gordon, Charles, 23

Gowon, Yakubu, 170

Greater Banda Island, 38

"Greater East Asia Co-Prosperity Sphere, The," 26–27

Greek majority in Cyprus, 83–86

Greenfield, Meg, 45

Grivas, George, 84–85

Guam, 59

Guinea, 21, 103–104

Guinea-Bissau, 111–112

Gulbenkian, Calouste, 89

Gulf States and the Peninsula: Bahrein independence, 87–88; British control of Aden, 90–93; Buraimi oasis, 89–90; Front for the Liberation of Occupied South Yemen (FLOSY), 92–93; Kuwait independence, 87, 218*m*; National Liberation Front in Aden,

92–93; Qatar independence, 88; Sultanate of Muscat and Oman, 90; United Arab Emirates, 88

Haiti, 27–28
Hammarskjold, Dag, 163–164
Harding, John, 85
Harrison, Francis B., 60
Hashemite dynasty, 24
Hastings, Warren, 16
Hatta, Mohammad, 48
Hawaii, U.S. annexation of, 27
Henderson, Loy, 153, 154–155
History of Christian Missions, A (Neill), 34
Ho Chi Minh, 46–47, 205; Indochinese Communist Party, 61, 152–154; nationalist activities in Indochina, 61–62, 152–154, 217*n*4
Holland: Boer settlements, 18, 110; colonies after Waterloo, 16; control and education in colonies, 31–33; economic impact of decolonization, 45–46; Indonesian independence, 55–59, 135–136, 219*n*2; New World settlements, 15; settlements on Ternate, Sumatra and Bantam, 15; Table Bay settlement, 17
Honduras, 27–28
Hong Kong, 26
Hopkinson, Henry, 84
Horizon History of Africa, The (Wallerstein), 35–36, 100–101
Horn of Africa, 22
Houphouet-Boigny, Felix, 103, 206
Hull, Cordell, 50
Hume, Allan Octavian, 65
Hussein, Saddam, 123, 198
al-Husseini, al-Haj Amin, 77
Hutu peoples, 108

Ibn Saud, 89
imperialism: corruption and favoritism, 37–39; cultural clashes, 33–36; legacies of, 29–30; maintaining control, 30–33; racial discrimination, 33–36, 124; religious clashes, 33–36; suppression of, 36–39
independence: definitions/descriptions of, 43–47; economic changes, 44–45; readiness for self-government, 45
India: Amritsar massacre, 38, 66; Bengal province, 68; British control of, 6, 30–33, 36; British geographic division of, 68–69; British war efforts, 51; Hindu-Muslim differences, 64–69; incorporation of nation-states, 44; India Act of 1935, 67; Indian Civil Service (ICS), 64–65; Indian National Congress, 65; Jawaharlal Nehru, 64–69, 128, 211; Jesuit efforts, 34; Mohandas Gandhi, 63–69, 205; Mohammad Ali Jinnah, 66, 69; Morley reforms, 66; Punjab province, 68; "Quit India" movement, 67–68; Regulating

Act, 16; steps to independence, 17, 63–69; suttee (widow sacrifice), 35; UN membership, 47
India's Struggle for Independence (Chandra), 65
Indochina, 13; French seizure of, 61–62; Indochinese War, 61–62; Japanese conquest of, 26–27
Indonesia, 54; Amir Machmoud, 56; Dutch "police" action, 57; East Timor division, 57–58; FRETELIN movement, 58; incorporation of nation-states, 44; Indonesian Nationalist Party, 56; Islamic population, 56; Marshall Plan, 52; military overthrow, 44; Mohammad Hatta, 48, 56; Muslim population, 56; rise of Sukarno, 56–59, 213; steps to independence, 17, 55–59; Suharto, 131; Sulawesi, 56; Sumatra, 56; Sutan Sjahrir, 56; UN membership, 47; U.S. role in independence, 135–136, 219*n*2; West Java, 56; West New Guinea (Irian Jaya) independence, 57, 58
International Monetary Fund (IMF), 131, 137, 139, 145–146, 192
Iran: Ardeshir Zahedi, 25; Ayatollah Ruhollah Khomeini influence, 72; claim of Bahrein, 87–88; Mohammed Mussadeq, 25, 72, 217*n*2; Mohammed Reza Shah, 25; Reza Shah Pahlavi, 25; SAVAK security service, 72; strategic oil resources, 71–72; Treaty of Turkmanchai, 24; wars with Russia, 24–25
Iraq: admission to League of Nations, 74–75; attack on U.S. Information Service, 148; British mandate of, 23–24, 74–75; British-imposed monarchy, 74–75; independence of, 73; in the Sykes-Picot Agreement, 73, 74
Islam, 19, 33–35, 56
Ismail, Shah, 14
Israel: state of, 77–78; UN and the question of Palestine, 184–186; Zionist claims of, 24
Italy: control of Libya, 23; independence of Eritrea, 96; Treaty of London, 73; treaty with Ethiopia, 21–22
Ivory Coast, 21
Iyer, G. Subramaniya, 65

Jakarta, 46
Jamaica, 101
Jamali, Fadhil, 149
Jamestown, Virginia, 15
Japan: conquests and colonization program, 26–27; expansion into Formosa (Taiwan), 26; German ports in, 26–27; invasion of Manchuria, 26–27; Russo-Japanese War, 26–27; surrender in World War II, 56
Java, 15, 16
Jewish settlement: Irgun and Stern Gang activities, 77; in Palestine, 76–78
Jinnah, Muhammad Ali, 206
Johnson, Louis A., 51

Jordan: Baghdad Pact, 75–76, 148–151; British treaty with Transjordan, 75–76
Jospin, Lionel, 106

Kameroon, 21
Karikal, 16
Kashmir, 31
Kaunda, Kenneth, 114
Kayibanda, Gregoire, 108
Kennedy, John F., 200–201; interest in Africa, 160–161; response to Third World leaders, 53
Kennedy, Robert, 160–161
Kenya: British protectorate of, 21; Hola Camp murders, 114; impact of World War II, 46; Kikuyu Central Association (KLA), 117; Mau Mau, 118–119
Kenyatta, Jomo, 35, 117–119, 207
Khama, Seretse, 116
Khomeini, Ayatollah Ruhollah, 72
Khrushchev, Nikita, 179
Kim Il Sung, 123
Kirk, Roger, 80
Kirkpatrick, Jeane, 177
Kissinger, Henry, 58; on New International Economic Order (NIEO), 136–143; Soviet and Cuban support in Angola, 116, 171–172
Kitchener, Herbert, 23
Kongo, 13
Korea, 26–27, 54, 154
Kowloon, 26
Kuril, 26
Kuwait, 87, 218m

Laos, 16, 44
Latin America, 17
Lawrence, T. E., 76
League of Nations, 74
Lebanon, 23, 73–75
Legazpi, Miguel de, 14
Leo X, 14
Liberia, 20, 160
Libreville (Gabon), 20
Libya: independence of, 81–83; Italian control of, 23, 73; Muammar Qadhafi, 82
Lippman, Walter, 49–50
Livingston, David, 34–35
Lumumba, Patrice, 107–108, 163–165, 207

MacArthur, Douglas, 46
Macauley, Thomas Babington, 45
MacBride, Sean, 188–189
MacDonald, Ramsey, 66, 217m2
Macharia, Rawson, 118
Machel, Samora, 115, 208
Macleod, Iain, 100
Macmillan, Harold, 45; on Cyprus problem, 85; independence for Northern Rhodesia and Nyasaland, 114; independence of Ghana,
100; "wind of change" in southern Africa, 109–110
Madagascar, 20, 104
Madras, 15–16
Magellan, Ferdinand, 14, 15
Mahe, 16
Maitland, Donald, 148
Majipahit, 13
Makarios III, 84–85
Malacca, 14, 16
Malagasy Republic, 38, 104
Malawi, 19, 114
Malaya: British acquisition of, 16–17, 62–63; Chinese control of commerce, 62; incorporation of Sabah and Sarawak, 63; Japanese conquest of, 26–27, 62–63; Malayan Communist Party (MCP), 62–63; steps to independence, 17, 62–63; Tunku Abdul Rahman, 23
Mali, 13, 94
Mandela, Nelson, 110, 175, 184, 208
Manila Pact, 128, 151–152
Mankekar, D. R., 188
Marcos, Ferdinand and Imelda, 124
Massawa, port of, 21–22
Mauritius, independence of, 104
Max Havelaar (Dekker), 30, 36
M'Bow, Amadou-Mahtar, 188–189
Mboya, Tom, 119
McGhee, George C., 163
McHenry, Donald, 178
McKinley, William, 59
McNamara, Francis, 103
Mehta, Pherozeshah, 65
Mellon, Andrew, 89
Memelik II, 22
Mesopotamia, 72–73
Mexican War of 1848, 27
Mexico, 14
Middle East in World Affairs, The (Lenczowski), 76, 79, 80
Ming Dynasty, 13
Mobutu Sese Seko, 161
Moghul empire, 13
Moluccas, 14, 15, 38
Mondlane, Eduardo, 111–112, 161, 209
Morocco, 22, 26, 82
Mountbatten, Louis, 68
Moynihan, Patrick, 141, 171, 186–187
Mozambique: Frente de Libertação de Moçambique (FRELIMO), 111–112; independence of, 112; Portuguese settlement in, 14, 17; resistance to Portuguese rule, 111–112; Resistência Nacional Moçambicana (RENAMO), 112
Mugabe, Robert, 115, 117, 168, 210
Muskie, Edmund S., 201
Muslim Brotherhood, 78
Muslims, 64–69, 78

Mussadeq, Mohammed, 25, 72, 217n2
Mutesa, Frederick II, 120
Muzorewa, Adel, 116, 168
Myanmar, 44
Myerson, Jacob, 139–140

Namibia, 21, 110
Naoroji, Dadadbhai, 65
Nasser, Gamal-Abdul, 148, 210; incorporation of
    Aden, 91, 92; independence of Egypt, 78–81
Near East, definitions of, 23
Nehru, Jawaharlal, 64–69, 128, 211
Netherlands. See Holland
Neto, Agostinho, 111
New International Economic Order (NIEO), 131,
    136–143
New Spain (Mexico), 14
New World Information and Communications
    Order (NWIO), 187–190
Nicaragua, 27–28
Niger, 21
Nigeria, 20; independence of, 100–101; U.S. aid
    to, 168–170
Nixon, Richard M., support of Rhodesia, 166–
    167, 221n3
Nkomo, Joshua, 115
Nkrumah, Kwame, 46–47, 113, 160, 211; black
    rule of Ghana, 97–100; Ghana indepen-
    dence movement, 32
Noel-Baker, Philip, 76
Non-Aligned Movement (NAM), 130–132
North Vietnam, independence of, 61
Northern Rhodesia, 19, 114
Nujomo, Samuel, 110, 212
Nyasaland, 19, 113–117
Nyerere, Julius, 116, 120

Odinga, Odinga, 119
oil: British access in Persian Gulf, 24, 25, 88–89;
    formation of Arabian American Oil Com-
    pany (ARAMCO), 89; Iran's strategic posi-
    tion, 25, 71–72; Iraq Petroleum Company
    (IPC), 89; Kuwait Oil Company, 89
Ojukwu, Odumegwu, 169
Omdurman, battle of, 23
Orientalism (Said), 125
Ottoman Empire, 22–23, 72–74
Ovimbundi, 13

Pakistan: British rule of, 31, 33; exclusion of
    Muslims, 67; military overthrow, 44
Palestine, 13; Balfour declaration, 76; British
    claim and mandate of, 23–24, 72–73;
    Camp David Accords, 185; Emir Feisal,
    76–77; "internationalized," 76–78; Jewish
    underground activities, 77; Sykes-Picot
    Agreement, 73, 74; UN partitioning of,
    77–78; UN Security Council debates
    about, 184–186

Palestine Liberation Organization (PLO), 184–
    185, 186
Panama Canal, 27, 49, 198
Papagos, Alexandros, 84–85
Pasha, Ahmed Maher, 78
Peace Corps, organization of, 53
Pearson, Lester, 138
Peking, 26
Percy, Charles, 140
Persia. See Iran
Persian Gulf, 24
Pescadores, 26
Philippines: after U.S. war with Spain, 59; Japa-
    nese conquest of, 26–27; Manila, 14; Propa-
    ganda Movement, 59; Roosevelt's trustee-
    ship of, 52; Spanish settlement of, 14; steps
    to independence, 17, 47, 59–62; Tydings-
    McDuffie Act, 60; U.S. military suppres-
    sion, 38–39
Plevin, Rene, 102
Pompidou, Georges, 106
Pondicherry, 16
Porter, William, 52
Portugal: acquisition of Brazil, 14; acquisition of
    Goa, 16; Catherine of Braganza, 16; decolo-
    nization of Angola, 43; education in colo-
    nies, 32–33; Gold Coast, 14; missionary ef-
    forts, 34; racial tolerance, 33; settlement in
    Angola, 17; settlement in Mozambique, 17;
    settlement on Ternate, 15; slave trading, 20;
    territories in southern Africa, 111–113
Powell, Adam Clayton, 129
Present at the Creation (Acheson), 51
Prize, The (Yergin), 131
Puerto Rico, 27, 59

Qadhafi, Muammar, 82, 123, 124, 198
Qassim, Abdul Karim, 87
Qatar, 88

racial discrimination, 33–36, 124
Raffles, Stamford, 15, 16
Ranade, Justice, 65
Reagan, Ronald, 173, 175
Real Case for Rhodesia, The (Chesterton), 165–166
Reign of Greed, The (Rizal), 59
Reinhardt, John, 33
Rentz, George, 89
Revolutionary Iran (Ramazani), 71, 72
Rhodes, Cecil, 18–19, 35
Rhodesia, 113–117; impact of World War II, 46;
    independent as Zimbabwe, 117; Lancaster
    House Conference, 116; raids into Mozam-
    bique, 112; unilateral declaration of inde-
    pendence (UDI), 114–115, 165–168, 221nn9-
    10; U.S. aid to, 165–168
Ricci, Matteo, 34
Richards, James P., 151
Riebeck, Jan van, 17–18

Rizal, José, 59

Roberto, Holden, 111, 171

Roberts, Edmund, 90

Roosevelt, Eleanor, 178

Roosevelt, Franklin D.: decolonization issues, 52; drafting the Atlantic Charter, 50–51; on U.S. involvement in Indochina, 152

Roosevelt, Theodore: actions for Panama Canal, 27; "Roosevelt Corollary," 27; "The Great White Fleet," 28; war with Spain, 59

Roosevelt: The Lion and the Fox (Burns), 51

Rusk, Dean, 161

Ruskin, John, 18

Russia/Soviet Union, 177, 179, 180; activities in Africa, 162; aid to Egypt, 79–80; Azerbaijan territory, 71–72; presence in Angola, 171–173; Russo-Japanese War, 26–27; Treaty of London, 73

Rwanda, 21, 107–108

al-Said, Nuri, 73, 149

Saloway, Reginald, 99

Samar, 38

Saudi Arabia, 24, 88–89

Savimbi, Jonas, 111, 113, 173

Scali, John, 139–140

Schaffer, Teresita, 192

Sékou Touré, Ahmed, 105, 160, 161, 213

Selassi, Haile, 22

Senegal, 20–21, 94

Senghor, Leopold Sedar, 212

Shared Hopes, Separate Fears (Gardner), 48

Sierra Leone, 20, 101

Singapore, 54; British acquisition of, 16; independence of, 17, 63; Japanese conquest of, 26–27

Skinner, Elliott, 159–160

slave trading, 19–21, 35

Smith, Ian, 115, 165–168

Social Cancer, The (Rizal), 59

Socony Mobil, 89

Somalia, 22, 94, 95–96

Songhai, 13

Soudan (Mali), 21

South Africa: African National Congress (ANC), 110; Afrikaaners, 110; apartheid and UN General Assembly, 180–184; British vs. Boers, 110; F. W. de Klerk, 110, 175; impact on Gandhi, 64; League of Nations, 21; Nelson Mandela, 110, 175, 184, 208; Republic of, 94; Sharpeville incident, 110; U.S. relations with, 173–175

South East Asia Treaty Organization (SEATO), 128, 151–152

South Korea, 44

South Manchuria, 26

Southern Rhodesia, 19, 116

South-West Africa, 21

Soviet Union/Russia, 177, 179, 180; activities in

Africa, 162; aid to Egypt, 79–80; Azerbaijan territory, 71–72; presence in Angola, 171–173; Russo-Japanese War, 26–27; Treaty of London, 73

Spain: favoritism in Philippines, 37; impact of Islam, 19; maintaining control, 30–31; New World acquisitions, 14; revolt in Cuba, 27; settlement on Ternate, 15; Treaty of Tordesillas, 14

Spanish-American War, 49

Spinola, Antonio de, 112

Sri Lanka, 14

Standard Oil Company of California (Socal), 88–89

Standard Oil of New Jersey, 89

Stanley, Henry M., 34–35

Stikker, Dirk, 136

Strait of Hormuz, 15–16

Straits Settlements, 16–17

Sudan, 21, 23, 79, 96–97

Suez Canal, 24

Suez Canal Company, 81

Suharto, 58, 131

Sukarno, 46–47, 56–59, 213

Sullivan, Leon, 174

Sykes-Picot Agreement, 23–24, 73

Syria, 23, 72–75

Taiwan (Formosa), 26, 54

Tanganyika, 21, 119–120

Tanzania, 119–120

Ternate, 15

Texaco, 89

Thailand, 44

Thant, U, 130, 177

Thatcher, Margaret, 116

Things Fall Apart (Achebe), 35

Third World: attitudes toward West, 123–127; Cold War effects on U.S. policy, 49, 147–158; conditions of imperialism, 29–39; definitions of, 1; gap between rhetoric and reality, 133; trade issues, 143–144; with Western media, 187–190; World Trade Organization, 144

Third World solidarity: Asian Relations Conference, 128; Bandung conference, 129–130; Congress of Oppressed Nationalities, 128; First Conference of Heads of State or Government of Non-Aligned Countries, 130; Group of 77 (G-77), 131; impact of World War II, 128; International Conference for Peace, 128; International Monetary Fund, 131; New International Economic Order (NIEO), 131; Non-Aligned Movement (NAM), 130–132; Organization of Petroleum Exporting Countries (OPEC), 131–132; Organization of the Islamic Conference, 132; Paris Peace Conference, 128; principles of peaceful co-existence, 129,

219*n*7; South East Asian Treaty Organization (SEATO), 129, 151–152; World Bank, 131
Thornberg, Max, 88
Thornberg, Richard, 126
Thousand Days, A (Schlesinger), 161
"Time of Troubles" (Clarke), 19
Timor, 14
Tobago, independence of, 101
Togo, Republic of, 21
Tonkin, 16
trade issues of Third World, 143–144
TransAfrica, 160
Transjordan: border with Saudi Arabia, 88–89; British mandate of, 23–24; British treaty with, 75–76
Treaty of Bogue, 26
Treaty of London, 73
Treaty of Paris, 16
Treaty of Tientsin, 26
Treaty of Tordesillas, 14
Treaty of Turkmanchai, 24
Treaty of Versailles, 21
Trevaskis, Kennedy, 91
Trinidad, independence of, 101
Tripolitania, 23
Truman, Harry, Point Four program, 145, 220*n*28
Tshombe, Moise, 107–108, 163–165
Tunisia, 22, 52, 82
Turkey: minority in Cyprus, 83–86; siding with Germany, 22–23; Sykes-Picot Agreement, 73
Tutsi peoples, 108
two Tunbs, independence of, 88
Tydings-McDuffie Act, 60

Uganda, 120; Asian minority rule, 120; British protectorate of, 21; Idi Amin, 38, 44; independence of, 120
United Arab Emirates, 88
United Nations (UN): Afro-Asian Group, 129–130; Charter of Economic Rights and Duties of States in the Economic and Financial Committee of the UN General Assembly, 140–143; colonialism issues, 178–180; election of U Thant, 130; Food and Agriculture Organization (FAO), 131; Kissinger proposal and the NIEO initiative, 141–143; linking aid to UN voting, 177; membership as independence, 44, 47; military aid to the Congo, 163–165; New World Information and Communications Order (NWIO), 187–190; Palestine question, 182, 184–186; partitioning of Palestine, 77–78; Resolution 3201 and New International Economic Order (NIEO), 137–143; South Africa racism debates, 180–184; Third World rhetoric and votes, 176–178; UN Committee on Trade and Development (UNCTAD), 142–143; UN Conference on

Trade and Development (UNCTAD), 131; UN Education, Scientific, and Cultural Organization (UNESCO), 187–190; UN Educational and Cultural Organization (UNESCO), 131; UN Environmental Program, 131; UN Industrial and Development Organization (UNIDO), 131; UN Security Council, 48; UN Special Commission on Palestine (UNSCOP), 77–78; UNESCO Resolution 4/19, 189–190, 223*n*55; U.S. and Third World in General Assembly, 176–190; U.S. regard for, 196–197, 201–202; Zionism and racism, 186–187
United States: access to oil resources, 50, 88–89; acquisition of Panama Canal, 49; aid to Africa, 159–175; aid to Nigeria, 168–170; aid to Rhodesia/Zimbabwe, 15, 165–168, 221*n*4; aid to Vietnam, 5, 151–155; approach to Third World, 3–7, 195–198; Central Intelligence Agency (CIA) activities in Third World, 25, 126, 165, 171, 172, 221*n*9; against Charter of Economic Rights and Duties of States in the Economic and Financial Committee of the UN General Assembly, 140; Cold War aid/assistance, 144–145, 161; Cold War influence, 53; colonial issues with France, 51–52; Congressional Black Caucus, 168, 169, 172; disillusionment with UN, 196–197; economic aid and Third World expectations, 134–146; end of Cold War, 5, 7, 8, 191, 192, 195, 199; legacy of Third World attitudes, 123–127; Marshall Plan, 134–135; military bases in Third World, 155–157; Monroe Doctrine of 1823, 27; National Association for the Advancement of Colored People (NAACP), 136; New International Economic Order (NIEO), 136–143; occupation of Philippines, 27; opposition to international banking reform, 145; priority to anti-Communism aid, 161; relations with South Africa, 173–175; response to Asian financial crisis, 192; role in breakup of empires, 47–53; sovereignty of Puerto Rico, 27; Spanish-American War, 49, 59; support of Angola movements, 171–173; terrorism against, 5, 197–198; Third World pressures and rhetoric, 47–53, 133, 176–190; trade and foreign policy goals, 192–194; trade barriers, 50; UN Security Council membership, 48–49; unilateralism and interventions, 198–202; withdrawal from UNESCO, 187
Upper Volta (Burkina Faso), 21
U.S. Committee on Africa, 160

Vajpayee, Atal Bihari, 124
Versailles, Treaty of, 21
Vietnam, *54*, 61; Bao Dai solution, 61–62, 153–155; Ho Chi Minh, 47, 152–154; military over-

throw, 44; North and South division, 62; U.S. aid to, 151–155
von Ketteler, Baron, 26
Vorster, John, 116

Waldheim, Kurt, 182
"Wars of Resistance" (Samkange), 35
Welensky, Roy, 114
West New Guinea (Irian Jaya) independence, 44, 57, 58
Western Sahara, 19
Wilson, Harold, 115
Wilson, Woodrow, 48–50, 74
World Bank, 131, 137, 139, 145–146, 197
World Health Organization, 178
World Trade Organization, 144, 192
World War I, anti-colonial pressure, 46–47

World War II: Greek-British cooperation, 84; impact on decolonization, 46, 128

Xavier, Francis, 34

Yanaon, 16
Years of Upheaval (Kissinger), 136–137
Yemen, 24

Zambesia, 18–19
Zambia, 19, 114
Zimbabwe: impact of World War II, 46; independence of, 19; Zimbabwe African National Union (ZANU), 115–117; Zimbabwe African Peoples' Union (ZAPU), 115
Zionism, 76, 186–187
Zorlu, Fatim, 85

DAVID D. NEWSOM is a former Undersecretary and Assistant Secretary of State and served as U.S. Ambassador to Libya, Indonesia, and the Philippines. After retiring from the Foreign Service, he became Director of the Institute for the Study of Diplomacy, professor and dean at the Georgetown University School of Foreign Service, and professor in the department of Government and Foreign Affairs at the University of Virginia. He is currently a senior fellow at the University's Miller Center. He is the author of *The Soviet Brigade in Cuba; Diplomacy and the American Democracy;* and *The Public Dimension of Foreign Policy.*